MW01233137

PRAISE FOR PAULA PRICE & HER MINISTRY

"Dr. Paula Price is astounding! Her wisdom in the prophetic is displayed so every reader will get an understanding of the prophetic dimension. Every believer should own a copy of this book!"

—Prophet Jeremy Lopez
www.identitynetwork.net

"It is a must read for everyone in ministry! The profundity is priceless! This handbook is truly a resource for all prophets, bringing enlightenment, revelation, and understanding to all who are called to be a voice in these times!"

—Pastors Michael & Carolyn Byrd
Embassy Center of Empowerment
Fort Lauderdale, Florida

"Filled to the brim with revelation and explanation concerning 'all things prophetic.' If you are one of those who refuse to settle for less than all God has for you…if you won't be intimidated by those who claim that God doesn't still speak today, then you'll love the answers and clarity you'll discover for this complex and often misunderstood subject!"

—Steve Shultz
Elijah List
www.elijahlist.com

"Dr. Paula Price has a unique and powerful ministry to the body of Christ. As an apostolic and prophetic teacher and consultant to business and ministry, she is filled with the wisdom of God."

—Stan E. DeKoven, Ph.D.
President, Vision International Education Network
www.vision.edu

"Dr. Paula Price's vast knowledge of the Bible coupled with her commonsense approach to life enables her to teach practical, in-depth wisdom for the Christian walk. She has an amazing wealth of knowledge and wisdom from God's Word. That coupled with her many years of experience as a corporate executive in the business world gives her the ability to apply God's wisdom in a practical, no-nonsense way that is both refreshing and insightful."

—Mark Gorman
Founder and President,
Leading Edge Network, International
www.leadingedgenetwork.org

"Dr. Paula Price is one of today's blue ribbon Christian leaders. Here is a person whose extensive experience, both in the business and church worlds, has equipped her to see and to understand the big picture with more insight than most others. I love to watch her creative mind discerning what the Spirit is saying to the churches and then moving boldly ahead to open new frontiers for the kingdom. I am privileged to be associated with Dr. Price and to have benefited greatly from her apostolic and prophetic gifts."

—C. Peter Wagner
Presiding Apostle, International Coalition of Apostles
www.apostlesnet.net

The
PROPHET'S
HANDBOOK

A GUIDE TO PROPHECY AND ITS OPERATION

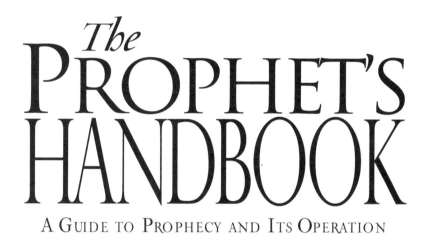

The
PROPHET'S
HANDBOOK

A GUIDE TO PROPHECY AND ITS OPERATION

PAULA A. PRICE, PH.D.

WHITAKER
HOUSE

Unless otherwise indicated, all Scripture quotations are taken from the King James Version of the Holy Bible. Scripture quotations marked (NIV) are from the *Holy Bible, New International Version®*, NIV®, © 1973, 1978, 1984 by the International Bible Society. Used by permission of Zondervan. All rights reserved. Scripture quotations marked (NKJV) are taken from the *New King James Version*, © 1979, 1980, 1982, 1984 by Thomas Nelson, Inc. Used by permission. All rights reserved.

THE PROPHET'S HANDBOOK:
A Guide to Prophecy and Its Operation
hardcover edition

Paula Price Ministries
7107 S. Yale Ave.
Tulsa, OK 74136
www.drpaulaprice.com

HARDCOVER ISBN-13: 978-1-60374-034-0 • ISBN-10: 1-60374-034-1
Printed in the United States of America
© 2001, 2008 by Dr. Paula Price

Whitaker House
1030 Hunt Valley Circle
New Kensington, PA 15068
www.whitakerhouse.com

The Library of Congress has cataloged the trade paperback edition as follows:
Price, Paula A.
The prophet's handbook : a guide to prophecy and its operation /
Paula A. Price.
p. cm.
Summary: "Shows the place and role of prophets in the church today and explains how to establish a prophetic company"—Provided by publisher.
Includes bibliographical references.
ISBN 978-1-60374-019-7 (pbk. : alk. paper) 1. Prophecy—Christianity.
2. Prophecy—Christianity—History of doctrines—21st century.
3. Prophets—Calling of. 4. Pastoral theology. I. Title.
BR115.P8P65 2008
234'.13—dc22   2007036413

No part of this book may be reproduced or transmitted in any form or by any means electronic or mechanical—including photocopying, recording, or by any information storage and retrieval system—without permission in writing from the publisher. Please direct your inquiries to permissionseditor@whitakerhouse.com.

1 2 3 4 5 6 7 8 9 10 11 12 ⱳ 16 15 14 13 12 11 10 09 08

CONTENTS

Part Two:
Guidelines for Establishing a Prophetic Company

PREFACE

G od is reinstating the office of the prophet as a standing institution in the New Testament church. The pervasive rise in occult activity, coupled with the church's naiveté in spiritual matters, are two of the main reasons why He must do so. In view of His divine agenda, questions concerning the office of the prophet and its modern-day functions in the local church are on many leaders' minds. Discussions are held regularly by church officials who ask how to engage prophets in the local church without surrendering authority over their sheep and control of the church's mandate. Their questions include how they should install their church's prophetic institution and administrate it effectively. They ask, "Is there some sort of ceremony that should be held for inaugurating those who occupy the place of the church prophet?" Furthermore, they wonder if there are professional credentials for prophets. If there are credentials to certify and authenticate them, who devises the criteria and how is the officer to be equipped to succeed? Should the church have its own prophetic training program, and if so, who delivers it?

Once the issues of installing the prophetic in the local church as an institution are resolved, the next most pertinent question becomes, "What are the prophets to do?" This generation wants to know how contemporary prophets are to be employed in their churches, and how they are to benefit and profit the church. According to Jeremiah 23:32, prophets exist in the houses of the Lord to profit them. That is a powerful statement on its own, because people rarely think about prophetics and profitability going hand in hand. Yet, that is what they are intended to do, based on the wording of 2 Chronicles 20:20.

The Prophet's Handbook shows how churches can multiply their harvests through a quality prophetic institution. It boldly delves into these matters and answers the questions above and many others essential to validating prophetics today and the officers and ministers who handle it. For the pastor who wants to know how to comply with the Lord's new and insistent prophetic move, this book can be an indispensable tool. No longer do devoted shepherds have to choose between ignoring the imposing unction of the Lord to open their churches up to the prophetic or risk exposing their flocks to irresponsible prophets. With this book, it is now possible to evaluate the prophetic messenger(s) you engage and confirm their eligibility and compatibility with your church before they are presented to your congregation. It is suggested reading if you are a prophetic educator, minister, or trainer. In this book, you get help as a pastor in developing budding prophets, redefining the seasoned ones, and educating the congregation on the subject as a whole.

The Prophet's Handbook frankly addresses pastors' concerns over installing the prophets they feel are assigned to their congregations. In response to the Lord steadily advancing the prophetic in these last days, this book clarifies for church leaders the best way to integrate resident prophet ministries in their churches. You will find it contains sound, balanced guidelines for the institution and regulation of the officer in the churches of God using His wisdom. This book takes you into the world of the prophetic and shows you how the prophet's ministry and mantle are invaluable for pastors and others. You receive details on the responsibilities, duties, and privileges of prophets in the house of God.

You are provided with suggestions for compensating staff prophets, training and qualifying them for service, fine-tuning their behavior, and fixing their range of authority. Also, there are guidelines for assessing prophets' performance and effectiveness, as well as strategies for managing difficult or untrained prophets. There is counsel for resolving conflicts with difficult prophets and advice on how to protect your flock from them. Emerging prophets in the church who read this book can find themselves, understand what the Lord is doing with and through them, and receive guidance on how to approach and work with their pastors in their new callings. Such information helps churches determined to have a quality and professional prophetic institution.

Candidly discussed are other prophet-related issues, such as the godly church prophet, prophetic protocols, parameters, limits, and government. Besides these, the most critical subject of all is treated forthrightly: the relationship between the pastor and the prophet. This vital discussion encompasses advice on the boundaries to be put on the prophet's interactions with the sheep and correcting errant prophetics. It talks openly about the necessary shifts in normal prophetic authority that must take place if a congregation is to be edified by the church prophet without sacrificing the pastor's position. Also covered are how and why the pastor is not subject to the prophet but is urged to create a cooperative alliance between the two mantles. The common recurring theme of the book stresses the importance of quickly establishing a functional pastor-prophet relationship. It is necessary that the first link in the prophetic institution's chain of events be forged between the pastor-prophet ministry. Such requirements are vital if the arrangement is to benefit the church's vision and edify its members.

INTRODUCTION:
THE SITUATION

Why was this book written? What makes it advantageous at this period in the Christian church's existence? There are three answers to these questions. The first one is the Lord's imposing and relentless revival of His prophetic institution to serve, recover, and secure His church in this era. The second is that contemporary prophets need to learn how the Lord operates prophetically as distinguished from how He moved evangelically over the past century or so. This distinction is vital if they are to respond to His heavenly initiatives the way their predecessors did, as Yahweh's voice to ancient Israel and the world. Many of the prophets answering God's prophetic restoration call have been trained by evangelists and pastors. Their ministries have been standardized and regulated by the Lord's *derived* mantles of pastor and teacher, which came from the apostle. As a result, His prophetic overtures are largely unfamiliar to prophets and therefore seem foreign and hard to accommodate.

The third answer is this generation's criteria for fulfilling God's mandate today. To begin with, modern prophets should first divest themselves of their society-imposed fear of backlash and become fearless. To face off with what awaits their readiness, they should become competent and shrewd enough to tackle what vies for this prophetic era's seats of authority. Prophets answering God's call today require unique training, government, empowerment, and organization to be used by Him the way He always has used His prophets since time began. The dark, archaic spirituality of the BC world now popularizing itself rivals this by blanketing the earth with its devious ilk in an effort to overshadow Christ's hold on it. Such a deadly vision more than substantiates the Lord's global reinstatement of the prophet's mantle. In the process it also impels prophets' need for high quality education to equip them to counteract it with the Almighty's wisdom and righteousness.

Moreover, witchcraft and demonism's invasion of the (heretofore) Christian world is especially ruinous because of its declared strategy, which is to syncretize traditional Christianity to blend its faith and practices with those of the old religions Christ deposed by the cross. Their effort appears to succeed in large part due to the New Testament church's slumber, a lack of biblical training, and an absence of spiritually sound exposure or experience with the supernatural. Fear of the dark drove the Christian church into a corner and sealed it off from spirituality, favoring instead an intellectual stronghold. The result has been the mainstreaming of primordial demonism that saturates every stratum of modern society.

Not since Christ restored the world to the Almighty after His triumph on Calvary has such a brazen effort to convert it to the old destructive gods and religions that felled ancient civilizations been so well-orchestrated. Over the last several decades, agents of this destructive campaign have worked feverishly to halt the spread of Christianity and to neutralize the Christian church's impact in the world. They infiltrated all of its systems and institutions to do so. Boldly these dark agents declared their campaign mission: to return the modern world under Christ's light and life to its BC era, and to return its dethroned gods to their pre-Calvary seats of power. Using the media, politics, education, and amusements such as cunningly downplayed video games, these forces condition their adherents to crave this movement. For nearly half a century, they stealthily waged war on Christianity while numerous Christians never caught on to it. Idealistically, they were deceived into embracing the romanticized notions of pagan dreams, surrendering themselves, their influence, and credibility to New Age, occult, and witchcraft movements. Without ever realizing it, seducing spirits beguiled many of our Christian ancestors into displacing Christ's throne with the virtually extinct deities of the old world.

Naively, many Christian churches and leaders, as well as many Christians themselves, adopted beliefs, practices, rituals, and other occult genres under the guise of religious freedom, God's love, and peace on earth—three objectives the Lord Jesus Himself personally repudiated as not His primary aims. Yet, because of the widespread abandonment of God's Word (see Luke 18:8) and the dumbing down of the Bible and its principal doctrines, the church has become desensitized to its calling and disconnected from its Founder. The redemptive grace Jesus brought to the planet is now taught licentiously, with God's people becoming libertines instead of His liberated sons and daughters. Admittedly, the strategy against true Christianity has been brilliant and its damnable results inarguably impressive to date, but God is not going to let it stop there. He set out on His campaign to win eons ago, and He is nowhere near ready to give up His fight. Insistently, over the last several decades, the Lord has been encroaching upon the secularists' stronghold, stealthily taking back territory promised and granted to His Son for His victory on the cross.

Mainly through the prophets, the Lord has been addressing the devil's attempted coup for some time. His initial step was to reactivate the mantles of His two prime ministers (see 1 Corinthians 12:28) of His new creation church in an attempt to curtail Satan's rampage. However, at every stage of His revival and restoration program, He consistently meets with a common obstacle, naiveté—the oblivion of those He summons to His true problem and its solution.

As a consequence of the church's myopic overemphasis on God's love, world peace, and religious harmony (even to the exclusion of His stipulated plan of salvation and sanctification), many of those answering the call to the prophetic today are conditioned to relegate the Lord's program to the world's political agenda. Incognizant of the battle raging against their faith's freedom going on behind the scenes, many are deluded by fantasies of what awaits them in God's prophetic ranks. They are misguided by incompatible training, and what they call prophetic service is drastically different from the age-old institution God established under Samuel. Many prophets' mantles are presently unprepared to face and overturn what lies ahead for God's people. Quite a few of them are unenlightened on what the word of the Lord is for this time in human history and cannot connect the Bible's prophecies with current events to recognize the work this generation needs them to do.

Modern Christian prophets, having been unprophetically trained, operate and think very much like evangelists.

They want to saturate the world with prophecy, exercise some spiritual gifts, and hold prophecy sessions the way evangelists hold altar calls. After these meetings, they send their audiences back home with nothing but a prophecy to fix their lives. In subscribing to this approach to ministry, many earlier prophets of this move overlooked that even a thirty-page prophecy is but a single moment (a day, hour, or year) in their hearers' lives. The absence of criteria, standards, protocols, and even a valid position description prevented them from discerning what else their hearers needed from them as prophets beside their predictions. Because, as first- and second-generation transitional prophets, they entered the ministry on the evangelist's fundamental credo, "Win the lost at all costs," often God Himself was included in their costs and risks. After their prophetic careers took off, these early messengers added the pastor's ministry mode to their service to maintain their ministries. While not all of them pastored, their mentality resembled nonetheless the fourth member of the Ephesians 4:11 staff.

For the sake of clarity, the aim and function of the pastor's office are akin to a nation's domestic agents. Pastors are the equivalent of the kingdom's household ministers. Based on this comparison, previous prophets took up the pastor's ministry type because the duties, responsibilities, outlets, and even compensation of their mantles' sphere were as yet unopened to them. So instead of functioning as divine communicators for God's kingdom, all prophecy became predictive and confined to the local church and its pastors, ignoring the world outside the church walls. Limiting prophecy to the local church left the world's interest in God and the supernatural to be handled by psychics, an attitude completely opposed to the ancient prophets' mind-set. They understood their prophetic charge to be to summon God's people back to His fold and faith because as watchmen, they were also gatekeepers.

True guardians of the Lord's gates equate to His spiritual border agents. They are not inclined to admit whosoever will come into the Lord's family or community (or to usher them into His presence) any old way. Unlike evangelists, the prophets' call is to filter and sanctify. They demand that candidates for Christ's blessings, deliverance, and other spiritual provisions reserved for His family of citizens come by way of Calvary. Prophets validate people's salvation and thus divine citizenship by requiring proof of their repentance and conversion. Entrants into Christ's eternal life should declare their faith to enter His kingdom as He stipulates. To remain in His house, they should live according to the Almighty's government in their lives. Jesus is not just the door to salvation, but He is the guardian of its entryway as well. Doors swing open and shut, and the Lord says in Revelation 3:7 that He shuts as well as opens the life's doors. (See Isaiah 22:22.)

Therefore, the Lord's converts are expected to prove daily to the indwelling Holy Spirit that their names remain written in the Lamb's book of life—Christ's eternal registry of redeemed souls. Prophets, as well as all loyal ministers of Jesus Christ, demand God's kingdom and church entrants renounce their faith and service to other gods and convert their entire public and private existence to the Lord Jesus Christ. Why? Because prophets are sifters. Their mantles filter and screen out what does not meet the criteria of heaven for its citizens. The evangelists may accept all who come, but it is the Lord's prophets and apostles who determine all who stay. From time immemorial, the Lord's representatives have accepted that He is holy and that only those who share His holiness can enter and partake of His family.

As committed officers of the Almighty's kingdom, prophets uphold His law of righteousness and refuse to allow any to escape sin's death sentence apart from repentance, Jesus Christ's justification, and His righteousness. True watchmen revere the Savior as the door to eternal life and will not allow those who would be transformed into His image and likeness to forgo His requirements. Prophets, as God's genuine custodians, are eternity's customs agents, permitting entry into God's kingdom only to those modeling His pattern of the perfect human and divine citizen. Ephesians 3:5 says that the Lord manifested the revelations that enable this work to be done in the saint to His apostles and prophets.

When Jesus came as the Great Prophet, just as His Old Testament predecessor Moses prophesied centuries before, He took up the very prophecies that predated and foretold Him. As a prophet, He spearheaded the Lord's plan to offer Israel's commonwealth blessings, privileges, and provisions to the whole world and competently executed the office with resolve, strength, solidarity, and skill. Resolutely, Jesus went about His ministry duties, manifesting the prophet's mantle to the full in every detail, for those who want to see it. He was then sent to take the world from the savage grip of darkness that abused it; and today in response to what Satanists want to accomplish in this era, the mission is the same.

The Lord once again revitalizes the mantle of the prophet to deliver His people and beloved planet from the barbarity of the fallen spirits that prey on them. From Abel to Christ, this is what the Creator did to either recover His people from devilish strongholds or authority over a geographic territory or sphere of humanity's existence. In this movement, His objective is both. The only difference is how the Lord executes this phase of His plan in modern times. Prophets are going to be used differently in this next dispensation, and because of it they will be more stringently regulated and directly managed by Him than ever before in the church's history.

Not deviating from His biblical precedents, in transitioning from this era to His next age of humanity, God's commencement of His program with the prophets stays with His well-documented, scriptural methods. From the Old Testament to the New, it is shown that God invariably marks creation's changes with His prophets. They are the timepieces that set the tempo and pace of His momentum. For example, in taking His people from the old to the new covenant, the Lord marked the change with John the Baptist, a prophet. When John appeared on the scene, the Lord's people were infused with paganism and demonics, and enslaved to other gods. So indisputable was this fact that the first encounter Jesus had with any power on earth was with the devil, *"who taketh Him up into the holy city, and setteth him on a pinnacle of the temple…into an exceeding high mountain, and showeth him all the kingdoms of the world, and the glory of them…in a moment of time"* (Matthew 4:5, 8; Luke 4:5). As the Prophet sent by God with a power greater than their own, He was able to free people from sin's grip.

To deliver His people after a long period of apparent silence, the Lord resumed His prior actions and set out to recapture the hearts and souls of His beloved family again. We can recognize His historical way of moving because the Lord stays true to Himself. He always regains dominion of His world and control of His kingdom through His prophets because He never did away with Amos 3:7, and the *"Scriptures must be fulfilled"* (Matthew 14:49). Scripture records God's prophetic episodes from Enoch to Noah, from Noah to Abraham, from Abraham to Joseph, and from Joseph to Moses. Joseph was God's prophet in Egypt, where Moses was inducted.

The mantle was resurrected in Samuel, who restarted God's prophetic clock and standardized the institution for Him under Moses' Law. Since him, the pattern has remained the same. When the earth is threatened to be overrun with Satanism and the potential for Satan to bully and abuse humans reaches proportions that recall Genesis 6:5, the Lord reacts by raising up His prophets to counterbalance the darkness with His light and life. When the Mosaic era was replaced with Christ, the pattern varied somewhat as Jesus instated and dispatched His apostles. This change too was initiated with the prophets.

Another impressive fact that makes this book timely is the advent of God's apostolic restoration. Keeping with His biblical pattern, since the New Testament's inception it has been noted that the Lord always foreruns apostolic reinstatements with the prophets. He does so because only His prophets can verify His emerging apostles. To be successful in this duty, this generation's prophets must possess a means of assessing, rightly placing, and regulating themselves to accurately and uniformly identify God's true apostles. *The Prophet's Handbook* facilitates their capacity to do just that, and much more. As a practical tool, this handbook allows kingdom leaders, especially apostles, prophets, and senior church leaders, to introduce and practice this dispensation of Christ's prophetics capably and responsibly. Using it as a guide, prophets and prophetic ministers can now be screened and intelligently made to understand what the prophet in God's service exists to do. An instrument such as this permits kingdom leaders to train, govern, guide, structure, and supervise their prophetic officers and affairs.

As a prophet, future prophet, or kingdom leader, you get from this book solid direction in the education, mentorship, coaching, and development of your prophetic people for your service. This compendium of guidelines, explanations, policies, strategies, and procedural regulations aids your administration and execution of God's supernatural spheres, being specifically created with the Lord's prophetics in mind. You hold in your hand today a powerful organizational, operational, and supervisory tool as a means of properly justifying the existence of the prophetic and instructions for establishing a prophetic company. This manual guides the assessment and screening all leaders should conduct with their prophets and prophetic candidates. It offers a prudent way to measure their capacity for reliable service and gives some clues to where each prophet's unique gifts would serve best. Equipped with this information, prophets can be better utilized in their organizations and properly placed in God's service. Now the prophetic can find its place and duty in all of the Lord's realms and enterprises. The examples and illustrations contained in this handbook demonstrate the powerful difference a well-tooled and organized prophetic institution can make in our times.

From situations to simulations, this instrument of quality prophetic service shows how to apply God's historical and spontaneous wisdom in modern societies. Its keen insights, profound truths, and pragmatic guidelines help any organization orient itself to the prophetic and ably install a quality prophetic division to preserve its existence. With the skills and abilities presented in this book, God's prophets, prophetic people, and their leaders can identify what best serves His interests and theirs to facilitate prophets' ministerial purpose in today's world. Sometimes a textbook and at other times a training document, this text is structured to enable you to institute spiritually and biblically sound prophetic bylaws and policies that actually function in the real world.

Next to your Bible, this will become a constant companion that you will strive to become well-versed in as a prophet to do your job effectively. Assimilating its wisdom into your readiness path enables you to excel in your prophetic training. Leaders will discover how to prove and verify their prophets using realistic methods, such as a probationary period. Anyone called by the Lord to touch this ministry in any way will feel equipped and secure in his or her actions and duties as a prophet. Those called to be chief, global, or supervisory prophets can feel secure in their oversight of those assigned to them.

Prepared under the auspices of the Holy Spirit with the Lord's Word as its wisdom, this handbook disseminates God's judgments, decisions, and decision-making policies and procedures on the prophetic so prophets and their colleagues can flood the earth with His mind. Expect to receive from this material insight into the Lord's motives and sovereign governance of this world. Knowledge gained from it gives the rationale of His government and encourages its incorporation in all prophetic tasks and duties.

PART ONE

THE CHURCH PROPHET'S ROLE IN THE WORLD TODAY

Chapter 1

OVERVIEW

The Overview covers the following information:

- How pastors can accept and manage the prophetic in their churches
- How to select and prove prophets for their churches
- What people want to know about the prophetic
- God's prophetic sphere
- Why all Christians should learn about the prophetic
- Prophetic subject matter
- About God's prophets and prophecies
- Full prophetic knowledge
- Are prophets for today?
- Dreaming, advance knowledge, and the prophet

Pastors wanting to fulfill the will of God concerning the prophetic in their churches regularly ask me how to go about it and what criteria they are to use to do so. They want to grasp the wisdom of installing and working with a church prophet beforehand in order to protect their congregations. Generally, pastors desire some reliable tools to evaluate their prophetic ministers (past, present, and future) and guidelines that enable their proper use of the ministry in the local church. Whenever questions arise over the matter, it is not resistance I most often meet, but confusion and curiosity.

Many pastors say they would gladly comply with the Lord in His present prophetic move if they could just understand how. They are rightfully concerned about how to install church prophets without disrupting their church order and unduly exposing their flocks to immature or incompetent prophets. They want to understand further how to set the mantle of the prophet within an existing church structure while keeping the balance of control and power intact. *Intact* means not letting pastoral authority be swept out of their hands by prophetic fascination. Frankly, I agree with them and hold similar reservations when acknowledging and developing budding prophets entrusted to my care. Before all else, I emphasize the importance of knowing the prophet's history. Factors like the character and ability of ministers should be thoroughly explored. Their background, prophetic track record, and relations with others, if they are not members of the congregation, should be investigated with care and discretion. Such information is helpful in gauging the potential success of prophetic candidates.

For example, it is defeating to use a prophet with less experience and expertise than the number of years the church has been in existence. It is also imprudent to use a prophet who has no heart for the sheep, whose time is spent doing anything but helping to nurture the flock of God. If the pastor is the only one who arouses the prophet's responses or interest, and he or she remains unaffected by everything else related to the church, then such a person may not be a good church prophet. He or she may serve well as an itinerant minister brought in at strategic times in the church's progress but should not be trusted with long-term prophetic duties or authority. Factors like these require meticulous attention to qualify the prophets themselves and protect those with whom they work.

The underlying aim of stringent investigation is prudence. It is necessary to assure the facilitation of the prophet's ministry in the church and to enable God's unimpeded access to the ears, hearts, and minds of His people. What makes this process indispensable is its ability to curtail prophetic incompatibility and expand the presently narrow ministry field of prophetics ordained by God to this generation. Beyond that, it furnishes earnest church officials with reliable measures for their developing prophetic institutions and promotes healthy prophetic growth, maturity, and stability at the same time. In addition, it protects this all-important ministry in the New Testament church.

This chapter gives you a quick overview of the essential elements of any serious prophetic discussion. It shows the important pieces of the puzzle for those seeking to learn about the prophet in God's church. As you review the pages to follow, you will get a true picture of the ministry, mantle, and operations of the church in snapshot form.

Following is an overview of what you should study to help you connect with the discussions in this book. The topics are:

1. FAQs—Frequently Asked Questions
2. Concerning the Prophetic

3. Key Terms and Phrases

4. About God's Prophets and Prophetics

5. The Full Spectrum of the Prophetic

6. Are Prophets for Today?

7. Am I a Prophet?

WHAT PEOPLE ALWAYS WANT TO KNOW ABOUT THE PROPHET AND THE PROPHETIC

If you are going to install a prophetic institution, enter the prophetic, and/or fulfill the office of the prophet, you need to be aware of the questions that lodge in people's minds concerning it. Below are frequently asked questions concerning the prophets and prophetics of the office and the officer, dreams and visions, and the validity of the mantle's operations today. Familiarize yourself with them, because the consensus is that if one is going to prophesy and expect to be believed, one should at least be able to answer these questions with clarity. Although not addressed in the listed order, the answers to these questions will unfold as you read through the book. Take time to jot them down as you come upon them. Check off each one as you get the answer to it.

FAQs—FREQUENTLY ASKED QUESTIONS

- What is a prophet?
- What exactly is prophecy?
- How does one become a prophet?
- How do prophets do what they do?
- If I'm not a prophet, do I still need to learn about prophetics?

- Why do we need prophets to tell us what God is saying when we have the Holy Spirit?

- How can psychics accurately tell the future?

- Are prophets really for today?

- I dream and know things in advance. Am I a prophet?

- Where does prophecy come from?

GOD'S PROPHETIC SPHERE

The most challenging thought to grasp about the prophetic is that the office is more than a prediction center. Since prophecy is where most people usually encounter the institution of the prophetic, they presume the gist of the office is exclusively prophesying—seeing and saying, predicting and interdicting. However, many things go into enabling a prophet to prophesy accurately.

WHAT EQUIPS THE PROPHET?

Before God releases the officer, He puts the prophet through an extensive training program. God's way of equipping someone for ministry is mainly spiritual. The prophet's function is largely supernatural, and people think there is nothing more to getting a prophet ready for the Lord's service than hearing and saying, "Thus says the Lord." For many people, prophetic preparation amounts to God isolating beginners and streaming prophetic dreams and visions at them. Truthfully, it is somewhat that way, but usually down the line a bit. Nonetheless, dreams and visions are how God usually presents Himself to the new prophet. The reason visions and dreams are the starting point of prophetic education is that God introduces Himself and awakens the prophet's revelatory faculties through them. *"If there be a prophet among you, I the* LORD *will make myself known unto him in a vision, and will speak unto him in a dream"* (Numbers 12:6).

Once the novice prophet is made aware of the calling, the Lord's preparatory methods shift to more stringent and demanding activities. *"The fear of the* LORD *is the instruction of wisdom; and before honour is humility"* (Proverbs 15:33) and *"Before destruction the heart of man is haughty, and before honour is humility"* (Proverbs 18:12) become the primary lesson objectives. Read the two short passages to discover the Lord's teaching objectives and then relate them to 1 Peter 5:10: *"But the God of all grace, who hath called us unto his eternal glory by Christ Jesus, after that ye have suffered a while, make you perfect, stablish, strengthen, settle you."* From these passages you can see that God diligently goes after the inherent and nurtured pride, arrogance, and independence of the young prophet since submission is the predominant requirement of prophetic service. Once this begins, things really heat up.

For a season, it may appear that prophesying is the last thing God wants of His new student. Resetting the newcomer's attitude, perspectives, and priorities to perform reliable prophetic services takes precedence over all else.

The initial classes are largely experiential, the curriculum multidimensional, and the tests excruciating. Yet the Lord finally does get His messengers ready for His service. The requisite areas of learning are spirituality, morality, integrity, discipline, and obedience. Integrated in their dynamics are ancient prophetics and history, revelatory techniques, and the scope of predictive prophecy. Trainers and mentors are selected from every area of human life, since that is the field the prophetic targets. The developing prophet encounters and interacts with every sphere of human existence so that the mantle is equipped to treat its every condition. Verbalizing may be the medium of administration, but the aims and outcomes of prophetic ministry are far more diverse.

QUICK STUDY CHART
Prophetic Training

Following is a list of prophetic subject matter that God teaches His prophets to make sure they are competent in their positions. Review it to comprehend the rationale of God's prophetic training path for you.

PROPHETIC SUBJECT MATTER

- The prophetic as the second most important office in God's supernatural branch of ministry
- The prophetic as an agency
- The prophetic as a commissioned office
- The prophet as an agent of the Godhead
- The prophetic as an agency with indelible functions in the church and the world
- The role and place of the second most important office in God's ministry
- The prophetic's agency status and authority
- The nature of a prophetic commission
- What happens when prophets become God's functionaries
- The prophetic's impact on Creator God's immutable creation codes

IF I'M NOT A PROPHET, DO I STILL NEED TO LEARN ABOUT PROPHETICS?

The answer to this question is an emphatic "Yes!" Everyone who is saved should know about the prophetic because that is how the church came into existence and how the Lord speaks to, and through, His people. The Creator spoke His plans to have a family, a people, and a nation for Himself long before any of it came into being. Those prophetic words acted on creation every day until the vision of God's heart came to be.

Based on God's method of bringing His word to pass in our times, by speaking and thereby causing what He said to come into being, prophecy apparently holds a high place in His mind. When the Lord speaks, His spiritual words encompass natural bodies, making prophecy the only way to get His eternal provisions from there to here. This is how it goes. First come the words, which are uttered outside time. From that seemingly insignificant act comes the natural body for them in time.

All that goes into making a vision a reality and materializing an idea are set in motion by this simple means. What leaves God's mouth is incubated and matured in much the same way an embryo progresses to a fetus and a fetus is born as a baby. Here is the main reason why much of what God says to and through His prophets is equated with impregnation, gestation, travailing women, and birth. The invisible process of God's word coming to pass is precisely like the visible process of conceiving and bearing a child. (See Isaiah 55:11; 61:11.) Isaiah 60:22 speaks of God's words having their time, and Jeremiah 1:12 answers this with prophecy's timing coinciding with His words' performance. Following are some significant words that are helpful to understanding this material.

IMPORTANT PROPHETIC TERMS

KEY TERMS AND PHRASES

- Agent
- Agency
- Biblical Prophetics
- Commission
- Divination
- Divine
- Dreams
- Foundational Studies
- Functionary
- Ministry
- Office
- Officer
- Official
- Prophecy
- Prophet
- Prophetic Attributes
- Prophetic Authority
- Prophetic Delegations
- Prophetic Features
- Prophetic Functions
- Prophetic Jurisdiction
- Prophetic Mantle
- Prophetic Ministrations
- Prophetic Skill
- Prophetic Studies
- Prophetic Sphere
- Protocol
- Protocratic
- Psalmist
- Seer
- Symbols
- Vision

Throughout this book, you will see these terms and phrases because they best define the prophetic. These terms are important for your grasp of the material and for identifying the language applied to prophetic ministry. It is suggested that you research them on your own and get familiar with their usage in general. A brief glossary of their meanings is in the back of the book. We encourage you, as you go through the book, to refer to them again and again to use their meanings in the prophetic office and its mantle while learning about the subject from your reading.

If you are a class, a learning group, or a prophetic study team, take time to explore the previous list of words and their relevance to competent prophetic ministry. You can find more specific meanings and applications of these words in my book *The Prophet's Dictionary.*

ABOUT GOD'S PROPHETS AND PROPHETICS

The list below shows you the substantial amount of information packed into this book. To operate as a professional prophet people can trust, you need answers to the list of Frequently Asked Questions of those who inquire of God through you. This handy resource is a constant companion in your professional ministry. When you complete this book and its recommended studies, you will be able to intelligently discuss the following:

- What the prophet is
- The nature of the prophetic institution
- Office/gift distinctives
- Office/vessel criteria
- Prophetic duties
- Prophetic territories
- Prophetics in the local church
- The proper prophetic lifestyle
- Twenty-first century prophetics and how the world and the church must be prepared

To get where God needs you to be prophetically, you need to understand the following:

- Prophets and the church
- Prophets and the world
- Prophets versus psychics
- Prophets of old
- Prophets today
- The proper prophetic lifestyle
- Prophetic features and functions

FULL PROPHETIC KNOWLEDGE

When one thinks about the full spectrum of the prophetic, the following should come to mind:

- Native prophetic abilities born in all prophets ✱
- Prophetic personalities that indicate the call to the office
- Supernatural attire, the invisible insignia of power and authority
- Angelic delegation
- Miracles and signs
- Prophetic dreams
- Prophetic order and protocol
- Supernatural orders
- Eternal reasons for the prophet
- Prophetic streams

ARE PROPHETS FOR TODAY?

Prophets are for today as much as anything else that has ever been. Here are some good reasons why prophets are and will continue to be needed by God for some time. Revelation 11 declares they will be active until the end of this age. The reasons are:

✓ God, the devil, man, and the world are all interrelated, and prophets are how each one contacts and conveys information to the other.

Start 22 Nov 08

- It does not matter how modern we appear, closer scrutiny shows we have not progressed so far after all.
- Technology names its work after the same demons the Lord has fought with since antiquity.
- Prophets still confront the same sin in humanity that has existed since time began.
- Television today, and the entertainment media in general, can do little without the same vulgarity that has pervaded the planet since time began.
- Sexual perversion—immorality, obscenity, homosexuality, and lewdness—runs rampant.
- Lust and greed are increasing.
- The devil and his children still operate in deception, delusion, sin, and perversity.

All in all, one can say the people of earth are still bound by the same sins that have always populated the planet. Heaven is still in control, hell still waits, Adam's seed continues to be formed, and the devil waits at their birth to claim them for his fate.

I DREAM AND KNOW THINGS IN ADVANCE—AM I A PROPHET?

Possibly, but remember, prophets are prophets from birth. God deposited their gifts in them from eternity and developed

[Handwritten note at top: I've always noticed difference b/t New testament prophet + seer. Thought both were prophets. Hum? ok? lets explore later]

them over time. What constitutes a bona fide prophet is the prophet's spirit, which will be discussed later. You may, however, be a seer. This can be so if you are an intense prayer warrior, relentless intercessor, or are highly responsive to spiritual matters. Under these circumstances, seers or intercessors can *[handwritten: Hum]* easily be mistaken for prophets when they are not. Psalmists too have been mistakenly declared prophets. In all instances, the common denominator is unusual supernatural interactions, responses, and information. What all three cases lack is the distinct enforcement power and spiritual authority intrinsic to the prophet's mantle.

More than just *seeing and saying*, identifying and combating, or hearing and singing makes one a prophet. The official prophet exceeds all these supernatural manifestations with powerful spiritual latitude. The prophet receives from God, upon completed training, significant license in the spiritual realm. The minister is also given a potent angelic guard that performs his or her words. With these, he or she enjoys a rank in God's kingdom to compel obedience to his or her prophecies over time, unlike the seer.

A seer, compared to the prophet, sees things with his or her inner being (spiritual eyes) beyond the five senses. A seer easily bypasses the natural eyes to accurately detect what is around him or her in the spiritual world. This ability is not limited to time and space. If you are a seer, you may also be a dreamer of dreams, although the two can be exclusive of one another. The dreamer of dreams is similar to a seer except the information received from the spirit world is only received by dreams or in a dreamlike state. Historically this method of revelatory communication has been deemed the most unreliable form of spiritual reception. Prophetic dreams mix too easily with the dreamer's emotions, personality, daily events, and life experiences, and can contaminate the message's purity. However, the dream remains nonetheless a valid tool of prophetic reception used by the Lord from time to time.

In the prophet, all the preceding faculties work together as one, operating either intermittently in an active prophetic environment or randomly in specific prophetic situations. What distinguishes the prophet is the officer's interpretative, translation, and application ability that enhances his predictions and empowers his faculties. Together these render the prophet's word more useful.

Hum? Kresha then is a psalmist
dreamer ~~~~~ who recieves through
of dreams dreams. Maybe even be
a seer.

Chapter Summary

1. Pastors are more confused and curious about the prophetic than resistant.

2. Pastors should use experienced and available prophetic types in their churches.

3. People's questions about the prophetic focus on ten issues.

4. In God's prophetic sphere, prophecy is more than seeing and saying.

5. Many tools are used to equip prophets.

6. Prophetic subject matter spans at least eleven areas.

7. Every member of Christ's body should learn about the prophetic.

8. At least thirty-two terms explain and actualize the prophetic.

9. God's prophets and prophetics require quality knowledge in nine areas and understanding in seven areas.

10. Full prophetic knowledge encompasses at least ten topical areas.

11. Eight reasons were given to say that prophets are for today.

12. Dreaming and knowing things in advance do not, on their own, make you a prophet.

Prophetic Action Items

1. Use the chapter introduction to help a pastor you know trust and embrace God's prophetic move.

2. Develop a ten-point checklist from what you read to screen a church prophet candidate.

3. Use the list of Frequently Asked Questions to help four people unfamiliar with the prophetic to understand it.

4. Use the prophetic subject matter Quick Study Chart to tell a non-prophetic Christian why he or she should still learn about the prophetic.

5. Blend the sections on Important Prophetic Terms, God's Prophets on Prophecies, and Full Prophetic Knowledge to answer the question, "Are Prophets for Today?" Include if dreaming and foreknowledge alone make one a prophet.

Chapter 2

CHURCH PROPHET IMPORTANCE

This chapter concentrates on the importance of the church prophetic. The chapter covers:

- The importance of the modern church prophet
- Why prophets?
- Believe not every spirit
- The antichrist spirit
- Spiritual equipment for prophets
- What makes prophets
- Are prophets for today?
- What is a prophet?
- The features of the Nabi
- How one becomes a prophet (see change instructions)
- Key prophetic distinctives
- The Prophesier's Quick Study Chart
- Why we need prophets when we have the Holy Spirit
- Theological doctrine
- Hidden dangers of self-prophecy
- Why God continues His prophetic institution

The importance of the church prophet in our present times cannot be overstated. Rising occultism, witchcraft, and sorcery create a domain of darkness in every stratum of society. Ignorance of the Creator's prophetics along with the church's resistance to the officer's reinstatement can be blamed. Add to that the church's apostate stance on critical spiritual and moral issues, and you see the conflicting duality. On one hand, these issues clearly set forth God's need for the prophet, and on the other, they answer why and how prophets are shunned and relentlessly persecuted.

Still, the rising tide of demonism, looming greater than ever on the horizons of our last days, means the prophet, as God's level-two power ministry, must be raised up and equipped to confront it. To better understand this, think about the worlds of Elijah and Elisha, two renowned prophets in ancient Israel during the era of the kings. Recall the state of affairs that motivated them and you see why God's only response to earth's deterioration today is prophetic reinstatement.

The light in Israel had virtually been snuffed out by paganism, and God's people no longer knew the real from the false. Their entire spiritual climate was black with demonic forces that had displaced Yahweh's truth and glory in their eyes. It started with Solomon but reached its zenith of destruction through his successor, Jeroboam.

If you remember, Jeroboam, who replaced Solomon as king of Israel, was extremely insecure about his new post as Israel's fourth king. He knew he was not of noble birth and really should not have been considered for kingship. Yet, Jehovah saw fit to install him, which He did by the hand of a prophet. After surveying the situation, Jeroboam imagined unreal threats to his kingdom. Terrified that he would lose his position if Judah continued to serve the very God who put him in power in the first place, he concocted a deadly solution. The account of the story in 1 Kings says his emotional insecurity drove him to rebel against the Lord and hand the kingdom, which Yahweh had caused him to reign over, to devils. His defection, entirely spiritual, was nonetheless deadly. Today we would call it a new religious movement.

Whatever the name, Jeroboam returned God's favor by plunging His treasured nation of Israel into a darkness from which it would never fully recover. In selfish paranoia, he created his own religious system, taking the country right out of Jehovah's hands, and delivering its dominion to the very gods (and demons) the Lord had rescued Israel from in the beginning. Jeremiah 2:11 calls it changing one's god.

Picking up from Solomon's defection, Jeroboam expelled the Levitical priests from the Lord's temple and put in their place those he chose out of his own heart. He installed all *Father!* who showed an interest in the job, thus shifting the order of priestly progression from its Aaronic dynasty to commoners. He further changed Israel's holy day celebrations from what God ordained by Moses to his own. The tragedy of his treason is seen in 2 Chronicles 11:14–15. Instead of ministering to and by the Holy Spirit that preserved and sanctified them, the new demonic priests now taught and promoted worship of devils. Read the account yourself to learn how the world of the prophets under Jeroboam was much like the world today. Repeating cycles of perversion and heathenism masked as New Age revelation solidify the need for the prophet more than anything else.

False teaching, perverted truth, humanism, and worldliness all crowd the consciousness of the twenty-first century church. Mirroring Jeroboam's era, large-scale classes publicize globally the ancient gods, goddesses, religions, and sorcery that history says destroyed every nation that worshipped them. The modern media, financed by the antichrist spirit in the world, crams those very Eastern religions down our throats as they proselytize for darkness.

WHY PROPHETICS?

The prophetic is the only prime choice because the Lord prepared it to stem the tide of demonism stalking our generation. What makes this so are the revelatory teachings of 1 Corinthians 14:32, Ezekiel 13:1-3, and Nehemiah 9:30. Together, these passages unmask a largely discounted reality concerning the prophet's makeup. The distinction sets the official prophet above the *prophesier*. It is the spirit within the prophet—not just the Holy Spirit but the unique prophet's spirit alluded to earlier. The prophet's spirit makes the prophet a prophet, whether or not he or she becomes born again. The Holy Spirit in a person furthers the distinction by establishing whether or not the prophet uses his or her spirit for the kingdom of God under the dominion of Jesus Christ. Otherwise, the capacity to receive prophetic revelations and the ability to prophesy are generic to the prophet's natural birth. See the ministry of Balaam in Numbers 23-31. He was not under Israel's covenant, and yet he was used by God to see with his spiritual eyes what God planned for the nation he was paid to curse. The prophet says that his eyes were finally now wide open. That means that it was in the instant that the prophet came in contact with His Maker that he knew for the first time the visions he saw then were real and those he saw prior to that moment were false.

The differences between the two spheres of operations—saved and unsaved—can be narrowed down to three definite things: spiritual authority, divine license, and enforcement power. If a prophet converts to Jesus Christ, his or her gifts are sanctified and inspired by the entirely new impulses and objectives of God's Holy Spirit. Now, because of the officer's love for the Lord, operating these revelatory gifts serves a higher purpose and targets a quality of life that exceeds the temporal and material, going all the way to the eternal.

BELIEVE NOT EVERY SPIRIT

Humanism scorns any hint of spirituality tied to Jesus Christ or the living God. The official prophet's signs incite powerful, divine intervention. Therefore, they cry out for an equally powerful prophetic treatment. As you may well see from our Jeroboam discussion, the same devils and sorceries are being proliferated today under the guise of spiritual enlightenment, personal empowerment, and independence from religion and the Creator. Many people, unlearned in the Word of the Lord, are seduced into thinking they are finding a better, easier way to God and/or redemption through these devious traps. They are being duped into believing they do not need Him because, as masters of their own destinies or fates, they create their own heaven and hell. These souls fall prey to the most fiendish of all seductions, spiritualism, because they lump all invisible and intangible encounters into one. Being enticed by metaphysical knowledge and psychic enlightenment, they drop their guard and are sucked into serving sin and death. What's more, many of those drawn down the yellow brick road to see the Wizard of Oz are Christians, or at least they claim to be. Such saints, in love with the idea of spirituality, overlook the reality that not every spirit is of God. (See 1 John 4:1.) Poor discernment and still poorer Bible education make them unable to tell whether something spiritual is of Creator God or not. Jesus, however, gave us a clue, and it is that clue that prophets decipher for us, as seen in John 6:45: *"It is written in the prophets, and they shall be all taught of God. Every man therefore that hath heard, and hath learned of the Father, cometh unto me."* Prophets decry the blurring of the lines separating godly and ungodly spiritualism. They reiterate Christ's words in the above verse, reminding us today that it is still all about the Lord Jesus Christ. One thing occultists hate and shudder at is the name of Jesus. That is why Christ distilled the whole of the redemptive strategy down to Himself and faith in His name.

YES AMEN !!

AN ANTICHRIST SPIRIT FUELS DEMONIC FLAMES

Occultism's insidious, renowned elevation in society's mind promotes sin and demonism blatantly through the most coveted icons of our culture. The ghastly and the ghostly have united to clutter the landscape of the invisible world with horrific powers with which mortal humans are not equipped to contend. Ungodly use of the supernatural and perversion of true spiritual power together demonstrate for us God's need for official prophets. The enormous spiritual enablement the Creator instilled in them drives back the hellish onslaught brewing to take hold of the modern world like never before.

To show these statements are not mere panic cries to defend religion and the church, ask yourself how much of what you encounter in your daily life smacks of demons, witchcraft, sorcery, and mysticism. The academic curriculum of public schools is flooded with them, while the truth of the gospel of Jesus Christ is denied equal exposure. Media ad campaigns and programming force ancient religions and pagan rituals on you and your children. The after-school and Saturday-morning cartoons we all once trusted are now agents of this crude and cruel crusade of occultism. And let us not forget the Internet and the technology world. Go surf the Web and see how often the names and teachings of ancient paganism are flaunted. Then you will know how drastic the situation is. The devilish campaign has been so relentless that it overwhelms many people and numbs Christians. Unaccustomed to such exposure to sin, they become so spellbound that they are at a loss for what to do. Some wonder if anything need be done at all.

Truthfully, many people sense something is drastically wrong with all this, but without *pneuma* (spiritual) education and training to enlighten their academics, they just cannot seem to figure out what *is* is. Again, here is where we need God's true prophets to shed light on the devices of darkness and instruct His people on the markers of true and false spirituality.

QUICK STUDY CHART
SPIRITUAL EQUIPMENT FOR PROPHETIC SERVICE

The prophet's work after the new birth in Jesus Christ brings hearers and learners alive due to the prophet's...

1. love for God.
2. commitment to holiness.
3. righteous zeal.
4. apprehension of divine truth.
5. acceptance of humanity's sin condition.
6. realization of the residual sin in the flesh of all believers.

7. understanding of the church's need to mature in God.

8. recognition that all mankind must repent and be saved.

9. allegiance to God.

10. determination to uphold God's truth on earth.

11. fearless rebuke of God's people to warn them of impending danger.

12. giving God's judgment on sin.

13. surrender to a total loss of independence and identity in Christ.

14. compliance with God's wishes—obedience, submission, or surrender.

15. seeking and receiving proper, God-approved training.

16. nurture and training of the flock of God.

17. peculiar human insight for prophetic service.

18. strength and conviction in things of God.

19. defensiveness about Christ and His gospel.

20. protection of God's kingdom and possessions.

21. zealous safeguarding of God's sheep.

22. reverence for God's sovereignty.

23. righteous respect for God's judgments.

24. disregard of worldliness in devotion to God.

25. contempt for worldliness in the body of Christ.

26. constant longing for a heavenly home.

27. aching for the redemption of God's lost sheep.

28. certainty of God's final judgment on man and earth.

29. eagerness to see the end of this age.

30. need for God's continuous fellowship.

31. strong sense of duty.

32. regard for the gravity of official ministry service.

33. knowledge of the scope of responsibility of prophetic office.

34. knowledge of the full impact of the office's demands and influence on self and the world.

35. comprehension of the outcome of prophetic work.

36. relentless hunger for God's presence.

These all sanctify and empower by the *chrio* anointing the basic traits and the character of all prophets irrespective of their salvation in Jesus Christ.

HOW DOES ONE BECOME A PROPHET?

Strictly speaking, one cannot, in the classic sense, *become* a prophet. According to Scripture, primarily Jeremiah 1, people are born prophets from their mothers' wombs. God merely awakens the prophet spirit in everyone called to the ministry. He does this by summoning them through visions and dreams. (See Numbers 12:6.) The idea that a person can just step into and occupy the *office of the prophet,* no matter how much the ministry is desired, is nonbiblical. While it is popular to lead Christians to believe that if they want to prophesy or serve as prophets, all they need to do is to want it badly enough, Scripture says this cannot happen. Prophets must have the spirit for the office. They must be able to receive and interpret divine communications, convey them to those of their era, and fortify their gifts with the license to enforce their words on the stubborn forces that would obstruct their manifestations.

QUICK STUDY CHART

WHAT MAKES PROPHETS TO BE PROPHETS?

Heightened by the salvation process, the following traits are called the natives of the prophet's makeup. They are:

1. **Propensity for visions and dreams**—Dreams of a predictive, revelatory, and highly insightful nature that are hard to forget or dismiss.

2. **Sensitivity to spiritual things**—Ability to pierce the spheres of the flesh and spirit, the visible and invisible layers of creation, to perceive God's truth in action.

3. **Comprehension of prophetic matters**—Grasping the apparently superficial to identify and isolate its divine, supernatural, and apocalyptic roots and/or to surface its predictive and revelatory elements.

4. **Apprehension of role and place of prophecy**—Giving credence to the subtle yet lofty position and imposition of prophecy upon human life and earthly existence.

5. **Awareness of God, most specifically Jesus' testimony, as prophecy**—Understanding that there is a Creator, accepting what happens in the now is the direct result of what He has ordained and inscribed on His handiwork from eternity.

6. **Capacity for revelation discovery**—The ability to pull back the veils of humanism and secularism to uncover the hallowed, holy truths of the Almighty in a given situation.

7. **Peculiar interpretative skills**—Seeing things at face value while instinctively applying the probe of the

Creator's truth to their meanings and outcomes.

8. **Extraordinary wisdom and human insight**—Knowing that the wisdom from above, as James' epistle says, is first pure, then peaceable, and easy to entreat. (See James 3:17.) As such, it is as the only answer to the woes and troubles of the world.

9. **Great sense of practical application**—Not being only a hearer of the Word of God, but also a resolute doer of its work, resolving life's thorny issues with heaven's eternal remedies. (See James 1:23.)

10. **Heightened spiritual discernment**—Recognizing that what is seen with the human eyes and discerned by human senses is merely the tip of the iceberg, beneath which the truth lies as a deeply embedded reality that must be weighed against God's creation laws as officiated by His protocratic government.

11. **Inordinate grasp of Scripture**—Regardless of the sacred writings subscribed to initially., it means to accept that to serve God apart from what is written as His will, programs, and conditions of that service is futile. Plainly, serving the risen Lord is vain without due regard to the written Word of God.

12. **Deep hunger for the knowledge of God**—Exemplifying the need for the Lord as the God of one's ministry and calling, above the need for ministerial expression and fame.

13. **Potential for inspired utterance**—Inexplicably speaking forth truths, wisdom, and maxims that can only spring from a higher source, because they show themselves to be obviously relevant, timely, and accurate in the situations that inspire them.

14. **Remarkable accuracy of divine communication**—A deep-rooted sense of important Creator truths. An unbiased and objective representation of the things of the spirit realm and of God.

15. **Strong literary skill**—An uncanny knack for writing what is discerned from the Spirit of God whether or not it is understood or seen as relevant at the time of its writing.

16. **Impressive elocution and oration ability**—The ability to say fearlessly what must be said on behalf of the Lord clearly, concisely, and persuasively without personal fillers, opinions, or bias, whether the communication is spiritual or practical in origin. This is so despite its evidential or implied power to alter the status quo.

17. **Unusual judicial aptitude**—The peculiar and rare ability to discern the difference between right and wrong on the basis of what Creator God ordained, sanctioned, shunned, and rejected; instinctively knowing how and why the good is more excellent than the evil.

18. **Notable organizational ability**—Apprehension of the reality that God is order, and to rightly represent Him and portray His highly intangible aptitudes, one must be organized and prone to orderliness.

19. **Outstanding leadership ability**—Comprehending the ministry as a position of trust and leadership where sound principles and practices of getting the will of the Lord into followers and performed by them is achieved.

20. **Influential government ability**—The wisdom to enact, legislate, and regulate the conduct, behavior, and

pursuits of the benefited groups without sacrificing the Lord's best interests.

If you are going to be a church prophet, or a prophet of any type for the Lord Jesus Christ, you should be naturally exhibiting the twenty traits described above. That is, they should not have to be instilled in you, but rather be refined through your prophetic education and service.

Why do you think the first thirty-six points and the last twenty points given are important to a prophet's ministry? When you consider your answers, review the lists again, and think about the problems or issues they address. Consider how the listed traits and characteristics translate to prophetic action that begets God's solutions. If you can see the practicality of the two, you are well on your way to understanding the prophetic and the ministry of the official prophet. These traits are covered more fully in chapter 13.

ARE PROPHETS REALLY FOR TODAY?

As we stated previously, prophets are for today as much as ever. As long as God, the devil, and man all stay the same, the need for the prophet continues. Revelation 11 says they will continue until the end of this age. These three and the world are all interrelated, and prophets and the prophetic law are how each one contacts and conveys information to and through one another. It does not matter how modern we appear; closer scrutiny shows we have not progressed that far after all. We have noticed how technology names its work after the same demons the Lord has fought with since antiquity. When you purchase many computer programs, not to mention computer games, you are met with the names of ancient demons in the guise of their mythological images. Beyond this, the Internet floods us with ungodly figures and practices, reviving them for a new round of age-old wizardry. In fact, the word *wizard* appears in nearly every computer program as if to compel us to embrace them in our society. For these reasons, God still needs prophets, especially since they balance the effects of psychics presently dominating their place on the supernatural front.

WHAT IS A PROPHET?

A prophet is a divine messenger of God (or any god). He or she is an official spokesperson for the deity served on earth. A prophet invokes the will, destiny, plans, and powers of God to manifest the spiritual and the supernatural in our world. Although prophets do this mainly by speaking, sometimes they resort to drama, theatrics, song, or other demonstrative modes to depict and otherwise manifest the word of the Lord—their sole revelatory objective.

According to *Strong's Concordance,* the Greek word for prophet is *prophetes,* the word most accepted by the New Testament church. However, in concept it falls short of the ancient origins of the prophetic in its usage and applications because the Greeks saw the prophetic predominantly in oracular contexts. By the time they controlled the world, religious and therefore spiritual extremes were being pushed to the background. Therefore, they stressed mostly the prophesying rather than the performance and provocative work of the ministry. Most of the definitions we use today to explain the prophetic come from their limitation of the office and its officers to this narrow field of revelatory activity.

The era of the Hebrews, on the other hand, had a fuller connotation of the prophetic as conveyed in their meanings of the word. Their term shows an expansive understanding of the mantle in all its contexts. Their word is *nabi*. Unlike the Greek perception of the prophetic, the Hebrews, who derived their use of the minister from the ancients who preceded them, saw the prophet as much more than a simple *predictor*. For them, the ministry had a power-wielding influence that affected destiny and dramatically impacted the world around them. The *nabi* can be traced throughout history, its functions documented as far back as man, religion, and God are recorded, after the Edenic transgression. The Israelites drew from these ancient models to operate their prophetic ministry under Jehovah God.

THE DISTINCTIVE FEATURES OF THE NABI

The confusion over what makes a prophet, and what signifies one as a vessel of prophecy, or prophesier, is understandable. When one is strictly guided by the definition of a prophet most commonly given, confusion cannot help but engender deeper confusion. If one defines the prophetic exclusively by giving the word of the Lord, then anyone who says, "Thus says the Lord," or "the Lord told me," may be a prophet. But when one takes into account the *prophetes-nabi* definitions, other important factors must be taken into account, such as, does the prophet invoke the gods? Is the necessary covenant that God ordinarily binds Himself to at work? Does the prophesier exhibit the signs and executions of an official? These questions help you see that much is needed by one who would declare himself or herself to be a prophet. The Quick Study Chart below gives a few more necessary points to consider when making the decision.

KEY PROPHETIC DISTINCTIONS

The *nabi* is expressly accepted as a divine agent of the supernatural world. The messenger's power is inherent in the spirit and flesh. The *nabi*, not unlike the *prophetes*, is *the* spokesperson for a deity—and so much more. This officer is also a teacher, predictor, and visionary who interprets dreams and visions, peers into the supernatural, and compels its invisible powers to perform and manifest themselves in the now. The *nabi* actuates spiritual powers to set in motion the events that take place in our world. (See Daniel 1-4; Zechariah 3; Amos 3:7.) All these actions are in addition to the prophecies many of our churches today are accustomed to receiving from modern prophets.

The definitions of both the *prophetes* and the *nabi* include "one who stands in the *restricted* office of the prophet." That means one cannot arbitrarily decide to become a prophet no matter how much he or she mimics the mantle's operations. However, *nabi's* meaning adds noteworthy dimensions that better instruct us on the ubiquitous range of the prophet's power and authority. Its meaning includes, from ancient texts, "one who invokes the gods." Hence, when Yahweh told Moses his mouth would be as God to Aaron, and Aaron would function as Moses' prophet—mouthpiece—to the people, both men fully perceived what He meant. (See Exodus 4:15-16.)

This says to us that if the prophet, local church or not, is without a deity who vows to perform the prophet's words, the title of prophet is invalid. The official title is how prophets accomplish what they do. The ancients understood this about the prophet sufficiently enough to include in their definition of the officer the power to "invoke, summon, and marshal the powers and resources of the gods." In our case, that would be the God of gods. The prophet, like any other authorized priest, does this by invoking the name of the god. The prophetic dimension differs in its sphere of enforcement.

Based on this information, we, as Christians who are the New Creation priesthood of the Lord Jesus Christ, invoke His omnipotence and authority by using His name and doing all that we do in His name. (See John 14:14; Colossians 3:17.) ✱ *Using His Name invokes His power* ✱

QUICK STUDY CHART

SUMMARY OF PROPHET AND PROPHESIER CHARACTERISTICS

THE PROPHESIER

The most common question of all is that of the difference between the prophesier—the one who utters prophecy—and the one who stands in the official stead of the prophet.

- The difference is the same as that between the official evangelist and the one who witnesses Jesus or shares the message of the gospel.

✓ Prophetic vessels are confined to the Holy Spirit's manifestations as spelled out in 1 Corinthians 12:3–11, while the prophet is not.

✓ Prophets are considered by God to be *officers* of His kingdom. That means they are *commissioned* by God and *delegated authority* that transcends the mere verbalization of a message.

- The vessel of prophecy is largely confined to prophesying and the spontaneous unction of the Holy Spirit.

THE OFFICE

The prophet as an officer, in contrast to the vessel of prophecy, is one who actually exercises all the functions and activities of the office with minimal divine restraint. He employs broad discretionary latitude.

- The immediate factor that sets one apart from the other is the presence of the prophet's spirit, discussed elsewhere.

- The prophet's spirit empowers and enables the prophet as an officer to move in and out of God's supernatural realms and territories almost at will, upon His release.

- The power and authority a prophet walks in and exercises are akin to that employed by the Lord's angels.

- Prophets have, based on the above, invocative, actuative, and demonstrative authority and power.

- Another major difference between the two is that the prophet also has enforcement power with that authority to provoke the performance of his other words in the earth. This is due in part to the supernatural contingent of angels assigned to the ministry.

MIMICKING THE PROPHET

Unfortunately, many people want to be prophets so badly that they intrude into the office's spheres with no capacity, aptitude, or resource for it. What happens in these cases is that they operate on their gifts rather than their New Creation spirits. This makes them susceptible to divining devils looking to give voice to their wills and actions in the earth through the power of a born-again soul. Unintentionally, and often unknowingly, these people become vessels of divination.

Since the deity performing their words is not the Lord Most High, such prophets become adept at divining from devils and thus operate more as psychics than prophets. Recall Balaam's words when he finally met the Almighty. He recognized a definite difference in his prophetic abilities. (See Numbers 24:15–16.) While he was operating his prophetics, he did so by the power of whatever divine spirit happened to be in his vicinity. While Balaam did not know the difference before the Almighty's enhancements, he surely discovered the distinction once the real God put a word in his mouth.

Generally speaking, the only one who can really identify and articulate that something is wrong with such prophetics is another New Creation prophet. This is according to the tenor of 1 Corinthians 14:29. Others may sense that something is wrong, but they are often unable to detect or express where the problem lies. It takes another professional prophet who can tell precisely how or why a prophetic operation he witnesses is wrong. Many prophets can only do so with sound, reputable prophetic training and education.

HOW PROPHECY SETS THINGS IN MOTION

Birthing spiritual products is a direct result of the word of the Lord in a person, agent, or force. God's auto-verbal acts and their processes are what the Creator calls prophetic. *Auto-verbal* means, in this case, that which is set in motion by a spoken word, to act by an embedded sign and power. When God, who is eternal, and thus outside of time, speaks to the world locked in time, that by definition is prophecy. Such speaking is what the Father calls *prophetic* because the message originates outside of the world's time zones (from eternity) and finds its chronology in humanity. Its events, once they leave the Lord's mouth, are encoded in creation's calendars, and reflect God's scheduled myriad of earthly events. By this means is prophecy set in motion in its appointed times and seasons. Review Solomon's words in Ecclesiastes 3:1–11 for biblical amplification.

Prophecy is set in time by way of the human medium who utters it. That medium may be a prophet, prophetic vessel, prayer warrior, intercessor, psalmist, or seer. While angels sometimes do this, prophecy still has to be empowered on earth through the utterance of the human voice. By their utterances, prophets activate their words' implantation in the life or sphere of life of the hearer. Here is what God means by Isaiah 41:4 regarding the generations.

WHY DO WE NEED PROPHETS WHEN WE HAVE THE HOLY SPIRIT?

Over the years, a misunderstanding of the scope of prophetic work has led many shortsighted Bible teachers to declare that the dwelling of the Holy Spirit in a life eliminates the need for the prophet—the official prophet, that is. Many have contended that the presence of the Holy Spirit within makes everyone who is saved his or her own prophet. Others add that the operation of the gifts of God as specified in 1 Corinthians 12:3–11 more than establishes the church's independence from the prophet as integral to fundamental New Testament ministry. Nonetheless, they are emphatically named in Ephesians 4:11 and 1 Corinthians 12:28–29.

Practically speaking, even though we have the Holy Spirit, people often cannot hear God clearly enough or frequently enough for themselves. Moreover, those who do hear God frequently find they misunderstand what the Lord is actually saying. How many times have you received a spiritual message that you could neither explain nor interpret? This is because God's language is different from our own.

The Lord's word and will are not obliged to our culture or its mores because His speech has otherworldly purposes in mind. Aside from His being Creator and the author of all language, God is Spirit; we are flesh. His being and world are of an order and complexity completely different from our world. God as Spirit means He is invisible and we cannot see Him. He must speak to us from His tangible media. His celestial nature means that when He does speak, it is without concrete means of substantiating His sounds and their meanings, or of sensitizing His words for our reception and interpretation. For these reasons, and due to prophetic inexperience, people invariably misunderstand what the Lord says to them. Their human filters, passions, and mentality, being conformed to this world, translate His meanings and intents to their personal advantage. It becomes easier to do this when they have little or no biblical knowledge and only devotional expertise with God's Holy Spirit. Think about the time that Jesus spoke to His Father and God answered Him in John 12:28–29. Some people heard the sound as words; others heard it as thunder. That is how it is today. For other examples, read John 8:41–43 and Hebrews 12:19–20.

In the passage from John 8, Jesus spoke to the religious leaders, presumably in their own language, yet the content of what He said completely escaped their spiritual understanding. This is similar to Yahweh's Sinai experience with His newly founded nation as retold in Hebrews 12:18–24.

In the Hebrews reference, the entire account is interpreted by the Holy Spirit from God's perspective. It seems the strictness of the Lord's word on the hearers back then was more than they could bear. The rigidity of God's word would not bend for what they perceived as unjust punishment on an animal thought too ignorant to stay out of harm's way. To those who looked on, an animal's death on account of infringing upon the Lord's holiness was nothing but Jehovah slaying an innocent victim. That it would die without knowing why was too harsh for the people to accept, so they begged Moses not to make them hear the Lord firsthand anymore. These examples point out the reasons why the prophet is needed in the local church, and how those who inquire of God should do so through them. People lack God's lofty righteousness, which Psalm 71:19 says is very high. Unless someone of understanding and wisdom brings it down to the earth realm's understanding, there is no way for people to grasp or regard it. When people cannot lay hold of the Lord's truth, there is less hope of their obeying what they hear from Him, or at least performing their obediences the way He intended.

Look at how differently you hear and understand information from how the Lord does. I once said to a group of people whom I was teaching that we can take years or decades to comprehend one complete thought from God. To make my point, I gave an example.

The Lord can start in January, delivering a word He needs us to follow by a certain time. Because of how humans interpret spiritual language, which is from the earth up instead of God's way, from heaven down, it could take a while. He will probably have to wait a year or more for us to understand what He said and the way He meant it. Take the following as a case in point. In January we pray and hear the Lord say, "Go." Our immediate response is to figure out what He meant. Did He mean go to the store, to the mission field, to the church?

What? After struggling on our own for a while, we finally settle down to get the rest of the message. We eventually return to the Lord to ask, "Where?"

Remember now, several weeks may have gone by. The next word comes: "Go to the place." Ah! We now have more information to go on, but there is still a final piece missing. You think, *Why won't the Lord just say what He means and get it over with? Why does He put you through these games?* Again, a few weeks of personal probing goes by, and then you decide you can go back to the subject with the Lord again.

At last He gets the entire sentence out: "Go to the church on the corner." You are stunned. *The church on the corner?* you wonder. *What church?* Now you are playing games because you know that there is only one church on the corner, and it is the little storefront one you would not be caught dead in. *God knows my heart,* you think. *Oh, I must have mistaken what He said. He could not possibly ask me to sink down to that level.* You inwardly regret pressing the point and wish you had not heard what He said. Since no one else heard Him but you, you begin the most dangerous of all prophetic games. You begin to twist the word you heard to cause it to say something you can live with. *Who is to know the truth anyway?* you rationalize. Three months have gone by, and you pressed the Lord into an answer you now do not like. Silently, you determine not to do it and put the entire matter behind you. What's next? Judgment.

God must send you through an assortment of excruciating, pride-breaking lessons for you to obey Him. He knew all along that you would react this way, but now that it is out in the open, He is forced to correct this flaw in your character and end your flagrant disobedience. It gets hard, and after years, what should have been a twenty-second inquiry and response has turned into a terrible test of wills, yours against the Lord's. Years go by, and you miss the blessing He had buried for you in that little, unattractive, no-name church. Still, the stronghold over your soul must now be broken. Could the prophet have made a difference?

Although you may not have listened to the prophet, the matter could have been greatly expedited by your hearing the entire command the first time. Perhaps you would have shaved three to six months off the search time and maybe been persuaded to obey in time to reap the reward of obedience the Lord had for you in the place you secretly despised before the window of opportunity closed. Prophets grasp God's thoughts and intents more quickly than others do. They are attuned to His way of communicating because that is how He constructed them, and over the years their training conditioned them to think His thoughts His way and not according to their own. Grasping, processing, and acting in Christ's mind comes more natural to prophets. That prophet's spirit we spoke of connects to God's consciousness and adapts to His communication style more readily than most. Let's look at some of the differences between how the Lord thinks and speaks and how we do, and how to discern the distinct differences the prophet makes. Review the Quick Study Chart below for a deeper appreciation of the difference.

QUICK STUDY CHART

GOD'S THOUGHTS THROUGH PROPHETS

If you are in a school, class, or prophetic study group, spend time discussing the statements here and explaining how they are important to what the Lord needs from the prophets in general, and those He sets in the church.

The prophet learns early that:

- God thinks in whole thoughts. We think in fragments.
- God says what He means in one statement. We often find it difficult to digest His statements all at once. It takes, in comparison, strings of statements to make our point. For Him, it's as fast as lightning.
- We understand the Lord and His style of communication bit by bit. God knows our thoughts and intents before the foundation of the world.
- God thinks and operates omni-creationally. We are primarily limited to His earthly wisdom.
- God approaches His handling of the earth from heaven down. We, on the other hand, process what He says and does from the earth up.

See Isaiah 55:8–11; Hebrews 4:12, 5:12–14; and Jeremiah 10:23 as a study session to see the difference between the two modes of thought—God's and ours.

Prophets are trained to help people grasp what God is thinking, saying, and willing for their lives from His perspective. Even with the Holy Spirit within us, our busy lives, difficulties, and crises can all cause us to misunderstand God at different times. It is then that we need God's prophets to inject His objectivity into our dilemmas. Prophets compel us to face the truth about ourselves, our motives, and our personal agendas. They make us, whether we admit it publicly or not, recognize when we are imposing our will on God to have our way. Prophecy makes it hard for us to explain away our manipulations under a religious veneer.

The Lord is pursuing a predefined outcome and a particular end product from His creation, and with His subsequent dealings with the human race. That is why He has offices and ministries. It is also why He has subdivided ministries. (See Psalm 103:19–21; Romans 8:38; Ephesians 3:10; Colossians 1:16; 2:15.)

A final thought on this subject is the two spheres of hearing God that set the prophet apart from the devotee. The prophet is trained by God to be His communication agent—a liaison. Being members of His high governmental staff, prophets speak as divine officials and not merely as transmitters or communication terminals. Prophets speak as public officials charged with upholding the Lord's statutes and legislations, assuring that His righteousness and truth are preserved and perpetuated, and that His encrypted word throughout creation is fulfilled. Prophesiers and Holy Spirit manifestation vessels are not privy to such high information. They are also not authorized to process it sufficiently enough to yield or enforce their words' activation or incarnation in the flesh. Moreover, the prophesier is not trained to overrun demonic occupation nor collaborate with angelic hosts. Lastly, for prophesiers to invoke the Lord's (actually angels') powers that are essential to prophetic success is difficult. Their license from God usually does not involve mobilizing the spiritual powers needed to perform God's will. They are usually not released to obey the prophet's voice.

When it comes down to it, prophesiers have neither spent time nor been granted the privilege of acquiring and perfecting such skills, so they lack the capacity to do more than voice what they see and hear form the Spirit. Expertise is what true prophets brings to their official occupation—expertise gained from trials, tribulations, extensive study, and frequent, sometimes harsh, correction by the Lord's Spirit.

THEOLOGICAL DOCTRINE NEEDS WISDOM'S PRUDENCE

As long as theology and doctrine separate themselves from human necessity and life application, wisdom will usually be lacking in the church's ministry applications. However, that is not the case with God. His Word and His requirements are not merely intellectual in object, although they are quite intelligent. God is pursuing a definite aim in our lives with His Word: that of His work, holiness, righteousness, and eternal qualification of the redeemed for everlasting life. For every principle, precept, function, and activity detailed in the Bible, there is a corresponding human condition, attitude, conduct, or belief that inspired it. Prophets easily grasp this truth. It substantiates their calling and defines their jobs. That is how they can tell you why the Lord called them and empowered their mantles. Prophetics are God's way of getting His word into society, and His will to work in its cultures. Depending upon their generations and the eras in which their words are assigned, prophecies are ignited by the mouths of God's prophets. Their ministries actuate and craft the prophetic words God implanted in creation for their times. (See 2 Chronicles 36:22–23.)

Remember, this pattern of the Lord goes back to eternity, as we have shown. Prophetics are how God brought His Son Jesus onto the planet. To underscore a New Testament place of beginning, it began with the angel Gabriel's word to Zechariah announcing the birth of John the Baptist. Six months later it repeated itself with Mary, who was also visited by the angel Gabriel. Both events were occasioned by the Lord's use of prophecy to fulfill the string of cryptic predictions that brought the promised Messiah into the world.

Centuries of prophetic words brought the Savior to earth. His conception was the culmination of God's constant stream of encoded, inflexible prophecies from the mouths of His servants. Their words shaped the events and birthed the people who eventually brought Jesus to planet earth.

Today, the church scarcely dares to think that Jesus arrived on the earth by the invisible vehicle of continuous prophecy spoken by the prophets over thousands of years. For prophets, this becomes crucial and validating information. It underscores their use by God. To respect and have faith in prophecy, you need to begin to think of it as more than sounds from highly spiritual people. You have to see with your spiritual eyes the teams of angels and the hosts of supernatural resources that go into action at the moment the words "Thus says the Lord" are declared by the Savior's legitimized prophet. *← confirmation*

At the beginning of the prophetic process, it seems the words are not going to happen, but if the messengers are true prophets of God with the prophet's spirit, then rest assured that the word will come to pass. In prophetic language, that says their words will *manifest* in their physical state in our world at the appointed time. What occurs behind the scenes of this world are the early stages of prophecy—its manifestation development. Prophets' words initially act as blueprints in gathering resources and agency activators that set the stage for the gestating process that births the message's physical form. An elaborate network of episodes and procedures go into action when a genuine prophetic word leaves God's mouth. Isaiah 55:9–11, referenced earlier, gives some insight into the chain reactions the Lord's word ignites to give earthly life to His prophecies. Study it and, with your study group, discuss how this looks, and may be recognized or acknowledged, in today's world.

SITUATIONS AND CIRCUMSTANCES THAT BRING US GOD'S PROPHETS

When the season for something the Lord has inscribed upon the tablets of creation arrives, heavenly blueprints begin to act in their earthly embedded codes. To understand this, think back to His engraving the Ten Commandments on stone. Those ten sayings had always been how the Lord governed human conduct on earth. They were just never legislated until He carved them in stone for Moses. The time had come for humanity to become acquainted with, and affected by, God's unseen creation governance. This principle holds true today.

It is at these times when God sends us another prophet or prophetic word. His aim is to transmit to us by supernatural means His words and will to kindle our faith enough to cooperate with His ordained circumstances. Sometimes they introduce what God is doing or will do. At other times they confirm what He has been telling us all along. Here is another reason why we need prophets. To be sure that we have heard from God, He sends us prophets to reiterate what He has been saying in our spirits. The prophets decode God's spiritual language and articulate it aloud for human comprehension. This is especially true when the matter is important to destiny and the divine will of our Lord. It does not matter if the word is positive or negative in our eyes; if it comes from the Lord, that makes it prophecy. Whether or not it is good *to* us, in God's mind and based on His pre-designed actions, it is good *for* us.

HIDDEN DANGERS IN SELF-PROPHECY

Since most people do not like to confront or hear the truth, many of them avoid it any way they can. This character trait means that with or without the Holy Spirit, they will certainly not be inclined to prophesy truth to themselves. When they inquire of God regarding a dire matter or something they really feel they must have, the principle of Ezekiel 14:14 will most likely kick in to skew what they claim to hear to their advantage. In urgent times or in moments of great need or desire, the conflict of interests becomes so great that their customarily sound discernment can fail as the drive to have their way overrides all else. If such people are honest with themselves and the Lord, they will admit their vulnerable state and seek God's answer from credible prophets. If their church has a properly functioning prophet institution, they can turn to such a group for quality guidance and accurate prophecy. That is why God needs prophets overall, and in His church particularly.

Prophets are a rare species when they are yielded to God. Because they can take God's truth for themselves, no matter how hard it is, they find it easy to administer that truth to others. Truly the law of "first partaker" is well ingrained in them prior to public service. The prophet is compelled by God to use this practice to ensure the prophecies' prime objective is always to minister to and for Him in truth.

WHY DOES GOD CONTINUE HIS PROPHETIC INSTITUTION?

Because we will spend eternity with the Most High God, we must learn all we can about how He does things in His world. While the need for prophecy may be altered in the future, its functional concepts go on, based on the rewards the Lord promised to those of the church who endure to the end. When you think about the Pergamos church (see Revelation 2:17), for instance, the eternal stone promised to those who overcome is symbolic of a revelation instrument. It equates to the Old Testament Urim and Thummim of the Levitical priesthood. In other words, that stone etched with the new name of the bearer designates who the bearer is in Christ's new kingdom, how he is to serve, and how he receives his instruction and insights from the Lord. Remember, we said earlier that prophecy is the communications medium of the spirit world. It is how its citizens pass thoughts, activities, plans, and the will of God to one another, between themselves, and to us. God's eternal protocol, being fixed in eternity, binds the earth to the same parameters for information exchanges between the two worlds. God will always retain the right to speak to His people. Actually, it is as much His duty as it is His right. He cannot change, and so throughout eternity He will, from time to time, utter things not everyone in earshot or in His realm can hear or comprehend. In short, not all of His mystique will fade just because we enter His world. Hence, some equivalent of prophecy will continue, as omniscience will not be granted to all citizens.

GETTING BACK TO OUR ETERNAL ROOTS

In anticipation of their eternal destiny and destination, the people of this world have to return to their Creator-endowed spiritual roots of communicating. Spiritual communication relies on more than the six senses. When one realizes that five of the six senses depend on the flesh and the sixth one is confined to the soul realm, it is easy to see how and why mankind was shut out of spiritual knowledge. It is also understood why the extent of the ethereal information we receive is limited to the *psuche* (psychic) realm of human existence. What is lacking in our reconnection to the Creator is a medium of *pneumatic* (spiritual) communication. Transmissions from the

Spirit of God to the spirit of man are outside the customary means imposed on us for receiving supernatural knowledge. This helps explain how witchcraft, sorcery, and demonology in general are, according to God, mere works of the flesh. (See Galatians 5:19.)

Since six is the number of man, and the five senses serve the body, that leaves only one sense to serve our immortal soul and nothing to expedite God's spiritual exchanges. That is, nothing exists until Jesus Christ's salvation reveals our spirits and obliterates the wall of partition that separates and veils the soul from the spirit. For these reasons, what mortals deem as supernatural is still light-years away from the Creator. The sixth sense and the flesh have more to do with the soul realm than the spirit, requiring humans to access another sphere to interact with God Almighty. The justification for this comes from Isaiah 26:9, where the Lord, through His prophet, identifies the difference between the activities of the soul and the spirit. The spirit is how one seeks and worships the Lord. Jesus confirms it in John 4:23–24. When it comes to the occult, since its practices are all products of the soul realm and the earth, theirs are works of the flesh. Furthermore, both passages give insights on how their powers came to be designated as fleshly works, despite their masquerading as spirituality. You only need to reread Revelation 12:12–13 to see the picture.

As much as the devil's clan wants you to believe that he is the height of spiritual power, in reality that is what he lost when he was cast out of heaven. He and his devils were left with only earthly power, such as that conferred on Adam until he lost the contest in Eden. Here is what the Lord Jesus meant when He said He saw Satan fall as lightning from heaven. (See Luke 10:18.) Satan fell from his celestial station into the spheres of the terrestrial, and terrestrial means earthly, worldly, and physical. To match Isaiah's description of true God contact, one must draw on the spirit. Any spiritual connection is provided by the most High God, according to John 1:11–12 and 3:5–8. Safe and secure eternal connections can only be made when one is born again. Distinctively, this means born from God alone. (Study John 5:24.) Apart from this Creator-provided method, all supernatural interactions remain soulish and fleshly.

HUMANS' SEVENTH SENSE

The New Testament, on the other hand, gives us a better analogy. It talks about the hidden man of the heart and the spirit man, and mentions the abolition of the wall of partition between them that the Savior accomplished for us on the cross. This means that the divider between the soul and spirit (see Hebrews 4:12) that veiled the latter from the former was disintegrated by the work of the cross. At least its legitimacy and necessity were disintegrated. All people must accept Christ and be born again to make it a reality for themselves. However, Christ's death allowed something to happen that had not been possible since Adam's fall: the communication and information exchange between both intangible parts of humanity's makeup—the soul and the spirit. Because of the work the Lord did on the cross, the spirit can now communicate to the soul and vice versa. Pure streams are possible, whereas before Christ, they were neutralized due to the eternal risks involved.

The name for the spirit's role in the supernatural affairs of the human life is "seventh sense." It speaks to spiritual knowledge and intelligence. What makes this true is that seven is the number of the spirit—God's spirit world—while six is the number of man and Satan. Better yet, it is the number of humanity's fusion with Satan via the fallen soul. (See Revelation 3:18; 1:4; 4:5; 5:6.) These show the difference between the sixth (soul's) sense and seventh (New Creation) spirit, and how they relate to people's supernatural faculties. Prophets are obliged to be cognizant of this truth to discern when an utterance originates from the Lord God or from one of His fallen creatures. The ability to do so is vital to revealing the dark side of the human heart, as Ezekiel 13:1–3 and 1 Corinthians 14:25 share.

What makes this knowledge relevant to prophets' validity is the reason they are seen as important to society and to the church. The prophets' importance to the world stems from the human inability to hear from and comprehend the communications of the spirit realm. God compensated for the barrier separating the soul from the spirit in most of humanity by endowing a select class of people with the ability to pierce the veil that blinds us to His world. In doing so, He permits their access to eternity's information streams. Essentially, this is why people need prophets.

In the church the prophets' value may not appear evident until one considers how biased humans typically are to our own views, feelings, desires, and pursuits. The institution of the prophetic counters this by conferring objectivity on the members of Christ's body so they get God's unbiased position on their circumstances and matters. Through His reliable prophets, the Lord impels truthful responses to our inquiries regardless of what we feel or desire, because He knows that the desire for our best is naturally seated in the soul realm. Salvation installed the Lord's Spirit of truth in you so the soul can finally tap into it to access the Almighty's life and wisdom. When the two, the spirit and soul, actively communicate and exchange information, the answers we receive from the Lord are accurate.

Ethical prophets force us to hear the word of the Lord on a matter, and if we are honest, to know and accept what we have heard as being from God. They bring you to the Christ of John 6:44–45, whose testimony is the Spirit of prophecy.

CHAPTER SUMMARY

1. Occultism is a major reason why the Lord needs the prophetic.

2. The spiritual realm is occupied and handled by many, many different types of spirit.

3. Fallen spirits that rival the Almighty are fueled by the Antichrist.

4. The prophetic is what the Lord uses to stem the tide of demonism stalking our generation.

5. Thirty-six spiritual qualities equip prophets to do what they do.

6. In addition to their thirty-six spiritual equipment qualities, prophets possess twenty distinct attributes for their service.

7. Prophets are for today because God, mankind, and Satan all stay the same; thus, the need for prophets continues.

8. A prophet is God's divine messenger who is defined by the two Bible words *nabi* and *prohetes*.

9. People cannot really *become* prophets.

10. Prophesiers are endowed differently from official prophets.

11. Holy Spirit-filled Christians also need prophets.

12. Self-prophesying is dangerous.

PROPHETIC ACTION ITEMS

1. Use the chapter's opening statements to outline a persuasive discussion that exposes the antichrist spirit

that rivals Christ's spirituality and explains why His prophetics are the only effective answer to it.

2. Illustrate a genuine prophet for those unexposed to the prophetics and those aspiring to enter it by profiling the minister using the two charts: Spiritual Equipment and What Makes a Prophet.

3. Build on task #2 by describing how one becomes a prophet.

4. Prepare a five-point rationale for why even Spirit-filled Christians need prophets.

5. Use the chapter summary discussion to depict what can be recognized as self-prophecy, its dangers, and its conflict with God's truth.

Chapter 3

A History of the Prophetic

In this chapter, you will read about:

- Mankind's relation to spirituality and earth's need for the supernatural
- Eternity's protocrats and their role in the prophetic
- God's seven protocratic spheres
- God's use of prophets' faculties
- The spectrum of the prophet's word
- The prophet's mantle
- What a miracle is and does
- Prophetic imagery and symbolism

Earth's Continued Need for Heavenly Assigned Spiritual Powers

Little has changed in mankind's relation to spirituality since time began. The earth still needs supernatural agents and human representatives to spiritually inspire its conduct. (See Job 32:8; Isaiah 11:1–5; Ephesians 1:17.) Prophets intermediate earth's transactions with God's spiritual citizenry. Sin, sickness, disease, error, lies, lewdness, and unbelief, as well as death and darkness, are all standing reasons for prophets' work in the world and protection in the local church.

The world's historical chronicles all cite primitive cultures' beliefs in an invisible force of powers backing the physical creation. In ancient times, it was accepted that they controlled all its activities and events. Exodus 23:23, Exodus 32:34, Joshua 5:13, Daniel 10:21, and Revelation 22:16 all show the truth of that belief. I have dubbed this force God's *supernatural protocratics*. As His spiritual powers of eternity, they see to the provisions He allocated to the earth. The apocalypse of Jesus Christ penned by the apostle John unveils them for us under the New Testament dispensation. In the Old Testament, many books did so, but none more poignantly than the writings of the prophets Daniel and Zechariah. Collectively, all biblical writings show us that what the ancient people believed was true according to the Creator. Angels were watching over them and taking care of their human matters.

Actually, it would make good sense on God's part to do so since He knew that humanity would be confined in their world primarily to what their five senses could touch. God knew Adam's fall meant that much of what He had created would be unknown and inaccessible to men. So, He answered the problem with prophets acting on eternity's behalf and in Christ's stead on earth to compensate for humanity's lost spiritual roots. The Lord enabled prophets' invisible selves to lead their world to discover that they were not alone on earth. His aim was to get people to perceive that all earthly events were the direct result of the supernatural initiatives of His powerful, invisible creatures. Hence, the principalities and powers in heavenly places spoken of by the apostle Paul in Ephesians 6.

To serve effectively as a prophet in this and the coming age of mankind, one must be educated in these truths, a requirement the prophets of Samuel and Elijah's day accepted. If the names and ministries of these Bible figures are unfamiliar to you, it is because you are not scripturally literate enough. As a prophet or prophesier, you should be knowledgeable of the historic roots of the prophetic to justify its need in today's and future generations. To appreciate prophets' present worth, you must relate it to their original value to God and people. Doing so implants Bible prophets' importance in the mind of the Lord's church.

The need for prophets is endorsed by the apostle Paul's revelation of God's invisible principalities and powers. These are the spiritual protocrats we spoke of earlier. Their presence tells God's apostles and prophets, the two most powerful officers of the New Testament church according to 1 Corinthians 12:28–29 and Ephesians 4:11, that they are not alone. These two officers are not only part of an elaborate earthly regime, but they are also supported by complicated and infinitely more powerful heavenly beings. Titus 3:1 says we are to obey them as well as those we see in the flesh. What are they? They were known of old as the seven *archons* of creation to the ancient world. You will learn from this section that they are suggestive of the seven angels of the New Creation *ekklesia*.

The apocryphal book of Enoch discusses eternity's supernatural *archons* in great detail, and until John's Apocalypse, they were scarcely uncovered in Scripture—but they are there. Zechariah's prophecy mentions them almost casually as the "seven-eyed priestly stone of the high priest Joshua." What subtle metaphors of the Lord Jesus and His church! Revelation 5:17 resurfaces those seven eyes, but this time they are on the seven horns of the Lamb and are defined as the seven spirits of God that are sent forth into all the earth. But how are we to know them as antiquity's *archons*? The answer is mostly by what they do. These are the powers that amazingly coincide with the seven churches of the Lord Jesus Christ discussed in Scripture—those seven spirits the Revelation tells us that eventually blanketed the earth, which ended up being divided into seven continents.

THE IMPORTANCE OF THE NUMBER SEVEN

Seven is an important number in Scripture; it is applied nearly five hundred times. In most of those cases, seven is used in religious, prophetic, and apocalyptic contexts. That makes it quite important to the Lord in setting time, in limiting events, and in other significant Creator ordinances. Beyond this is the obvious—there are seven days per week, and the seventh day is doubly important, being the Sabbath. Now this is biblical genre we are talking about, not occultic. God decreed the number as the unit of completion, thoroughness, and spiritual dominance. Among these is the most profound of all, those seven spirits before God's throne. However, what they do or how they govern may not make sense to you. The following is a list of what those seven powers oversee as first eternity's seven *archons* and today the seven angels of the New Creation *ekklesia*. Their names and areas of effect are followed by a brief description. Bear in mind as you read them that no society or culture on earth exists without every one of them functioning, no matter the names by which they may be called. I call them the seven spheres of creation over which God's spiritual protocrats rule.

QUICK STUDY CHART
GOD'S SEVEN PROTOCRATIC SPHERES

- Worship and ritual
- Family and community
- Business and commerce
- Mammon: money and economy
- Government and administration
- Military and warfare
- Education and communication

No matter where one goes on the planet, or in what society one sojourns, he or she will find that these seven spheres of human life prevail. Here is a brief explanation of each one.

1. **Worship and ritual**—The worship and ritual system ordained by a deity. This is based on the character, functions, abilities, and authorities of the spirit worshipped, and coincide with the ways the deity or spiritual power was designed to access or employ God's supernatural resources. Unwritten protocols establish that worship and religious observance are the only ways for humans to access God's higher powers and their resources. These are crafted and imposed upon the citizens of our world by the spirits that govern them or their territory. Under the New Creation church dispensation, Melchizedek, the priest who met Abram after the slaughter of the five kings, is the principal officiate of this realm. He resurfaces

in detail in Hebrews 7. He too is connected with Christ's church, as its eternal priestly order over which the Father God made Jesus High Priest. The Lion of Judah's *ekklesia* priesthood is derived from this lineage.

2. **Family and community**—The sphere that replenishes the earth. It conforms to the Lord's procreative mandate to multiply. Every culture has families and a multiplicity of families to create communities, tribes, nations, etc. The household culture that evolves from obedience to God's command to *"be fruitful, and multiply"* (Genesis 1:28) makes this a perpetual sphere in creation. Every institution born to man arose as a result of the family.

3. **Business and commerce**—Population growth generates needs that different citizens' gifts and talents must supply. These form the basis for an exchange system that over time establishes business and commerce. What one person makes translates to what another buys, because he or she sees it as valuable or essential. Buying and selling systems emerge as makers charge sellers something of value for their goods and services and pay them to discover and connect with those who need them. Marketing was born to get the right merchandise to the right buyer.

   According to Proverbs 8–9, Lady Wisdom, a principality herself, rules this sphere of human resources. Later, we see that it was, and is, Christ all along. In Him are hidden all the treasures of wisdom and knowledge. (See Colossians 2:3.) Deuteronomy 8:18 says this sphere releases a specially endowed ability imparted by God under covenantal circumstances. The prophet Isaiah wrote that it was the Lord who taught His people to profit. (See Isaiah 48:17.)

4. **Mammon: money and economy**—A thriving commercial system eventually develops a currency that turns into a monetary system. The places where money is stored are called banks, and their management of money in relation to the goods and services made constitute the sphere of finance. It is what Christ called *mammon*. When communities grow and accumulate wealth and riches through exchanges, a spiritual principality manages this function that goes all the way back to eternity and Lucifer's kingdom, according to Ezekiel 28. The natural counterpart to this supernatural function from Ezekiel 28 is found in Psalm 107:23.

5. **Government and administration**—Rules transformed into laws control citizens' wrongdoing, curb destruction of the land, and preserve its best interests. Once drafted, the laws comprise the people's constitutional code of living, successfully establishing orderly government. Notice that the first thing the Lord did when He brought His new nation into existence was to issue a law for them. Judah, based on Psalms 60:7 and 108:8, is God's lawgiver. The New Creation church, like its founder Jesus Christ, who sprang from the tribe of Judah as Lord of all, emerges from all these references as the Almighty's lawgiver. This conforms to Isaiah 7:6–9, which places the Creator's governmental system squarely upon Christ's shoulders.

6. **Military and warfare**—A government's power and authority, sure to be challenged by lawbreakers and that makes enforcement necessary. Preserving the

government and protecting its community is done by a military—communal, civil, and national force. These include a land's police and armed forces. When Joshua was to take over Moses' rulership, he was inaugurated on two levels. (See Numbers 27:19; Deuteronomy 31:14.) After his inauguration, the Lord introduced Joshua to the spiritual power that would see to his military conquests. Joshua 5:13–15 says a spiritual man appeared as captain of the Lord's armies. That host never left Israel, as 2 Kings 6:17 shows. Deborah, a military judge under Jehovah's hand, experienced them also. (See Judges 5:20, 23.)

7. **Education and communication**—Productive citizens make a society profitable. However, they must learn skills, talents, and trades to contribute to its wealth. Education equips a community to afford what it needs to buy to survive. Communication addresses the basic need to transmit thoughts and understand others. A uniform way of transmitting thoughts, feelings, and ideas creates a communication system. An organized means of assimilating the community's logic, wisdom, skill sets, and abilities form the basis of a viable education system. Since education must be communicated, the two pair to form a comprehensive outreach sphere.

These seven features are found in every society and are jointly administered by their respective heavenly and earthly principal agents and by the prophets. It does not matter how crude, primitive, or sophisticated the system, these all prosper within a thriving civilization.

Prophets are made aware of their principalities early in their training. God sees to it that they know and can recognize the spiritual forces that truly govern and control our world. Take as a case in point the watcher over Nebuchadnezzar and his kingdom in the book of Daniel. Zechariah 3:1–9 gives an example of this in action, as do Ezekiel 9:1–11 and 2 Chronicles 20:20.

Spend time as a study group or class identifying human activities and provisions that coincide with the functions and influences described in the seven spheres.

FUNCTIONAL DIVISIONS OF THE PROPHET'S OFFICE

Based on the recognition of God's creation spheres, and consistent with this premise, the prophet's office is divided into similar spheres that reflect these invisible powers and distinguish prophetic personalities and anointings as assigned by the Lord. Interestingly, since they track with the seven spheres of creation, by studying them you can identify a prophet's distinct prophetic concentration. Prophetic divisions benefit the particular area of prophetic treatment dispensed through the Lord's various prophetic mantles. No matter how versatile, prophets generally concentrate themselves into discrete areas of the human experience. Thus, prophetic assignments are the footprints of creation's spheres and are supported by Scripture. For instance, take Daniel's ministry. It is easy to see that the sphere of prophetics his mantle concentrated on was *government*.

Other examples are Ezekiel and Isaiah, who seem to have served the sphere of the *ecclesiastical*. Amos fits the category of agriculture, or in our terms, the *laborer*. Moses' call centered on *monarchy*, while his brother Aaron's mantle settled on the *priestly*. Deborah and Joshua manifested their prophetics as *military* leaders. The prophetess Huldah appeared to concentrate on *education* with Elijah and Elisha, whose mantles doubled as *power* prophets. Agabus and Silas both showed themselves as prophets called to *apostolic companionship,* while Gad, Iddo, and Shemaiah were *seer* prophets. Samuel emerges as a *shepherding* prophet, David's Nathan a *temple* prophet. Jeremiah illustrates a *reformation* prophet. Isaiah's mantle doubles as our *evangelistic, redemptive* prophet. Daniel is reflected as a *presidential* prophet, and Zechariah as an *apocalyptic* prophet.

It is helpful to note this diversity of prophetic giftings to recognize where you fit in God's revelatory service or to identify the prophetic sphere of those prophets who serve you in God's kingdom. The chart below outlines the typical distribution of prophetic work.

Contrary to what most believe, prophets do more than just walk around prophesying every day. If they are to do their jobs, they must leave their prayer closets and serve the Lord's best interests by ministering to His people. Below are some of the elements that go into prophetic work. As you can see, they broaden the traditional, narrow stream of the ministry considerably.

QUICK STUDY CHART

GOD'S USE OF PROPHETS' FACULTIES

- **Visions**—Open-sighted divine communications.
- **Dreams**—Divine communications received while asleep.
- **Symbols**—Translation of icons and emblems that represent something God wants to use in prophetic language.

- **Parables**—Communication of prophecy using daily life imagery.

- **Similitudes**—Divulging supernatural knowledge by way of comparisons and contrasts.

- **Words of wisdom**—Conveying prophetic insight and applied understanding for God's practicality in everyday affairs.

- **Words of knowledge**—Declaring something God knows to another that is unable to be known or discovered by natural means.

- **Prophecy, prediction, and revelation**—Unveiling the Lord's hidden information and truths, regardless of the era, and foretelling them as prophecy.

- **Divine decrees**—Actuating and turning the events of this world so they line up with the embedded commands and programs of the Lord.

- **Declarations and commands**—Provoking the will and works of God to the extent of overriding the works of darkness and altering the normal course of life's events without prophetic intervention.

- **Intercessory prayer**—Intervening with God and His spiritual activities to alter undesirable occurrences in the world.

- **Supernatural intervention**—Positioning oneself through prayer, service, and sacrifice between impending catastrophe and its victims to reverse the enemy's assault with the Lord Jesus' authority.

- **Spiritual watch care**—Patrolling and stationing oneself in one's assigned prophetic ward to guard and prosper those in one's prophetic charge.

- **Spiritual guardianship**—Encircling a territory either by divine assignment or church position as the supernatural power force to stay the hands of judgment and/or obstruct demonic infiltration. Exerting the prophet's authority to enforce the will of the Lord on human situations.

- **Praise war**—Conducting formal or informal spiritual worship sessions to facilitate the spiritual battles behind the scenes that one's prophetic guard is engaged in on behalf of those within the prophet's watch.

Practice identifying and simulating each one of the above after creating a scenario that depicts it. Conclude with the most obvious talents or traits a prophet would need to perform them. Justify your results with explanations of your decision-making rationale.

QUICK STUDY CHART
SPECTRUM OF THE PROPHET'S WORD

From what we have discussed so far, you can see that being a prophet is hard work. But there is more. Here are a few more things prophets must be occupied with that many of them do naturally, though only a few can explain why or how.

- **Tongues and interpretation**—Supernatural prayer in the Spirit that transforms itself into the tongues of angels and sometimes the ancient tongues of old spiritual powers.

- **Discerning spirits**—The ability to see physically or discern intuitively the presence of God's invisible creatures, angels, or demons.

- **Psalms and poetics**—The activation of the aesthetic side of the prophet's mantle that resorts to songs, rhymes, and rhythmic sounds to release or give the word of the Lord.

- **Seers**—Interaction with the spirit realm as a visual deliverer of messages from the Spirit of God.

- **Dreamer of dreams**—Receiving or confirming the word of the Lord as revealed through dreams and night visions.

- **Supernatural stratagems**—Meetings with God in special prophetic sessions (awake or asleep) to get His mind and plans on the tasks He is presently dispensing to His prophetic staff.

- **Spiritual offerings, sacrifices, and servitude**—Performing, confirming, and instructing others in God's true spiritual service requirements and their methods, value, and benefits.

- **Spiritual warfare**—Joining by prayer, praise, or intercession God's invisible forces deployed to the earth to compel the fulfillment of His word, or to invoke their actuation through prophetic power.

- **Power sieges**—Relentless praise creates supernatural barriers around the enemy's camp to halt his progress.

- **Power confrontations**—Confronting sin, error, heresy, and perversion with the authority of the prophet's mantle and standing off with the works and forces of darkness to defend the church, faith, and flock of God.

- **Discernment of heresy and heretical messengers**—Detecting and correcting erroneous teaching, trendy doctrine, or Scripture dilution; marking and publicizing what is emphatically errant teaching as measured against the word of the Lord in Scripture.

- **Prophetic drama**—Portraying the word of the Lord in action, set to music or dance; depicting the invisible activities of eternity in public theatrics to demonstrate to worshippers what the Lord is doing behind the scenes.

Illustrate the signs that manifest each one of the above and the particular situation that calls for it.

THE PROPHET'S MANTLE

One captivating thing about the prophet's ministry is the mantle that an officer wears. It designates him or her as God's servant. Outward garments worn by servants reflected every ministry position in times past. They were important, and no serious worker would start a tour of duty without wearing a mantle. It is much different today. The attire donned in earlier times was meant to convey the essence of the worker's profession, his or her sender, or principal, such as in the case of a soldier, judge, or surgical physician.

In the case of most ancient officers, the sender was a deity and was therefore invisible. The god's invisibility made it necessary for physical symbols to depict its power, authority, reputation, and image to followers. As the book of Leviticus shows, this was usually done with clothing and power tokens. Swords, clouds, stars, lightning bolts, animal figures, and such were crafted to portray the deity's attributes. Jehovah did as much with His priesthood. In every culture, these had to be made to show the people their gods and identify their workers as members of the deity's staff. Call to mind on this subject the Lord's meticulous instructions to Moses about the priest's garments, His tabernacle, and its furnishings.

Thus, the servants of Baal in the Old Testament wore distinctive garb that reminded his worshippers of the god to whom they belonged. Headdresses worn were usually etched with an image—an animal, fish, or lightning bolt—to symbolize the inherent presence and power residing in the deity's minister. With goddesses it was no different. Their servants too dressed in attire that represented them and their kingdoms and portrayed the power they possessed and wielded. For instance, Ishtar's priests often were transvestites who wore feminine clothing to imitate their goddess.

When the Lord God Jehovah established Himself as Israel's God, He took great pains to tell the Israelites how they would and would not look to the other nations. Likewise, His priests were admonished to adorn themselves exactly as He commanded with no variation whatsoever. No fertility emblems that imaged pagan gods were to be worn before Him. The people were not to look at the priests' attire and be inspired to resort to their pagan rituals and orgies. Again, the purpose was not only to depict Yahweh, Israel's God, but it was also to not misrepresent His image to His people and cause them to serve another deity in His place. Often, during humanity's darkest eras, priests of one tribe's gods dressed up like the gods of their enemies to infiltrate their temples, spy out their wealth, and plunder their goods. With the sacred and profane being so tightly fused in those days, it made a good warfare tactic for a takeover. Naive worshippers, moved by sight, easily succumbed to these ploys.

Today we would call such outfits that depict a line of work, rank of authority, or religious statement, "service uniforms," and they would be the equivalent of those worn by modern civil, religious, and military workers.

MANTLES SIGNIFIED THE PROPHET

Throughout all history, the mantle signified the prophet. Every prophet dispatched by a deity wore select garments that brought to mind his stature and epitomized the nature of his messages as delivered to him by his or her god(s). Elijah's hairy garment is a good example of this; John the Baptist inherited it. While we all know such outfits may not be needed under the New Testament era, their symbolic counterparts do apply. Otherwise, how else could John the Baptist have been recognized as the resurgence of Elijah's mantle?

A MANTLE

A mantle, first of all, is a cloak, a covering, and an emblem of authority or power. It denotes an office's insignia of service. The specific Hebrew word for the prophet's mantle is *addereth*. It comes from the root of their word *addir*. Together the two words mean, and inform us, of the following things about *mantles* in general, and the *prophet's mantle* in particular.

QUICK STUDY CHART

WHAT A MANTLE IS AND DOES

Addereth and *addir* refer to the *prophet's mantle,* and together mean:

- A covering, a cloak, a garment, a mantle
- A mantle as the source of sustenance, establishment, power, glory, and honor that come from serving in ministry
- That which causes fame, generates might, and creates worth and nobility as a result of public ministry

- The manifest splendor and magnificence of a delegate, official, or agent of a deity imparted and bestowed as part of the attraction equipment essential to successful service

From the above it is easy to see the prophet's mantle as more than just a cloak or covering. Symbolically, it communicates to the spirit world everything the prophet is and has as a representative of God's kingdom and signifies that he is God's messenger. Thus, the prophet's mantle as a work resource is a power tool, a protective garb, an insignia of authority, and an emblem of divine license. It is a guard against the elements, a stylized uniform, and a statement of service. Its saturation with the Lord's anointing over time, as with Elijah's mantle that Elisha inherited, integrates functional portions of His omniscience, omnipotence, wisdom, counsel, and might. Isaiah 11:1–5 itemizes the qualities and powers inherent in the prophet's mantle, which is a figure of the anointing. What a spiritual mantle's presence upon a person identifies is tantamount to the officer's badge and its radiance. Its density speaks to the wearer's degree of authority and inherent power.

I once ministered to a young woman I had just met. As I began to pray for her to give her the word of the Lord, suddenly, right before my eyes, there appeared a huge, gold, badge-shaped shield. It covered her whole chest from shoulder to shoulder and from her neck way past her midsection. Seeing it told me that every vital area of her life was doubly protected by God. I did not know immediately what she did for a living, but the badge, more like a shield, indicated she was a woman of present or future power in God. It was thick, and it said, in essence, "guarded by God." It had taken hits because there were many dents in it, but oddly they were distributed evenly and looked more like engravings than damage. I later learned the woman was of considerable rank in the military. This vision has happened to me more than once.

On another occasion, I delivered the word of the Lord to a young man, also a stranger to me. Again, I stood before him to prophesy and saw all these occupational signs. I was initially confused and thought, *I cannot figure what God wants to focus on with this man.* Suddenly, in the midst of the panorama of work symbols, an officer's hat appeared. I knew he would be an important person in the military and that in his preordained position, along the way, he would have ample opportunity to acquire the skills needed to be effective. The path the Lord had him on meant that he would have to do many seemingly odd jobs that appeared unrelated to one another. But ultimately, his experiences would all converge, and once he completed his course, he would serve the Lord in high rank in ministry, as well. Without the imagery of well established occupations or practices, it would be hard to set God's lively stones in their rightful place in His body. Also, knowledge of such imagery further helps in vision and dream interpretation. They say silently what the Lord needs His messengers to voice publicly.

As you can see, mantles reflect more than rank in the Creator's service callings. They indicate the learning path of the wearer, the ultimate position, and the assortment of preparatory training skills that would finally comprise the mantle's power and authority. Using various imagery, prophets' mantles signify their range of ministry and the predecessor their calling descended from, as in the case of Elijah and Elisha, and Elijah and John. The mantle and its condition coincide with the message the prophet concentrates on and the position he or she holds in the eyes of the sending deity on account of what a prophet's predecessor experienced. Sometimes, what seems tattered to humans is celebrated by God as triumphant.

Prophets' mantles were more than adornments to decorate them for service. They were viewed as the reflective power of God and thus worthy of honor, respect, and reward. When a prophet's word failed or the prophet wanted to be recognized, what distinguished him was the cloak he wore. Often, disappointed monarchs or peers would tear a prophet's mantle to signify the prophet's word was not backed by any spiritual power. This is what occurred between Jeremiah and Hananiah in Jeremiah 28. The coarseness of Elijah's and John's mantles was meant to indicate the harshness of the word they preached and the cost of that word to themselves and their hearers. Isaiah and Ezekiel, two prophets stripped of the customary prophet's mantle, were not exempt from this explanation in that their nakedness represented their message. Their nudeness imaged the outcome of an angry Jehovah who was about to strip His precious country bare. The prophets' symbolism said that its inhabitants would be attired as fugitives instead of kings and priests.

PROPHETIC IMAGERY AND SYMBOLISM

Aside from knowing the functions of the prophetic office and its diverse manifestations, prophets also need to understand the way God speaks and why. Divine communication often comes in the form of symbolism and imagery. Pictures or signs say visually what is spoken audibly. God is able to speak in all His nations' tongues, but to assure that His word and works are understood in all tongues forever, He uses these two with His agents and workers. Their use is what we mean by the language of the Spirit, and its words are based on His creation. They make the Bible fit age to age.

When the Lord speaks in visions, He uses His own language in the form of imagery. Creation elements and objects make God's thoughts visible. For instance, mountains represent governments and high celestial powers. Hills symbolize high stratospheric powers. River imagery equates to flows and streams as in information or revelation, and trees stand for nations as the Lord's plantings. Chariots exemplify war and transportation vehicles, while horses depict warfare, service, competition, and travel. Symbolic language is necessary for God because it transcends time. Nature images tend to represent both perpetuity and timelessness. Human instruments bespeak a particular era or trend and thus are transitory.

Since human language varies from culture to culture, creation symbolism sees to it that what God says over the millennia of earthly existence is always relevant. Think about it. A bird is a bird, known around the world with different names. Winged creatures mean the same thing to every civilization. Likewise, animals, land and water, foliage, dirt, sun, moon, stars, and such all mean the same thing to every generation. God uses them when He wants to depict a human behavior that is analogous with a lower creature, or a spiritual one. It is the same when God uses angelic imagery. Their ordained station is as significant to the message as the creature itself, being heavenly rather than earthly. Weather, family, males, females, and children, regardless of what they are called in a particular country, nonetheless conjure the same image in people's minds. It is for these reasons that imagery serves

God's spiritual communication purposes so well around the world era to era. Prophets are very attuned to this reality and are taught by the Lord to grasp what He says no matter what sign or symbol He uses.

Divine symbolism also works well in dreams and visions. This is because pictures are self-explanatory and relate to the dreamer's world. Dreamers are instructed by God using images and symbolism typical of their everyday life. When prophetics are at work their transmissions are from God. They use His ways of talking to His creatures in their terms. If a trucker is to really heed what the Lord wants to say, then he or she hears God's message in trucking terms. If the word comes in a vision, the Lord captures his attention by using a highway, road stop, or payload imagery. In like manner, if the Lord needs to get a cook's attention, He will use food, recipes, cookware, and utensils, as well as hungry or satisfied eaters.

Visions are a little different from dreams. They are more like broadcasts that depict the mind and happenings of God in His expressions irrespective of our comprehension. Visions tell God's story God's way and leave their interpretation and translation to the recipient to obtain from His Spirit. Visions are not interested in our trends, idioms, slang, or language, and many times appear outdated. The Lord resorts to contemporary terms when they help Him make His point. Otherwise, the words and terms He uses are drawn from the things He made: the earth, the heavens, air, water, and so forth. Good prophetic training says prophets must become adept at God's wording and eternity's vernacular. To see that they do, the Lord begins prophetic education with a deep study of His prophets' writings. He walks newcomers through the words He spoke long ago and causes trained prophets to zero in on His own interpretations. Once the prophet gets the hang of this, he or she is ready for more advanced lessons in symbology and later prophecy formation. This continues until the learner is skilled in divine communication and prophetic enforcement.

In the next chapter, the ancient premise for modern prophetics is presented.

CHAPTER SUMMARY

1. Humanity is tied to the Lord's spirituality and the supernatural.

2. Prophets mediate earth's interaction with God's spiritual citizenry.

3. Earth and its institutions are guarded and supplied by the Lord's spiritual protocratics.

4. Seven is an important spiritual number.

5. There are seven protocratic spheres.

6. The prophet's office has functional divisions.

7. Historically, mantles have always signified the prophets.

8. Prophetic imagery and symbolism are how God speaks.

PROPHETIC ACTION ITEMS

1. In groups of three, develop a prophetic commentary on the Scriptures used in this chapter. Structure it to evaluate the prophetic implications contained in these Scriptures to validate prophetic service from God's perspective.

2. Look up the word *protocratic* as used in the secular world. Apply its basic wisdom to God's spirituality and New Testament prophetics.

3. Relate the protocratic sphere to modern societal structures and institutions.

4. Group the fifteen faculties of the prophet from the Quick Study Chart on pages 90–92 and imagine a

spiritual or revelatory situation each member of your group would serve.

5. Locate four Bible prophecies that exemplify this chapter's discussion on prophetic imagery and symbolism.

Chapter 4

RESIDENT PROPHET
MINISTRY ORIGIN

In this chapter you will read about how Israel's prophetic order began.

- The Lord balances His spiritual powers
- Samuel, the priestly prophet
- Samuel's mantle: a church prophet ministry model
- Benefit of church prophets in every church
- Regulating the prophetic

HOW ISRAEL'S PROPHETIC ORDER BEGAN

The Bible tells us when and how Israel's official prophetics became an established institution in God's principalities. It was at the dawn of Samuel's tenure. He was the first prophet under the Mosaic kingdom to institutionalize the order. Presumably taking his pattern for the institution from what was in existence in his day and that which predated his country's prophetics, Samuel set out to refine the ministry to serve the Lord. By now we know that the ancient *nabi* officiated every nation's religious history over the centuries. Every religion, it seems, had its prophet, seer, shaman, priest-craft healer, or teacher who administrated its supernatural resources and mediated its access to it. These, it would seem, comprised the fundamental elements of a religion regardless of the god the institution was formed to serve.

Consequently, the priesthood having been established and the prophetic having been initiated by Moses in Israel's deliverance, it was Samuel who was chosen to supply the remainder of the kingdom's spiritual components. Samuel also inaugurated the judgeship system under the direction and rule of Jehovah. In respect to the *nabis* of old, present chronicles show that only Israel's prophets rose to lasting renown and became the enduring standard of reputed prophetics for modern man. Their words are still active today and many readers can attest that they came to pass or are yet coming to pass.

Although Joshua was considered a prophet, his service was mainly militaristic, as the kingdom had yet to be established in Israel's control. Until that time, however, the priests, using the Urim and Thummim, answered prophetic revelation on spontaneous issues and questions requiring God's answers. Of course, this excludes the supernatural manipulation by the occult prophets such as Balaam, who dominated the ancient world during Moses' and Joshua's time. Accepted and respected as a social order, the demonic ministrations of the supernatural that preceded Israel's prophetic institution held largely uncontested sway throughout the world, civilized or uncivilized. The first stunning challenge it received came from Moses in his deliverance of the nation of God from Egyptian bondage. By Samuel's time, the Lord Almighty had carved Himself a place and an enduring reputation in the world, even if His people had lost sight of it. (See 1 Samuel

3:1, which talks about how rare widespread revelation was in those days.)

By the time Samuel was old enough to serve the Lord, Eli's sons' perversion of the priesthood and rank abuse of God's people paved the way for a division of the two functions, the priest and the prophet. Furthermore, their defilement of God's offerings in the process forever settled the separate operations of the two offices, according to 1 Samuel 1–3. Their repugnant behavior caused the people to fear Eli's death and resist his sons' dynastic inheritance of the priesthood.

The combined resentment of the people from the sometimes violent abuse they suffered at the hands of Eli's sons set the stage for God's final division of His two spiritual powers. The wisdom of the principle may be better appreciated by looking at Ecclesiastes 5:8. The priesthood, being deformed, had no higher official to oversee it. God's disillusioned people had no human recourse to appeal to aside from Eli, who had already refused to discipline his offspring. Later, Samuel proved to be no better at parenting his progeny than Eli had been. When Samuel's service was nearing an end and it was time to pass the torch, his unruly sons revived Israel's earlier fears and moved the nation to ask for a king to counterbalance priest and prophet abuse.

The people again questioned the character of leadership they would get from Samuel's sons. By the time he passed the institution of the *nabiim* on, the two functions had permanently split, with Samuel inaugurating Israel's first king.

THE LORD BALANCES HIS SPIRITUAL POWERS

To create and maintain a godly balance of power, the Lord always groups His hierarchical officials in varying levels of ministers that oversee each other. That is what Ecclesiastes 5:8 means. This structure allows them to rectify abuses and inequities in His kingdom, and it is not exclusive to the church. Such was the case with Eli, Samuel, the prophetic, and the priesthood.

To assure the revelatory provisions of God were not monopolized by a single group, the Lord distributed spiritual power among the two existing official revelatory institutions He ordained in that day: the priest and the prophet, respectively.

Bible accounts indicate that God's prophetics as a ministry had been practically muted during the nation's developing institutions from Moses to Samuel. The end of Joshua's era also ended the fixture of established prophetics and the godly use of spiritual power. Divine utterances were loosely delivered by whatever prophet was available. The priesthood curtailed the legal exercise of God's supernatural exploits to the priests' personal advantage. Their dominance caused the prophetic to fade into the background, eventually becoming nostalgic window dressing on the nation's spiritual landscape.

Priestly ministry, concurrent with this move, rapidly became presumptuous. The young nation's secular, political, and social dominions each took its natural course and shape as Israel grew. Only the prophetic remained fetal in nature. It alone lagged behind as an important professional class in Israel's culture. Blending with the priests' teaching mandates, it became locked into their interpretations and applications. Spontaneous utterances were rare because they were hindered and eventually suffocated. The manipulations of Eli's sons reflect this. (See 1 Samuel 1–2.)

Since no concrete provisions were left by Moses to found and extend his prophetic initiatives into the cultural life of the new nation, the priests developed the function as they saw fit. Moses had made provisions, however, for the prophetic's eventual reinstatement. (See Exodus 18.) Nevertheless, he prepared no definite guidelines for its emergence among the ranks of the Lord's officers. It took God's displeasure with Eli's ministry and His judgment on his immoral priesthood to change all that, and He did so with Samuel. God instigated the new move, spearheaded by Samuel, that would perpetually have both prophet and priest regulating each other.

To introduce His change in response to the nation's degeneration, God sent an unnamed prophet with a word to Eli the high priest. He declared that Eli and his posterity would be permanently obliterated because of the depravity he endorsed in the land. Not long after this, the Lord awakened the prophet Samuel's spirit to undertake the mandate of *institutionalizing* the prophetic. His charge included restoring Israel's pure worship and perpetually guarding against the potential excesses of the priests in the future. (See 1 Samuel 3.) It took a prophet to do it because a prophet had brought them into existence and a warrior prophet had settled them in their new land. Thus, the premise was set. The Lord initiates everything by His prophets.

SAMUEL, THE PRIESTLY PROPHET

The task of instating a standing moral council of prophetic officers was given to one born expressly for that purpose. Samuel's very name says so. It means "name of God" or "God's name" to show how his work would again exalt the name of the Lord in the lifestyle and worship of His people. It is noteworthy to point out how the Lord chose Samuel for the judgeship.

Providentially called to be a prophet and to restore the nation's worship to its covenant God, Samuel was reared by a priest in God's tabernacle. The young man was equally well-learned in all his assigned callings. He was knowledgeable of the ministries of the priesthood, nurtured as a prophet and judge, and groomed for governmental leadership. Thus, Samuel would be both separator and bridge in the nation's new move. His appointment would paradoxically merge and divide its priestly and prophetic functions for integrity and efficiency. As Israel's first judge, he functioned symmetrically as Israel's priest, prophet, and governor-general.

Samuel's appointment first closed out the priesthood's terrorist reign as supreme power in the land. He then ushered in the joint reign of prophet and priest under the interim system of judgeship that preceded Israel's shift to monarchy. Deborah, in Judges 5, was the only other *prophet* accredited like authority. She performed all the functions Samuel did in her service, acting as commander and chief, as well as gubernatorial prophet in the land. Ascribing the title *judge* to Deborah's office gave her the same authority and status Samuel enjoyed. A complete portrait of his ministry provides a credible service model for today's prophets assigned to individual churches.

SAMUEL'S MANTLE: A CHURCH PROPHET MINISTRY MODEL

Samuel's mantle of judge, prophet, and priest comprised the transition team of that era, which concluded the old order, regulated priestly authority, and installed a new institution at the same time. His first official act was to issue the decrees that judged Eli's house, broke Israel's ties with the occult, and established himself and his order as the nation's head of state. Following this, Samuel taught the nation about holy and unholy service and corrected the errors of the priests' ministry. Samuel meticulously reeducated Israel about the office of the prophet and elevated its previously incidental function to an official rank in the ministries of the Lord's land.

Samuel led Israel's people to war as their general, arbitrated their controversies as a judge, instructed them in divine service and worship as a priest, and established a school to structure and standardize their prophetics. Samuel's work extended to inaugurating the royalty and nobility of the land, qualifying subsequent prophets, and verifying and empowering new leaders and officers with God's approved authority.

One thing is evident in this profile. Samuel pointedly depicted the diverse functions and activities of the prophet installed in a church more than any of his predecessors did. He was a commander in war, an intercessor in covenant breaches, and an officiary at all the nation's ceremonies. From this, it is easy to see the question of dedicated prophets assigned to every congregation for God is not strictly a matter of wisdom. It is an ordination that goes all the way to the heart of necessity, seeing to it that every gathering of God's people in His name reflects the full complement of His officers and agencies. It allows the Lord to manifest and demonstrate His fullness when He is with His people. If a ministry wants to become and remain biblically correct, then every gathering is to contain a representative of three out of five of the Ephesians 4:11 officers. The apostle as founder, as well as the evangelist, may be itinerant. In addition, church gatherings, based on 1 Corinthians 14:19–32, should have in attendance a minimum of two to three prophetic voices. God's integrity and diligence say that this is usually the case, even if the prophets are not allowed to speak out in service.

Benefit of Church Prophets in Every Church

If a church and its leadership want to succeed in their vision and divine mandate, then opening themselves up to the credible prophetics of God is a good start. If a church wishes to excel in its purpose and ride the crest of sustained victory, establishing its own church prophets or a resident prophets' institution is how to do it.

Before going further, I want to acknowledge that many people object to the title "church prophet." For those who do, the term *resident prophet, staff prophet,* or *sanctuary prophet* works just as well. Regardless of the name you use, the title applies to prophets of congregations, whose main duties and spheres of influence concentrate on a local church and its congregation. They are likely to be your shepherding prophets more than anything else.

Our discussion here is not especially addressing itinerant prophets serving a number of churches in a circuit, much like the one Samuel traveled. Here, our attention is primarily given to one in a church called to the prophetic, sent by God to become the prophet of the church. Since not everyone is called to the national or international realms of the prophet's office, it is wise to deduce those assigned to other levels are called to cover individual churches and ministries.

Prophets of the church, as an ordained institution, spiritually and sometimes practically, guard and protect local congregations. When requested, they also provide the same benefit for various itinerant ministers. Under these circumstances, their function acts more like a mentorship.

In the local congregation, the prophet's ministries are mostly limited to exercising the Lord's authority in the work he is assigned to and locally releasing His power from the world of the supernatural to enhance it. The ever present spiritual strength of the Lord is what the church prophet brings to the local church. His or her presence ensures that pastor and congregation alike reap fully the new covenant blessings promised to every New Creation child of God in the Lord Jesus Christ—the very thing that Satan and his hosts seek to divert from the Lord's churches. Prophets bring balance to the prophetic expressions that flow through the church. Furthermore, they add a fuller dimension of spirituality to routine prophetic service customarily handled by whosoever will.

Moreover, these officers standardize the proprieties of the office and regulate its practices and developments. Well-trained and seasoned staff or resident prophets bring competence and prophetic mastery to the churches they serve. When operating in harmony with the other ministries of the church, the accomplished prophet can swiftly elevate his church's rank in the spiritual realm. Easily, he or she can increase resources and release previously held up funds to flow into the church. Prophetic intercessions can reduce community hostility, win the favor of civil authorities, and disarm principal agents working against the ministry. Beside this, the church prophet can enrich the overall spiritual and natural state of the ministry in areas too numerous to mention here.

REGULATING THE PROPHETIC

As widespread prophetics are relatively new to this generation, the prophetic is ever evolving as a valid church institution. Finding its reputable place among the Ephesians 4:11 officers of the New Testament church and establishing its parameters and protocol is a massive, ongoing venture. Here lies the ground for sound prophetic *guidelines*. They are intended to steer the processes pastors use to install prophetics in their churches. A thorough treatment of this process and its most prudent procedures is found at the end of this book.

To help you perceive the official nature of the prophet's rank and the mantle's status as an office, a discussion of the prophet's standing in the supernatural is in order. We start with the link between the prophetic and an agency in the next chapter.

Chapter Summary

1. Samuel founded and established Israel's prophetic institution.

2. Samuel, a prophet, was raised by Eli, the high priest.

3. The kings eventually became a counterbalance for the prophetic.

4. Samuel typifies the church prophet.

5. Church prophets help their churches succeed in their divine mandates.

Prophetic Action Items

1. Conduct a thorough study of the prophet Samuel's ministry to relate it to the ministry of a church prophet.

Chapter 5

THE PROPHETIC'S
AGENCY STATUS

In this chapter you will read about the prophetic—an official agency of the Godhead. It covers:

- God's divine communication medium
- Agents and officers—what they do
- Prophets as agents
- Why agencies and agents exist
- The agency principal
- Agency/principal relationship
- The agency agents
- Legitimate commissioning
- Role of the agent and agency in the church
- The agent as an officer
- Prophetic agency as God's principality
- The apostolic—God's earthly principal stronghold
- How prophetic movements begin
- Prelude to apostleship
- Ministry leader apostleship

THE PROPHETIC—AN OFFICIAL AGENCY OF THE GODHEAD

A ll study on this subject points to the status of the prophetic as an agency. The word *agency* denotes a business and its operations. An agency is an official entity that administrates and executes the duties and responsibilities associated with a delegation, usually called a commission. Commissions are usually handed out by governments and monarchs. The fact that, even in today's world, they must be petitioned for and approved by the government in the land reflects the fact that this practice still holds true. The word *official* is a key term that asserts order, permanence, perpetuity, and solidarity as the result of an agency arrangement.

The attachment of the word *official* to anything means it is backed by a governing power authorized by a higher one to support, oversee, and police the activities of the agency. This role includes the guarantee of its agreements and the warranty of its services and provisions. To add this definition to the function of a commission sheds a great light on what the prophetics is and means to God.

The word *commission* is used regularly in Scripture to designate those who are sent out on an errand for a specific purpose by one in authority. The distinctive feature of the commission over the errand-runner or routine messenger is the authority that accompanies the dispatch. To be recognized as an agency, the idea of a delegated commission must be real.

A commission, broadly speaking, is an authoritative, power-wielding entity that rules or governs subordinate entities. Commissions are born when the originating powers or forces that initiated the business or activities that necessitate an agency hand down portions of their activities to delegates to represent their interests in other religions. Those who are commissioned are charged with prescribed duties. When we speak of a delegation in the context of agency service or commissioned action, its meaning is larger than what is customarily understood in routine work circles. An official delegation's service is much broader and carries infinitely more weight. It includes deputation to an assignment under an authority. Take a moment to study those words and you will see what is really meant by the term *delegation*. All of this information means prophets and the prophetic are ranking officials of the Lord's government, representing it to the people rather than vice versa.

God's Divine Communications Medium

The prophetic is a divine agency of the Godhead. It is how the Lord God keeps in contact with His world. Instead of telephones, headsets, wires, and satellites, the Lord uses dreams and visions and angelic visitations from the spiritual creatures assigned to the planet. As the Creator's eternal communications medium, the prophetic doubles as an effective administrative instrument. Through prophecy God dispenses His truth, enlightens His people, and issues His judgments in the earth. Prophecy declares God's plans and actuates His words and will in their seasons. All this makes it so much more than a predictive tool, establishing it as His rod of correction, staff of rulership, and creative implement, too. With these, prophecy also acts like a trigger mechanism with signals that call into action the embedded commands of the Lord dormant in creation until their time. The greatest example of this is the Revelation of the apostle John. The entire event, unfolded to him by Christ's angel, is but a series of prophetic spurs that rouse and initialize the words of God asleep in creation until their preappointed time.

Prophecy is how God extends His hands to the world and causes what He wants to appear in it to do so on time. Thus, it further serves as His inducement arm. The Old Testament word for the ministry used in Hosea 12:10 links prophecy to the hand of God, translating the word ordinarily used for hand (*yad*) as "ministry." Together, this says that prophecy is the Lord's means of invoking the powers and agencies responsible for exteriorizing His word and manifesting His power and will in action on earth.

Beyond this, the prophetic serves as God's avenue of divine enactment and legislation, according to Galatians 3:19 and Hebrews 2:2. As instruments that invoke the terrestrial agencies, angels, principalities, and powers of creation, prophets participate in their summons via the medium of prophecy. (See Ezekiel 9:1–11 and Zechariah 3:1–10.) Other words for *agent* are listed below to give you an idea of the scope of the function in God's mind and that of any legitimate organization. An agent is:

- Executive
- Administrator
- Judge
- President
- Minister
- General
- Chairperson
- Governor
- Guardian

- Custodian
- Prelate

AGENTS AND OFFICERS—WHAT THEY DO

In relation to the prophet, agents and officers exercise and exert the delegated authority they derive from the Godhead. Based on the language of 1 Corinthians 12:28–29, prophets govern by ruling and administration beneath God's sovereignty. Ideally, they do so according to His divine canon (written law). Aside from legislation, prophets organize the operations and structure of the New Testament church, taking part in its discipline as needed. That is, collectively, instinctively, or punitively. The instructional mandate typical of prophets in general and church prophets in particular further requires the prophet's mantle to be apt to teach. Prophets should be equipped to teach people about the supernatural, the divine world, and their spiritual heritage in Jesus Christ. Also, New Testament prophets are the ones most equipped to transmit apostles' doctrine to the remainder of the fivefold for them to disseminate. Apostles make good sense to prophets because this mantle is the one that certifies them.

Advancing the reasons for the office's continuance, prophets still judge according to the Lord's Word of truth. They manage His executive administrative affairs, supervise those in their care, and guard the body of Christ against demonic infiltration or worldly overflows. As ministers, prophets develop the saints in Christ's spirituality, officiate over its priestly tasks in the earth, and enforce the righteousness of God. As protectors and servants, prophets cover, shield, and encircle their congregations, interceding for them as necessary. As governors, they regulate and manage the church's supernatural interactions and sift the false from the true. As intermediaries, prophets interpose themselves between the Lord and His people, and prevent dark powers from overtaking them. Lastly, and perhaps most importantly, prophets intercede for God's people.

Intercede is a word that many people only partially understand. Besides praying for others, it means intervening in their matters with one's own authority and position, invoking God's influence while doing so. Zephaniah 2:7 (NKJV) applies this word to a special, divine visitation where God acts on behalf of His people as the word of a qualified agent. Prophetic prayer performs just this function. When one intercedes for another, he is actually interposing himself between the victim and his or her problems or crises. Prophets, as God's intercessors, first and foremost accomplish exploits of this kind in their prayers and wage combat for the churches they cover. (See Jeremiah 15:1 and Ezekiel 14:14. Both passages show God's regard for the prophet's intercessory prayer on behalf of His people.)

In addition, practically and economically speaking, the high intercessory duty of the prophet disburses God's economy, as we have seen from 2 Chronicles 20:20, and dispenses His covenant provisions. Thus, the prophet's powerful status in the realms and spheres of God authorizes the release of the resources and possessions hidden in His treasuries and those of other creatures. An interesting fact about this mantle attribute is that every worker in God's kingdom has his own treasury in eternity from which streams the supernatural supplies of his service. Each minister is given a storehouse of weapons, finances, abilities, talents, and skills with which he or she serves God and meets the needs of His people. Prophets' treasuries are usually quite stocked. This is because they are to release and deal out great portions of it to those who come to them. Loaded with more than material blessings, the prophet's mantle contains spiritual and miraculous resources that overturn everything the devil and his angels may throw at those they surround. Likewise, Elijah and Elisha were both so endowed. Elisha knew that Elijah's mantle was both powerful and wealthy. Therefore, he understood that he was getting more than a cloak or a uniform. He recognized that all the power and benefits that ever streamed from Elijah were resident in that hairy garment. When he asked for the mantle, he knew that it would more than just cover him; it would transform, empower, and enrich his life and service to God as long as he lived. Had he only gotten a word from Elijah or the laying on of hands, he would not have been nearly as potent in his ministry. The power that remained in that mantle is revealed through the Bible's record of Elisha's early exploits in 2 Kings.

PROPHETS AS AGENTS

Like all the fivefold officers of Ephesians 4:11, prophets are officers, and that makes them agents. The prophetic as a divine agency makes those who stand in the position agents. By now you understand that an agent is a representative of a principal, usually a sovereign land, monarch, or government. Agents and their agencies serve as ambassadors, consuls, delegates, intermediaries, and the like. When you think of the prophets and the prophecies that come from the messengers' mouths, recognize that their position with the Lord authorizes their prophecies and assures their performance. It is this license from God that frees prophets to exercise His power, enforce His will, and perform (or cause the performance of) His Word.

A prophet of God, as His agent, transacts the Lord's business the same way an agent of an insurance company, government official, or military officer does. As recognized representatives in good standing, a company or government's agents, according to their contracts, bind their organizations to the performance of their word. As long as prophets obey the Lord's Word and respect the bounds and limits of their ministry covenant, the prophecies they give cannot fail. Understand that exteriorizing the Lord's spoken word in the natural world is not only how prophets are so designated, but is emblematic of their fundamental reason for existing. If God does not honor a prophet's word or substantiate the messenger's work, then the person is not a prophet in actuality. The person needs to be neither feared or trusted until God does.

The key to prophetic honor is in all the prophets' words. When they consistently come to pass, the proving deity they represent backs them in all professional regards. This requisite alone ordains that prophetic preeminence should take time, preferably decades, because new prophets' prophecies can take a while to come to pass. However, the time lag between a prophecy and its fulfillment can make people not accept someone as a prophet for years. I have met people to whom I have given a word contact me five, ten, or more years later. They confess they did not receive my word at the time, or rejected it as just me. What amazes them after so many years is that the words I spoke, regardless of their reaction to them, were performed by God. What amazes me is that He not only performed my word in time, but He let them know that it was according to the prophecy I gave that He did so. This ought to encourage many young prophets. Be patient, because matters of life take time, and even if you know your word was right on when you gave it, rest in the fact that God will confirm you. The idea that prophetic confirmation is always a quick event is misleading. Sometimes, the best part of your training is in learning to wait in faith.

WHY AGENCIES AND AGENTS EXIST

An agency exists to administrate the affairs of the commission, bureau, or business that brought it into existence. It expedites its affairs, executes its commands, exercises its authority, and accomplishes its purposes and aims as prescribed in the agency agreement. As instruments (one synonym for the word *agent*) of principals, agencies are empowered by their principal to intervene on their behalf, intercede for their best interests, and direct and govern their affairs. What an explanation. Prophets, then, are to see to God's business and not their own. Their words are to uphold and expedite God's purpose for sending them, and not what they want to be. Prophets must become aware that they are God's agents, and their ministries are His divine agency.

A prophetic agency, in or outside the church, is ordinarily interposed in the principal's territory or settled in a remote territory amid the population it exists to serve. Its call is to establish the principal's authority and strengthen his or her holdings in distant lands. Think about how the prophetic is to accomplish this on behalf of the Godhead and the kingdom of heaven on earth. As with natural or secular agents, so it is with God's spiritual ones. Chief prophets are assigned by the Lord territories over which they rule and spheres of ministry within which they serve.

According to the pattern set by Samuel, they generally have a diverse mix of prophetic staff members to facilitate their agency assignments. In ecclesiastical matters, prophetic delegation and dispatch pertaining to the church's realm on earth. Prophets under these circumstances become the embodiment of God's executive authority beneath His apostles, although always as their collaborators. Any genuine apostle will have a strong multifaceted prophetic staff to work alongside him. In this way, the prophets are the first and most potent authorities the apostle can rely upon.

EXTENT OF AGENCY POWER AND AUTHORITY

The word *authority* means the lawful right to enforce obedience, the legitimate power to influence or direct the behavior of others—usually subordinates. The exercise of authority involves instruction, command, censure, and discipline. Hebrew terms for *authority* convey words and sentiments that ascribe majesty, glory, honor, renown, and even ornamentation to our basic understanding of the word. The ornamentation refers to the badges and other insignia of authority. These all signify the exalted station of the one placed in authority over others. Additional words and meanings include the accompanying grandeur, appearance, and excellency that impose their forms upon the one so installed. These are inherently contained in the office to which the authorized one attends. The sum of these words explains the weight of authority and its effects on those upon whom it is placed.

It is not difficult to see how, based on the above, authority originated with God; nor is it hard to understand its effect in Moses' inauguration of Joshua, one example of prophetic authority transferred and at work. As a matter of fact, whenever Moses was instructed by God about inaugurating anyone, he was told to do so by taking the authority that was upon himself in the form of the spirit, and place it upon the inaugurated one. Here is the spiritual significance behind the laying on of hands in ceremonial promotions and appointments. The goal of the act is the impartation of the spiritual properties of the promoter through the act of delegation. Once completed, the act is seen by heaven to transfer or transmit agency authority on the one touched. That impartation invests a person with the power of the office into which he or she steps.

Agency authority extends to setting and enforcing laws and mandating prescribed behaviors. This consists of permitting and prohibiting certain acts perceived by the delegated representative as harmful, detrimental, or nullifying to his or her principal's best interests. Agency guardianship extends to the agent's assurance of the institution's perpetuity. Thus, the agency as the delegated command authority is to sway and influence its realms, territories, and regions to the advantage of the commissioning principal.

THE AGENCY PRINCIPAL

An agency is not legitimate without the head person who ordained its existence. That head person supplies the agency's authority. The name for such a person, we have said, is a principal. A principal is a chief or head who empowers the agent and agency to act and speak on his or her behalf. As a principal, he or she initiates and governs the delegate charged with carrying on business and administrating its vision in its name. This is particularly applicable when more than tasks and assignments are involved in the sending. Usually agency commissions carry with them the connotation of authorizing satellite (replicas) of the principal's headquarters in the distant location.

The principal is first in the line of power in a delegated arrangement. As such, he or she is the ranking authority who inspires, authorizes, and endorses the agency and all that it discharges. Moses' inauguration of Joshua to succeed him exemplified this type of delegation in action, as did Yahweh's empowering and dispatch of Moses with a transference of His power delegated like authority to Joshua at the direct command of the Lord, who may be seen as the sending principal of Israel. (See Numbers 27:23.)

When the Lord inducts and dispatches His prophets, He does so as a principal and makes the prophets, indeed all His ministers, functionaries representing Him in the world. For a heightened respect of the prophetic and all the ministries of the New Testament church, adequate enlightenment must be given to their charges, those who are to see their orders as delegated commands from the Lord and not just as sermonizers or predictors.

Besides sending, principals are persons and groups who authorize, underwrite, and guarantee their agencies' right to exist, to do business, and to legally act in their remote territories. The verifying factor is that the one who delegated the authority and who sponsored the agency must have sovereign power and/or lawful jurisdiction within the territory the agency serves. A principal, as one in authority (a person or nation), spearheads the actions or movements that generated the agency's presence in the land. The Bible calls them heads (*arche* or *archon* in the Greek), among other things.

AGENCY/PRINCIPAL RELATIONSHIP

True agencies are chiefly accountable to their principal. They hold to his or her dominant views and ideals on the mission and its assignments, and execute all tasks, operations, and duties the principal's way, despite any private views or personal opinions they may hold. The agreement between the principal and agent, ideally, extends to the best means of carrying out these for the principal as well. The four aspects—mission, assignments, tasks, and duties—are all integral to an agency. Without them, an organization and its institutions have nothing to practice, no business to transact. Agencies' remote administration and government, along with their workers, called agents, are therefore illegal. Activities conducted under these circumstances may be construed as anarchic and dissenting without a lawful principal. This can also be the case when the principal has failed to define for the agency its parameters. Apart from them, the legitimacy needed for agency occupation and profitability are void.

Here is where the prophetic receives its legitimacy. Christ, being the Head of the church and the Lord over creation, gives the prophet his or her legitimate right to act in all the world. It is Christ's authority that is delegated to—and exercised by—the prophet; not his or her own authority, as many suppose. *The prophet, as an agent of the Godhead,* is to pursue the content of the delegation handed down by Christ. Although that delegation is mainly spiritual, its success in the physical world ends up being material. The reality of definite consequences for dereliction of duty spans the Bible. What gives most prophets their boldness against the Lord is a shortsighted self-will. Such prophets believe the Lord has little recourse for their disobedience and have become too familiar with His long-suffering grace. They take liberties not accorded to them as His representatives. These messengers see God as out of sight, out of mind, and out of control. However, the Lord has dealt with this before, according to Psalm 94:7, and He does not change.

As the institution settles its organization and strength, He will address these matters through the faithful prophets He installs.

Since the rewards and penalties for service and disservice to God presumably come later, many ministers feel they can take what they want now and bear the consequences later. Scripture, however, tells us that is not always the case (see Matthew 7:13 and the Lord's parabolic contrast of the good and faithful servant versus the evil and faithless servant), not to mention that they merely suppose they can painlessly suffer whatever consequence they imagine He assigns to their misconduct.

THE AGENCY AGENT

It is the agency's founding or initiating principals who commission authorized representatives for a discrete purpose. The commission is the embodiment of what defines the agency's work. It encapsulates the purpose for its dispatch, delegates authority, and authorizes their business, services, and dispensations as related to the founding purpose. All must be clearly defined for the operative or functionary (two more synonyms for agent) to complete his assignments. Because agency assignments are usually apart from their principal's residence or headquarters location, the word *dispatch* heads the list of what a commission entails.

The sending away aspect of the assignment requires principal deputation that sanctions the commission and its agency representatives. In written lawful and often notarized documents, the principal states how the agency is to legally perform in his name in distant territories. It is the power of the commission that gives the dispatched (sent ones) the permission to execute the commands and charges of the principal as defined. An agent, as a representative of the commissioner, acts as an instrument employed by the principal to be virtually the principal away from the hub or headquarters location. Prophets in this capacity are equated to Christ as long as He is in heaven, as seen by the Lord's words to Moses in Exodus 7:1. That is the essence of His Matthew 28 Great Commission that 1 Corinthians 12:28 and Ephesians 4:11 qualify for His ministerial staff.

LEGITIMATE COMMISSIONING

One important thing worth mentioning about a commission is the present-day church's acts of commissioning. The church has taken up the practice of nonchalantly laying hands on people in informal ceremonies to commission them to go forth. To what or where is not always clear. Under certain circumstances, such a practice, done in the name of Jesus, is not inherently wrong. It can, however, be dangerous. Casual acts of commissioning can be somewhat misleading and can activate spiritual forces and warfare the newly commissioned one is not prepared to confront. This is especially true when the person commissioned has had little preparatory training and limited information on the nature, purpose, and aim of his or her commission. To perform the ritual as merely a religious rite strips it of its powerful inaugural impartation. What's worse is that it releases mediocre performers to perform a critical function as they see fit.

For a commissioner to have power to dispatch agents, the factors stated above must be established. The commissioner must be a legitimate principal. He or she must have sovereign or legal authority within the realm of the commission to be economically, spiritually, or otherwise able to support the agent—the one on whom hands are laid for dispatch. Thus, the commissioner must be higher or at least more highly endowed than the one being sent forth. The reason for this has to do with the sure difficulties, hardships, and obstacles the agent will face while on assignment.

The commissioner should be able to finance, shelter, protect, and extend his or her reach (and aid) to encircle the agent. He or she should be more than capable of undergirding the remote agent's activities in the distant territory. There must be sufficient license to authorize, anointing to empower and impart, and resources to sustain the operative in the remote location. These necessities demand the commissioner be more than a peer or subordinate.

The commissioning body or individual's word should be respected and heeded in the place where the agent is sent. The legitimacy of the commission and the reputation of the commissioner must be impeccable for the agent to serve effectively or to have the power to enforce the principal's commands. Additionally, a letter attesting to the legitimacy of the agent and the authenticity of the commission is necessary. Study for insight the account of Peter and the other apostles' dispatch of Paul to his ministry to the Gentiles in the book of Galatians. Review also their reception of him when he was brought to them by Barnabas for the first time. Re-examine as well their protective escort of Paul when the Jewish authorities sought to kill him for his defection to Christ. All these examples show that the principal must have the status in the natural and supernatural realms to assure the agent's survival and success.

Certification should be based on observed or presumed spiritual exploits. It should include training, practice, and exposure to the rigors of the office. Approval criteria should be specifically tied to what the prophet's office and mantle exist to do for God. These should be more than discernible. They should be measurable according to the position's pre-scribed duties and functions.

The official rank of the principal or commissioner (some-times this authority is delegated) must legally and practically exceed that of the agent. Principals must have jurisdiction in the assigned territory for the acts and the dispensations of their commissioned ones, or agents, to be official. Officialdom is significant to an authentic commission. Those employed by an agency are its officials, as the words *officers* and *agents* too are synonymous.

Being an official also makes the agent an intermediary who bridges negotiation and settlement gaps as an envoy or deputy stationed in the land to conduct business for the prin-cipal. In this stead, he or she forms diplomatic ties between the two in a distant location. This statement is significant as distance, remote government, and management are integral to most agencies' purposes. In this way, some agents double as ambassadors on the principals' behalf. One synonym for the word *ambassador* is *minister.* This word brings the subject of our discussion to the church and shows how the preceding explanations pertain to the prophetic.

You see, prophets are second-ranking *officers* of the fivefold ministry unfolded by Paul in the book of Ephesians 4:11 and 1 Corinthians 2:28. As officers of the church, they are immediate ministers of Christ's gospel and its legitimate governmental and power agents. Governmental agents uphold their states and their laws in the places they are assigned. They teach, train, encourage, and guide the citizenry's obedience to those laws to preserve the state's wholesome existence. While all fivefold have this responsibility, it is on whose direct behalf that they do so that makes the difference. Apostles and prophets, as high officials, would equate in rank as officers of the federal government. The evangelist and pastor would be seen as state and local authorities. The teacher, depending on the mantle type, could be seen as both.

Role of Agent and Agency in the Church

In the church, ministers are servants of God. As His servants, ministers fill one of two roles. They can be lay servants who serve the Lord not necessarily in an administrative, governmental, or executive capacity, or they can be officers. The latter term applies to the positions outlined in Ephesians 4:11 by the apostle Paul. Their names make them officers with agency authority and responsibilities.

Being sent by the Lord Jesus certifies their service as a dispatch or a commission. For our purposes, this discussion centers on the latter definition, that being the officer of the fivefold offices. Official fits because occupying an office intrinsically makes one an officer. First Corinthians 12:28–29 settles this for us, as does an etymological study of the term and application of the word *officer.*

The Agent as an Officer

An officer can be an executive or director, a manager or a vice, a general or a chief. If you studied these words thoroughly, you would immediately see *the prophet as an agent of the Godhead, and his or her service (or ministry) an agency of the kingdom of God.*

These conclusions are reached from the sum of the explanatives given earlier for the term *agent*. Prophets, along with the other Ephesians 4:11 officers, do in the spirit realm supernaturally for the Lord and His kingdom what diplomatic, civil, and political authorities do for their earthly organizations.

Prophets administrate the heavenly treasures of the New Creation government. They officially handle the dispensations of the supernatural released by God to His church. Prophets furthermore exercise the Lord's spiritual authority on earth to keep the balance of power between the darkness and light, the lie and the truth. They authorize and empower the church's ministries and supply God's heavenly provisions to His people by decreeing, declaring, and teaching what the Lord gives them to dispense to their spheres.

As agencies of the Godhead, prophetic officers are licensed to maintain the Lord's control and to communicate His divine approval and good fortune to the body of Christ; again, this is not unlike what earthly agents do for their agencies. They stabilize, advance, and enlarge the kingdom of God and manage official kingdom ventures on His behalf. Prophets execute their commission, charges, discharges, and duties as commanded by the Lord using primarily His word—spontaneous, written, and revealed.

What makes this knowledge essential for the advancement of the prophetic is its realm of application. The prophetic agency is one of the many powers of the kingdom that establishes strongholds for the Lord Jesus Christ. The totality of these strongholds, along with their powers and forceful authorities, constitute the church's grounding as His ordained principality, according to Ephesians 1:15–23. Prophetic wards are set up to stream God's eternal light and divine truth into the world to reverse death and overturn its edicts in the lives of those touched by it. As the power force of the Lord's lone earthly principality, Christ's church prophets are to see that His churches profit and do not bankrupt the planet.

PROPHETIC AGENCY AS AN OUTGROWTH OF GOD'S PRINCIPALITY

A principality is the territory of a prince's dominion. It is the sphere of domain and authority of the offspring of a king. The offspring, insofar as God is concerned, are His born-again children. As His servants, ministers are most specifically the church officers Ephesians 4:11 identifies. The church's install-ment as God's eternal principality reversed the coup Satan pulled off in the garden of Eden with Adam, who surrendered his position as head of God's ancient principalities. From then until now, they have been world-dominated or manipulated. The sons of darkness have held sway over the main of the world's holdings. Only when the supernatural forces of God in the spirit realm merge with the vessels of His Spirit on earth is the balance of supernatural power affected. Refer back to our discussion of God's spiritual protocratics. (Also, see Dan-iel 10:21, Ezekiel 9, and Romans 8:38–39.) Thus, the darkness is restrained and modified by the light. Here is where the pro-phetic fulfills its role and gives way to the apostolic. A brief discussion of the apostle is in order if the Lord's prophetic and the apostolic moves are to interact successfully.

THE APOSTOLIC—GOD'S EARTHLY PRINCIPAL STRONGHOLD

John's gospel tells us the prophet foreruns the apostle. The apostle is the human investment of God's principal pow-ers and their dispensations. One of the two most important synonyms for the word *apostle* is the term *principalia* for our word *principality*. The second one is *plenipotentiary*. The terms collectively show the scope of apostolic authority in God's world and reveal the weight of responsibility Christ puts upon them as officers. Jesus Christ's direct summons and commissioning of apostles makes them His principalities on earth in their respective sub-realms and spheres. As such, they exhibit and exercise the omnipotence and sovereign power of God the Father as given to the Son of Man.

Before the apostle can do this, however, he or she must have the Lord's ordained ministry path prepared by the prophet. This is what John the Baptist did, as told by Luke in his early chapters. Luke stated that a prophet on the order of Elijah would come and turn the hearts of the fathers to the children, and the children to the fathers. This is a fulfillment of John's goal; it is essentially to prepare the people to receive and participate in the next phase of the Lord's plan.

As forerunner, John's task was to clear the heart path of the debris, fallout, and calamities the people had grown accustomed to living with every day for the Messiah. John preceded Jesus, as was foretold, preaching the word of repentance and baptizing with water to foreshadow the Lord's baptism with the Holy Spirit. When John effectively recognized and confirmed Christ as the Messiah, the focus of ministry activity shifted from him to Jesus.

After that, the normal course would have been that John's disciples submit to Jesus, which some of them did. Once this happened, John would have served as chief prophet under Christ, the Great Apostle, and participated in helping the world understand and adopt to His message. This all could have happened if John had not lost his head. The Lord allowed this because the Old Testament prophet's economy had to give way to apostolic leadership and governance. Under this dispensation, the apostles assume that place above the prophets, as is their right.

How Prophetic Movements Begin

Prophets usually start their movements with calls for repentance. They invoke the people of God to renounce their sins and abandon their secular and humanist contests with the Most High and Holy God. Elijah's Mount Carmel contest was no less than this. Prophets do this today to prepare people for the coming of the apostle, who prepares them for the coming of the Lord.

Prelude to Apostleship

When the truth and righteousness of God have been reinstalled, the ground is ready for the apostle to come forward with the next phase of God's plans. Here is where previous moves that limned the upcoming apostolic move take shape. Prophets begin the arduous interpretive process of linking the now word of God to its preceding move to propel saints forward into what God wants to set in motion. Thus, the mold is sculpted for the architecture of what the Lord will do next. The apostle then takes up his or her place as the present generation's principal stronghold of the Lord Jesus Christ in human form. Ideally, the two team up and take the next leg of the ministry's journey onward in the race, with the prophet paving the way before every step.

As you can see, a close working relationship between forerunning and subsequent prophets and apostles must be forged. That is the only way prophets will internalize and help apostles inculcate their apostolic revelations as part of a team. Very close and strategic team meetings must happen between the two to unfold God's plan and see to its continued success.

The apostle's house (the church, its affiliates, and intra-extra ministries along with its congregation) then serves God as a territorial stronghold. Furthermore, it becomes a supernatural watch station for the Lord, one of His jurisdictional precincts. It is where His territorial angels (similar to those over the seven churches in Revelation) are assigned to serve. Now you can see what the opening words of the Lord's revelation to the seven churches indicate. The superintendent of that spiritual precinct, the church, is the church prophet. The pastor functions as its governor when the church is not answering to an apostle. In this context, the pastor is over the prophet. If there is a bishop over the church, or an apostle, the pastor fills his or her role beneath him.

MINISTRY UNDER APOSTLESHIP

The apostle or bishop licenses pastoral performance, which is nevertheless still above the church prophet. The bulk of the church's spiritual weight and authority is *delegated,* according to God, to the prophet of the church by the pastor. God's ideal, however, is that the two, the pastor and the prophet, form a bond that makes delineation of each one's authority and roles incidental and not paramount.

THE CONTROVERSY OVER OFFICE VERSUS GIFTING

Of the many issues hindering the prophetic and God's rightful restoration of it to mainstream Christian service, the question of the gift over the office is the most troublesome one.

Hardly anyone affected by the prophetic today fails to question the difference between the two. Is the gift more than the office? Should the prophet's ministry be regarded as an office, and if so what does that mean to the church's hierarchy? Is hierarchy of God, and where is it in the Bible? How does the prophet's position affect the historical place of pastors?

On it goes year after year, with the argument over what validates a prophet and makes this type of minister different raging on. Distinguishing the prophet from the prophesier (the office from the gift) is critical and that is what this section does. The best way to separate and distinguish between the two is with a look at the societal systems that are already in place—those we are all conditioned to respect.

Here is a case in point. We have all heard about gifted singers, dancers, or athletes, and how many of them exhibited above average ability or talent from childhood. The musician, for instance, who just sat down and taught him or herself the piano. The athlete who picked up a ball and never seemed to miss a basket from the first throw. The artist who took up a pencil and sketched what was seen, with no direction or guidance whatsoever. People such as these come in all fields, but they all share one thing: an exceptional ability to do what they were formed to do, effortlessly and with only minimal outside intervention, if any. These are the gifted ones, the prodigies; the amazingly talented minds, hearts, and souls that make their mark on the world early in life. Being credited with genius deemed to be worthwhile in adulthood, these young ones are usually mentored from the day of their discovery to protect them and their gifts until both can benefit the world. They are nurtured, coached, and guarded until their natural talents can be honed to a fine art.

Unfortunately, no such wisdom characterizes those who happen upon the prophetically gifted soul. It seems that the moment anyone displays any impressive special ability in the area of the prophetic, he or she is immediately whisked to center stage and the front of the line. The prophet's ministry may be presumptuously practiced by whomever, with no requirement, special aptitude, or approval system whatsoever. Merely by saying, "Thus says the Lord," and having it come to pass (perhaps once or twice) gets these people promoted and rashly installed as prophets. No wonder the church fails to take the office seriously, or to recognize that there is indeed an office for prophets at all. So insignificantly is it viewed that anyone claiming a word is from the Lord is often granted immediate access to the body and entrance into its official spheres, usually with no questions asked. For the most part, those declaring a call to prophesy are believed and trusted based on no actual criteria. No proving, training, or apprenticeship is employed, just the ability to say something predictive and perhaps remotely profound.

That is not how the prophets of old saw this function, nor is it how they entered and executed their office. The ancients of their day were not bedazzled by the gifted; they demanded wisdom, reliability, proof of infallibility, and a solid track record. Our predecessors would never acknowledge a person's right to the prophet's office merely based upon a word. The Lord, through Moses, condemned this attitude and meticulously outlined the features and effects of His ordained prophets, stressing to them that there was a marked difference between the official and the gifted.

Indeed, the office is superior to the gift because it predates every other biblical ministry. From the time of Abel to the present day, the prophet's charge was a special one that only those suited to its service could bear. The office determines its official entrants, not the other way around. As with any public service or means of serving the public, the offices are created for the benefit of their authorities and their community, in that order. The empowering authorities' best interests are to be served continually and the public to benefit from that service is to be provided for and protected. The offices have their own duties, descriptions, standards, performance guidelines, and entrance criteria that serve as eligibility requirements for those who enter and serve in them. Compatibility with the office's stated qualifications must be exhibited upon entry and proven sustainable over time.

The Lord spelled out the qualifications He required in detail for those who would voice His mind to His people in early Israel. Stringent qualifications and extensive training paths were always stipulated for the one appointed to represent another. You could not just stand up before the public and serve them without credentials that showed you were authorized to do so by a higher authority. In those days, no one was officially accepted as a public voice or agent apart from demonstrating his or her possession of these qualifications. The same cannot be said about today's gift-obsessed church. People sing, write, draw, lead, and minister at will. They are encouraged do so freely, and to exercise their gifts as amateurs, appearing primarily as entertainers.

Here is the difficulty with this practice: these gifts are not regulated and cannot be, because they are outside of an official (office) capacity. They are freelance, independent expressions of one's natural talents available to be used at the owner's will. That is not the case with an office. Offices are dictated by those who establish them. The entity that delegated a measure of its mission or commission to an agency sanctions the official use of a particular gift or talent on its behalf. It usually starts by setting the parameters, boundaries, purposes, functions, and objectives for its agents' proposed duties and responsibilities. Once this is done, the distinct talents, abilities, skills, and experience needed for successful execution are then defined, to become, in turn, the service qualifications for those authorized to act on its behalf. To employ the most qualified people for the job, screening takes place to attract and gather the skills, talents, and gifts that best match the position's qualifications.

You can see now how and why more than talent and gifting are necessary for official functions. Professional entities require skill, experience, training and education, aptitude, and the proper attitude for their positions. They want more than a person who can or will do the job. They want the one who can be relied on time after time to do it well, according to their standards and to the protection and promotion of their best interests.

Our Lord and Savior Jesus Christ wants the very same thing from His prophets. He spoke repeatedly about getting the right people for the right tasks and using them according to their abilities. That is what the parables of the talents and the mina stress, as does His admonition to first count the cost of an endeavor to assure that what one starts one is well able to complete. When it comes to being God's voice, these standards could not be more important. Spiritual gifts, like natural gifts, rely on offices; giftings rely on officials for validity. Because validity comes with privilege and power, the responsibilities that counterbalance them are great.

To qualify for the opportunity or right to affect others with your gift in the name of an agency, you must be qualified by more than your talents. You must meet the criteria of the office. In this manner, the office must regulate the gift; otherwise, how can its existence and effectiveness be assured? What other means does an office have to guarantee that what it was created to accomplish for its creator can and will be done by the best person for the job? Therefore, the office itself discerns whether or not a gift is compatible with its own charge. It is the office that decides who is able to withstand its rigors and when a candidate is ready to perform effectively as a qualified representative of the agency it serves. The office determines and dictates the agent's schedule, readiness, behavior, conduct, measurements and standards, latitude, rank, and authority. Gifts, by themselves, need none of this kind of oversight. Based on these principles, the office invariably conforms or evicts its gifted entrants. Apart from the office, the gifting, on its own, only scarcely affects the world outside of its immediate admirers. It is not until the officials of its field of endeavor recognize and engage its services that the gift can perform in an official capacity. That is how it is with the prophetic.

The reason prophetic ministry has been so disturbing up to now is because the gift has been too often elevated, used, and exercised apart from (and above) the office. That left the prophetic gifting to operate with no guidelines, oversight, standards, entry criteria, or evaluative measurements. It also had no remedy or recourse for any damage it caused. Nothing really existed to assure accuracy, integrity, relevance, or purpose fulfillment. Those qualities are only available in an office.

The prophet's office has been in existence since Abel. (See Luke 11:49-51.) Its long-standing existence predates what we have come to accept as spiritual gifting. Generally, when this term is applied to any spiritual activity, it is referring to the gifts listed in 1 Corinthians 12:7–11. However, that is a misnomer because the word that is taken popularly for gifts in that passage does not pertain to the independent operations of individuals, but to the arbitrary manifestations of the Holy Spirit. Perhaps that is where the problem began in the first place. Nevertheless, Scripture establishes that long before the latest gifter came along, the prophet's office existed and was professionally occupied by those whom the Lord chose. It does not matter how much the prophetic may have been ignored over the years of the church's existence. Its office may have remained vacant, but in God's mind it was never defunct. If this next generation of prophets is going to get it right, they are going to have to relegate the gift to the office and demand that the prophesier and other prophetic gifts be regulated and administrated by official prophets.

CHAPTER SUMMARY

1. The prophetic is an agency.

2. Agencies include an official and a commission.

3. A commission governs subordinate entities.

4. Prophetics are God's divine agencies of the Creator's communications.

5. Divine communications release God's prophecies. They declare God's plans and actuate His words and will.

6. Prophets are God's divine communication agents.

7. Agents are officers of the Godhead delegated with Creator authority.

8. In addition to prophesying, prophets also intercede.

PROPHETIC ACTION ITEMS

1. Conduct a study of agents and agencies and use your information to design what you conclude your prophetic ministry should be. Include policy, protocols, practices, and operations, if you can.

Chapter 6

THE CHURCH
PROPHET'S ROLE

In this chapter you will read about the difference between church prophets and itinerant prophets. It covers:

- God's plan for the church prophet
- *Shamar* prophets
- General church prophet tasks
- Avoiding prophetic monopolies
- The watchman duties of the church prophet

HOW CHURCH PROPHETS DIFFER
FROM ITINERANTS

To understand the church prophet's role, we start by giving some fundamentals on the position. Our goal is to validate church or resident prophets by defining their role in the church. Of course, the best place for us to begin is in Scripture. The following material comes from an extensive study of Hosea 12:13. The passage reads, *"By a prophet the LORD brought Israel out of Egypt, and by a prophet he was preserved."* The relevance of this teaching centers on the two words used to describe what Moses the prophet did, and continued to do, in the life of the people God sent him to deliver from Egyptian bondage. Implications behind Israel's exodus and Moses' subsequent guardianship over the delivered people of God shed light on the prophet's constant work following deliverance. Its inclusion in Hosea's discourses instructs us further, beyond what we learned about Samuel's ministry, on how the prophet may be utilized in the local church. From these meanings, it may be deduced that every church needs a prophetic guard. That is a force of seasoned prophets that create the shield of defense that keeps the church clean, pure, focused, and out of Satan's reach. This shield takes the first hit, akin to what a government's guard would do. Guardianship is the primary and standing purpose of the church prophet. Without one, the church is vulnerable to humanist and demonic victimization and can easily lapse into its original bondage to carnality. The cares of this world and the pride of life overtake it.

Two words that are used in this passage show what ancient prophets did. Together they enlighten us on the functions of stationary prophets in today's church, jointly giving us a sketch of this officer's work in the modern church. The two words are *alah* and *shamar*. In this discussion, we concentrate on the Hebrew word *shamar*. It means "to guard." Regarding the prophet, these definitions are a good guide for those who cover our churches with their prophetic mantles and mandates in the twenty-first century. *Shamar* clarifies their functional activities and responsibilities in local congregations.

God's Plan for the Church Prophet

God intends that church prophets watch, guard, protect, fence in, patrol (heavenly and societal realms), war, pray, and intercede for their assigned churches. These responsibilities include their constant purview of Christian doctrinal and theological outpourings in their generation. Church prophets should not conduct their offices in a vacuum. They should be aware of new teachings and movements taking place around them so they can endorse or renounce them. In doing this, they spiritually and supernaturally guard the Lord's church as long as it is on earth. Our description of the ministry of the contemporary prophet as taken from the book of Hosea involves the prophetic in all of these functions because of *shamar*'s meaning, as defined in the next section.

SHAMAR PROPHETICS

The word *shamar* means "to keep and guard safely; to preserve and protect." Think about this prophetically to see how one so assigned achieves these in the church. Speculate on the probable duties, responsibilities, and position description needed to accomplish this as an official prophet.

As a spiritual entity on earth, the church enjoys the bulk of what is performed or accomplished for it in the realm of the spirit. Such officiations are executed by the prophet, who uses mostly supernatural means, such as prayer vigils and intercessions, spiritual warfare, and divine revelations. By nature, prophets employ these tactics for modern interpretation and translation of the old to the new, or vice versa, for their local congregations. At first glance, the above spiritual duties seem pitiable and insignificant in comparison to human initiatives because they are essentially ethereal in context and nature. Further study reveals an inherent potency in these methods that, when compared to earthly blessings, makes many carnal or humanist tactics impotent in contrast.

Thus, local church prophets should, above all, endeavor to attend prayer sessions held by the church. How else can revelations imparted to prayer groups be balanced and validated by them as credible witnesses? Also, in no way besides actual participation in the congregation's prayer vigils can church prophets effectively and intelligently battle darkness for the flock. This ceaseless endeavor is incumbent upon them because prophets' powerful spirits easily release blessings and victories to the church that may otherwise be held up by demons. Their dynamic presence is respected by them on account of the prophets' numerous clashes with these powers during their training years.

As a recruit, the well-trained prophet successfully learns how to guard and keep the territory God gives to a particular church body. The church prophet who does not participate regularly in a congregation's corporate prayer life is a guard disconnected with his or her purpose for being on the wall, and unenlightened on the mien of prophetic ministry. Many prophets object to this duty because they feel themselves and their anointing to be too potent for the lay member. They prefer to get their intelligence on the congregation strictly from the Holy Spirit. While there is much to be said for this approach, it is not enough to shore up the wobbly faith of struggling leaders and members, and it does little to affirm the prophets' interests and concerns for their hopes, goals, or predicaments.

Church prophets should regularly participate in, and spiritually see to, the officiations of church sacraments and special ceremonies, such as weddings, christenings, and baptisms. In this capacity, church prophets should stand by with a ready word from the Lord on the celebrated event. Likewise, their presence immediately preserves the protocols, practices, and executions of the services and keeps God's aims at the heart of it. As supernatural agents of the Godhead in attendance, church prophets ward off ungodliness, error, abuse, and neglect when they are competently trained.

GENERAL CHURCH PROPHET TASKS

Churches and their leadership should be well versed on how and where to employ their church prophets. For instance, consider the christening of babies. All babies born into the world have a divine purpose, which can be revealed to the parents by God's prophets. The church prophet's role, then, is to divulge that purpose to the parents before negative world influences have a chance to subvert or inseminate the child's destiny with its Christ-less alternative. Ideally, parents will use the prophet's revelation to nurture the youngster in God's divine purpose. Children in the church should have as ample a time to hear from God about their lives as the adults do. Having trained prophets minister to them as practice is a good developmental exercise. Church prophets should be in attendance at, or soon after, a youngster's conversion or baptism to minister the Lord's word on his or her new life and to cover him or her with the mantle of the church. The way a child's parents were nurtured may naturally attempt to overthrow the will of God in a child's life, so the Lord's higher powers must intervene early to prevent needless upsets and diversions that take youngsters, novice ministers, and newcomers to Jesus Christ off course. The revelations of the church prophet can place newcomers to Christ on their predestined paths and settle them in their New Creation destiny.

Church members can also benefit from this resident ministry from time to time. If church members were able to hear from the Lord prophetically in their home church regularly under the auspices of their pastor, then fewer saints would be seduced to follow questionable prophets' ministries or resort to psychics to hear about their futures. Another important function of the prophet is prophetic counsel. This embraces more than prophesying; it is advisory prophetics that blend present insight, future wisdom, and divine revelation with prophetic acumen.

Beyond this, the church prophet should be part of the clergy representatives in membership crises like death, illness, calamity, and so forth. The prophet's word ensures that the demons involved in the attack are halted and do not tread past their assigned or permitted bounds. Read over David's penalty for counting Israel and how the Lord told the angel on assignment in the judgment when to draw back his sword. The account is in 1 Chronicles 21. Another good activity for the church prophet is accompanying church members who have to face and interact with world authorities like judges, police, and so forth. The respectful presence of the church prophet interceding in the background and upholding the will and word of the Lord in the matter can soothe otherwise explosive situations. Above all else, the church prophet should be present and involved at the church's major outreach functions, and it goes without saying that the mature ones should collaborate on the church's business matters. If you read 1 Kings 22:6–13, Ezra 5:1, and Nehemiah 6:7, how this all works is elucidated.

AVOIDING PROPHETIC MONOPOLIES

It should be said in conclusion that the church prophet institution should not be limited to just one prophet. The one chosen to *superintend* the ministry of the local church should be free to identify, nurture, and induct others into the ministry to help shoulder the workload. Also, having more than one prophet reduces the possibility of prophetic monopolies in the church and allows the congregation to hear from God from more than one dimension.

Pastors should seek to establish the ministry of the church prophet as an ordained order that includes prophetic representation from all the relevant spheres of the church's life.

THE WATCHMAN DUTIES OF THE CHURCH PROPHET

Going back to the word *shamar* that we have been discussing, it further means "to watch over as one who guards cattle or sheep," a definition that sums these up in the prophet. *Sheep,* in this case, refers to the flock of a congregation. In the Lord's church, it refers to church members. You may already know that another word for the prophet is *watchman.* It symbolizes the patrolling and guardianship activities of the officer in the supernatural realm. Thus, the watch center of the church prophet's territory coincides with a church's divinely appointed sphere.

Watchman duties are accomplished through the prayer, intercession, and petitions of the prophet on behalf of the church. They entail activation of the prophet's mantle to invoke and marshal the spiritual forces assigned by God to keep the balance of power and tilt the scales in the church's favor at the prophet's word. Furthermore, they comprise the many reasons a prophet should be installed as the superintendent of the church's overall *prophetics*, and as head of its spiritual guard, particularly the prayer group. Such a guard would consist of the prayer team, special intercessors, dedicated psalmists, seers, and, of course, subordinate prophets. The *watchman* application spotlights links between what prophets do spiritually and what a similar officer would do in the natural realm. Thus, the word *shamar* gives prophets the status of spiritual guards, warriors, supernatural enforcers, and keepers of the churches of God. (See Jeremiah 17:16 and 50:6–7 as examples.)

Additionally, our word *shamar* identifies a prophet who encircles (or surrounds) to retain and attend to, as one does a garden. The prophet's spiritual authority acts as a fence or garrison around an assigned congregation to shield it from harm, attack, or demonic trespass. Protection from trespassers, as meant here, includes protection from the spoilage, destruction, invasion, and threats that result from spiritual and human trespassers in the church. There are times when heretical types or wayward renegades join a church just to sow seeds of destruction in it. The watchful eye of the resident prophet can spot these people and bring spiritual discomfort to bear on them so they are ill at ease among the flock and quickly leave. This tactic is always engaged by occultists in the church's neighborhood.

On the other hand, in congregations where the prophetic is refused, the same situation can have disastrous results. By the time church leaders become aware of the sly manipulations of roaming renegades, it is often too late. Usually excessive generosity, overt assistance, and frequent volunteering at the outset obscure their tactics. Therefore, the ulterior motive that brought them to the church is submerged beneath a veneer of good deeds—charity work. Witches and other destructive occultists rely on this tactic to infiltrate and contaminate the churches they target for attack. Months, years, even decades can go by before the scheme is uncovered without a discerning and well-respected prophetic eye. In the meantime, countless souls may be lost to the church because of the free course given a saboteur of darkness. A solid screening program with a significant probationary period could reduce the success of such attacks.

For an additional example of the detriment of a prophetic void, see the effect of Elisha's death on Israel in 2 Kings 13:14–21. The account gives a biblical picture of how the absence of the prophet is used advantageously by the enemy. Notice how the band of raiders attempting to invade the area was successful only after Elisha's death. The *spiritual void,* better yet *prophetic void,* left by Elisha's demise enabled their attack on the land to finally succeed.

SHAMAR UPHELD BY KINDRED TERM

Our *shamar* teaching is supported by a kindred term that validates its truth. It is the word *natsar,* and it legitimizes the watchman status of the prophet in the contemporary church by expanding previous church prophet responsibilities.

The resident or staff prophet is to spiritually and practically engage in activities that protect, preserve, maintain, and observe the quality of the church. Prophets are instrumental in helping a church secure its basis for existing, its stability, and its congregant growth. They are obliged to observe and spiritually nurture its communal life. This even includes inspecting worship and recreational forms, educational doctrines, and kingdom practices to ensure they are consistent with Scripture and compatible with the nature of the Godhead in conduct, perspective, and manifestation.

Natsar prophetic functions surround the church as they would a well-guarded city. That makes the prophetic guard a human wall about the church and a spiritual shield by which the Lord hides the congregation from attack. The prophet's covenanted spiritual authority intervenes for the church as the mantle cloaks it to conceal its vulnerabilities. In this way, the stationed church prophet fortifies the church he or she covers as a fortress in God's high places. In this capacity, the prophet protects the house from the bondage and strongholds of idolatry, spiritual intimidation, and ecumenical compromise. Prophets quickly spot even secular holds and humanist philosophy lurking in traditional church doctrines unseen by most. (See Jeremiah 4:16 for a better understanding of God's mind on this duty, which is also what Nahum 2:1 talks about.)

The preceding discussions establish that prophets are fighters. This is the nature of the mantle and the requirement of the task. Prophets must be fearless, determined, resolute, and protective. If not, they end up being mere newscasters who announce what is going on with no godly effect whatsoever on the events happening in the church. Obviously, character and temperament flaws such as this can be harmful without divine restraint, which is why prophets must be painstakingly obedient and fiercely loyal to the Lord. However hurtful the job may be at times, prophets are dangerous if they have not surrendered their hurts and disappointments to the Lord. Those who do not turn to the Lord risk raiding, intentionally or not, His treasures. When this happens, these prophets cease to be servants and frightfully become supernatural mercenaries using powerful abilities to finance their whims or reward themselves for all they suffered. Read God's answer to this improper prophetic attitude in Micah 3:5.

Despite the risk, prophets overall, when well trained, are worth it. Pastors, in light of this information, ask yourselves if you could use some added spiritual help and increased supernatural covering for those entrusted to your care. If so, you are ideal candidates for a church or resident prophet institution.

In the next chapter, I will present information to guide shepherds and church prophets in their discovery and installation of this ministry. Also outlined are more valuable uses of the church prophet in a local church.

CHAPTER SUMMARY

1. Hosea 12:13 amplifies prophetic service.

2. Two words, *shamar* and *natsar,* expand prophetic duties.

3. The church prophet performs at least eight specific functions.

4. The word *shamar* identifies the guardianship duties of the prophet.

5. Local church prophetics require several standard tasks.

6. Local churches should avoid prophetic monopolies by installing prophetic ministries that represent the entire body.

7. The prophet's guardianship duties fulfill the mantles' watchman actions.

8. Micah 3:5 depicts improper prophetic attitudes.

PROPHETIC ACTION ITEMS

1. Show how prophetic guardianship should be carried out and the particular human issues or conditions that necessitate it.

2. Depict how you would recognize Micah 3:5 in action.

3. Project what type of screening and readiness programs today's prophets need in order to be effective.

Chapter 7

THE CHURCH PROPHET

In this chapter you will read about the church prophet and how the Bible's ancient models apply today. It covers:

- Church prophet submission
- Church prophet leadership interaction
- Church prophet lifestyle and posture
- Benefits of church prophet submission
- How church prophets are financed
- Standard position of the church prophet

CONTEMPORARY APPLICATION OF ANCIENT GUIDE

Y ou have been introduced to the validity of the church prophet in the local church. The office and officer were discussed from the perspective of Hosea 12:13 and the Hebrew words *shamar* and *natsar*. Here we pick up the study from that point.

From what you read previously about the *shamar* function of the prophet, you now understand how church prophets are to fulfill spiritual and practical functions. It can be said, for comparison's sake, that their *watch care* functions closely resemble those of resident watchers in certain secular institutions, such as fraternities, sororities, rehabilitation houses, and similar institutions where personnel are assigned to oversee, tend to, and safeguard residents.

With the prophet, it is more significant because his service has governmental and priestly, as well as predictive, elements attached. Any overseer of a communal dwelling or gathering place whose position is more than custodial, to use an earthly example, fits this category. Observing the functional preoccupations of such custodial care superintendents clearly illustrates this aspect of the church prophet's spiritual purpose.

ALL-IMPORTANT CHURCH PROPHET REQUISITE—SUBMISSION

In the church house, a prophet's authority is subject to the pastor for the duration of the assignment. The reason for this is simple: the church and its members were given to the shepherd, not the prophet, unless the prophet is the pastor. Read about Gad and Nathan's service under David's reign for how this works.

RESIDENT CHURCH PROPHET AND LEADERSHIP INTERACTION

Nathan and Gad were of David's *nabiim* institution, although Gad was a seer and Nathan a nabi. They served as resident or stationary prophets, as discussed earlier in the book. Nonetheless, their presence, assignment, or spiritual authority as staff prophets did not negate David's regency over the land. Although their words had great power and induced the supernatural, their positions did not subjugate or supersede David's reign. The two royal officers served him as counselors, seers, intercessors, sages, and prophetic warriors with authorized voices in the supernatural. They worked in tandem with each other for the good of each one's assignment and their mutual service. Both prophets' greatest contribution was their official license to invoke the nation's potent spiritual powers and responses in this world. If you read Deuteronomy 32:9–13, you see that the Lord established Israel in a spherical as well as natural high place. Covenantal relationship with the Most High God brings with it the benefit of abiding in His highest realms. David understood this, as may be seen from reading his words in 2 Samuel 22:34. He saw those of his cabinet as spiritual high powers assigned to his reign, as they were with Saul, and he did not limit that cabinet to only secular authority.

When Saul and Jonathan were slain, David understood that they had fallen from their high places and their deaths were most likely the consequence of their spiritual weakening. Job 25:2 fortifies this truth by declaring that the Lord makes peace (indicating His sovereign authority) in His high places. Read with this Psalm 18:33. For future teaching on the subject so it makes more sense to you, think about "God's highest places" reference in this light. Read Psalm 18:33, Isaiah 14:14, 2 Samuel 22:34, and Habakkuk 3:19. They all share the same idea of what is meant. Prophets need to grasp this concept since they are the physical embodiment of God's high place representatives in their churches. It does not change in the New Testament because all of its writers that address the subject speak about the influence of the heavenly places and our inheritance contained there.

Spiritually, such high place references, tendered by the Hebrew word *bamah*, define the clouds and the highest waves of the seas. This word speaks to the heavenly and celestial spheres of God as much as it refers to the high powers of the earth and their corresponding authorities.

The two prophets' (Nathan and Gad) spiritual high places occasioned their positions of authority with David. Their mantles gave the king direct and immediate access to the spontaneous will and word of the Lord on routine and unexpected matters. For this function to be fruitful, it is obvious that prayer must be a great part of the watch duties of the prophet that serves a church.

Remember, intercession and prayer, not merely prophesying, are priority jobs of the prophet. Without a disciplined and potent prayer life, church prophets would rely on their *soulish realm* for revelation. They could then risk prophesying out of their own hearts (Jeremiah 23:16) or their own spirits (Ezekiel 13:1–3) what is called *divination,* as discussed later. The perceptions of the leader and the whims of the flock can prevail in these cases more than anything else. Worse than this is the church prophet who fails to read the Scriptures regularly or fails to seek the Lord for daily prophetic ministrations. In these cases, Jeremiah 23:13 is the outcome. The spiritual principles and laws of creation see to it, because what is written in Isaiah 66:4 and Jeremiah 23:13 can be the only consequence.

CHURCH PROPHET LIFESTYLE
AND POSTURE OF THE CHURCH

Prayer, separation from the world, and devotion to God are the phase-one acts of prophetic preparation. After these, a rigid adherence to the Spirit and Word of God alone ensures church prophets consistently deliver the pure words of the

Lord to those in their care. Neglecting such requisites and fraternizing constantly with the household are the greatest dangers to prophets' accuracy. Here is why.

Excessive mingling with those they serve can cause prophets' devotion to their charge to overrule the will of the Lord in certain situations. Hearing too often their problems, needs, and plights firsthand can so arouse prophets' compassion or opinions that they can confirm what the Lord may not have ordained. The incident of King David's desire to build a house for God in the book of 2 Samuel 7:1–29 makes this point.

As you can read from the account, the prophet Nathan's constant interactions with David caused him to give David a word from the sphere of the obvious. He prophesied the obviously predictable when asked by David if he thought God would be pleased if the king built Him a house in which to dwell. Nathan told David to go on and build God a house, because his experience with the king had shown him how pleased Jehovah was with king David. In the prophet's mind, God's good pleasure was so abundantly evident in the king's life that He could not possibly deny David the honor of building Him a temple. After the prophet gave God's consent to the king, he was later sent to reverse his word following a vision he received that night. It is a good thing the prophet Nathan was not too proud to reverse his word with the king and give the real word of the Lord on the matter. Many prophets today would not do so for fear of professional embarrassment or being labeled false prophets.

Instead of allowing the king's sacrifice to be spurned by God and wasting his time, money, and energy on what would not have pleased the Lord, Nathan boldly gave the king what he learned was the true mind of God regarding his plans. In this case, revelation could have been jeopardized by familiarity and both could have been dangerous. Thanks to the humility of the prophet, it was not. Nathan's willingness to admit his mistake meant the king's desire was denied for hallowed reasons only. Due to David's military career, which involved much bloodshed on God's behalf, building a house for the Lord was assigned to one of his sons, Solomon.

This example shows that for the church prophet in particular, the line between friendship and familiarity can easily grow thin and fade. Warm feelings and the fortified trust that grow between the prophet and the pastor could eliminate boundaries and relax standards to the point where the prophet's mantle in the church becomes merely a spiritual prop. It can also be the other way around. The pastor's authority in the union may get so weak that the prophet disregards it in favor of what he or she is certain the Lord is saying.

When familiarity takes hold, the pastor can claim to have a church prophet, but over time he may nullify the messenger's value to the church and its leaders. I have been in such situations in the past. When the struggle between the two mantles remained unresolved, the only thing left for the pastor and church prophet to do was to sever ties. To all concerned, this case made the decision to dissolve treasured relationships or withdraw from comfortable fellowships for professional reasons difficult. Being aware of the gravity of my office and the conditions under which such relationships were formed, I recognize when God's motivation for my being in someone's life is jeopardized or compromised. I not only distance myself when familiarity begins to border on contempt, but I also do so for the benefit of the person greatly in need of God's prophetics.

It is quite easy for prophets to get to the place where they commune with someone so much that the person forgets who the prophet is meant to be in his or her life.

At these times, joint prayer sessions yield little objectivity as the prophet begins to sit on important information received from God. Intimate acquaintances start to question the veracity of the words prophets receive because of perceiving the messenger as being too close to the situation. On the other hand, the prophet worries about threatening the friendship if he gives his pastor-friend a word he or she will not like. As the days go by, the prophet grows more timid by the friendship, fearing pastoral retaliation. The pastor and the church's spiritual covering begin to disintegrate. Wisdom dictates under these circumstances that the problem be brought out into the open and discussed frankly. If the suspicions of the prophet are true and his or her usefulness to the pastor is finished, good decisions should be made as the two accept that the prophet's time with the ministry is up. Although this can surely prove painful, it is nonetheless quite prudent. As the severing process gets underway, responsible plans should be made to make the transition from the old to the new prophet as smooth as possible.

Even with this likelihood, which need not be viewed with negativity, God still would like to provide His Davids of today with the same benefit as their ancient predecessor by installing like prophets in all His churches. Truly the church needs a solid, competent, masterful *nabiim* institution operating in Christ's integrity. The Lord yearns to give His pastors the advantage they need over darkness by assigning a potent *spiritual watch-force* to guard and defend His churches from their onslaughts.

As operatives of the divine kingdom of the Most High, prophets' spiritual authority in the church's realm should easily supersede that of the kingdom of darkness. Not restricted to the supernatural alone, the church prophets' activities that effectively impact the spirit world can effortlessly overcome the edicts of human kingdoms as well, another value they bring to the church. According to Scripture, the prophets of God should *profit* those they serve, not merely themselves. A prophet's mature presence in a land says that prosperity on all fronts should be at the church's disposal over time.

THE BENEFIT OF VOLUNTARY CHURCH PROPHET SUBMISSION TO THE CHURCH

While it is true the prophet is the second-ranking Ephesians 4:11 official, those assigned to local churches voluntarily submit to the shepherd to cooperate with the will and purposes of God. Their decision to do so allows them to collaborate effectively with the head of the church on matters pertaining to the Lord and the church, and enables all concerned to yield the peaceable fruit of obedience. Humble church prophets take care not to usurp the pastor or to attempt to draw away the sheep as disciples after themselves. They shun the very appearance of evil suggested by these behaviors before the membership, deliberately giving the pastor due regard in every public instance. From their hearts they know they are in the church on divine assignment and their job is to uphold the pastor in every credible way. In addition, submissive church prophets make sure the sheep do not see them as alternatives to the pastor or attempt to pit the two against each other, prophet versus pastor. Church prophets do not shepherd the sheep they cover and guard outside the pastorate. Committed and insightful church prophets protect and develop the members and keep them in the Lord's spirituality.

I once had a prophet of a church whose agenda was wholly contradictory to mine. I called a meeting with this novice to try to get to the bottom of a similar problem. I thought that if I discussed the matter with him personally, he would see the value of a functioning collaboration between us. It did not work. You see, as long as the prophet was free to lead, prophesy, and perform, everything was fine. When I imposed boundaries and guidelines on him, his attitude turned sullen.

In the meeting, the young prophet became belligerent and informed me that he was not giving his life to ministry; he had a life outside of it and he would not permit me to tell him what to do. Taken aback, I let him know that the two perspectives were mutually exclusive of the prophet's office. His life was no longer his own and a church prophet assignment, like a mentorship, presupposed his being told what to do. My words had no effect. The prophet countered by adding that he would determine when he would or would not obey me. I was stunned, as I had never imagined these disorders brewing in this person's belief system. He had come to me from under a reputable and well-known prophet, and I assumed the person had these basics of prophetic character resolved. He did not.

After a few more "I'm grown and don't need anyone to tell me what to do and where I can go" tantrums, the prophet informed me that he had to seek God on my request. I had asked that he give me advance notice when he would be leaving town or skipping a service, and that was his response. Naturally, I saw that the entire arrangement had grown dysfunctional and said as much. My answer to our young prophet was that any position with any organization would require such notification and that the issue at hand was not a matter of adulthood or childhood. It was a matter of accountability—professional accountability. I realized that this young prophet would be embarking on a long road to learn two very primitive prophet lessons: obedience and accountability. If it were not for the insight into what the Lord was going to have to do to teach him that the two go hand in hand, and that one cannot be without the other, I would have been more disturbed. As it was, I was grieved as Samuel over Saul because, knowing God as I did, I saw that it was going to get rough for this young learner. Rather than wait for the prophet to pray and get God's answer, I severed the relationship by releasing the novice from my tutelage. I knew this outburst masked deep-rooted problems springing from other issues that hindered his ability to grasp the most elementary of prophetic principles.

Cases like this show why church prophets should not be installed who have problems with accountability, with reporting to the pastor as instructed, or with performing their duties according to the pastor's directives. These all amount to insubordination and will culminate in a church insurrection. After a while, that is what happened in my case. The young prophet, convinced he was ready to go it alone, gathered a number of other neophytes and began to teach them. Ironically, the very obedience he required of his new followers was lacking in himself. I am sure many pastors have been in this place, and the sagest answer I can give you is to cut ties early, quickly, and decisively to avoid infecting the rest of your germinating leaders, should a prophet be unwilling to listen and learn from you.

I am reminded at this point of those churches whose staff prophets have diverted the flock's attention from the pastor to themselves. In some instances, the act of treason was so great that even the tithes due the church were diverted to the prophet. I have experienced this myself. A prophet, afraid he will not get the opportunity to do his ministry, attaches himself to a church for only one reason. That is to ingratiate himself to the pastor long enough to seduce the spiritually hungry or immature members with his prophetics. Once the prophet's ministry has dazzled the susceptible members of the church, the prophet creates a situation where he can retaliate against the pastor for an artificial hurt by abruptly leaving the church, freeing himself to launch his ministry with the pastor's flock. Beckoning disgruntled members he has inflamed over time, the prophet sets up a ministry to rival the church and convince its membership to support his work. He instructs them to bring their tithes to the prophet's meetings to finance his rebellion. This is error, as Scripture records that no prophet, or other itinerant minister, is authorized to receive congregational tithes and offerings due the church he serves. Moreover, the Lord expressly forbids local church servants, ordained or not, to splinter a church down prophetic lines. It should be underscored here that tithes generally go to the priests (shepherds) of the household and not to the church or itinerant prophet unless they are tithes the prophet's ministry has earned. If the prophet is the priest (pastor), or serving in a similar purpose in a tither's life, then he or she is authorized to receive the tithes. To do otherwise could have a congregant's giving go unrecognized by God.

Aside from the previous situation, prophets receive and are entitled to offerings and support for their labors, but not the tithes from the church to which they have been assigned without the pastor's approval. Prophets truly sent by God will encourage congregants to surrender their tithes to the church and not to themselves for the sake of obedience. They will also urge church members to remain under the covering of their pastor and not to seek prophetic experiences outside the church. You will know a God-groomed church prophet by how he or she leaves. If the prophet leaves the church quietly, informing only the pastor and refusing to incite other members or leaders to leave with him or her, then this is a godly and trustworthy prophet.

HOW CHURCH PROPHETS ARE FINANCED

A staff prophet should be compensated regularly like any other permanent or long-term employee of the ministry. A regular salary is necessary if the prophet is to forgo traveling ministry to serve one church. If not, the danger of his abandoning his post to provide for himself is great, and this endangers both the church and its head unnecessarily. I strongly urge pastors to properly compensate their prophetic staff, particularly their chief and assistant chief prophets, just like they would any other full-time servant of the house. As soon as it is practical, the staff prophet should be compensated routinely like any other employee of the church or work. It cannot be stressed enough that if you require your prophet to remain in the church and to dedicate all prophetic resources to it, your pastor must compensate him or her sufficiently enough to do so. Such compensation need not come directly or exclusively out of the church budget, and it may be only partly allocated from church income. But pastors should allow their staff prophet to hold prophetic meetings, seminars, classes, and such under church auspices where he or she can attract offerings. The cost of such meetings should be borne by the prophets themselves with fees assessed according to what their personal ministry can afford. The prophet should also tithe from the money raised from the church's covering.

Under these conditions, it is helpful to urge the congregation to pledge to support the local church's prophetic institution as they would any missions team. The reason I stress prophet compensation so stringently is because of my experience with pastors in the past. On numerous occasions, I have heard them criticize their supposed church prophet's itinerant ministry. When I ask them if the prophet is paid like any other staff member, most say no. I then ask how they expected their prophets to serve their churches and still provide for their needs. The answer is usually a shrug or a quick change of subject. Prophets, like teachers, deacons, and praise leaders, must be put into the church's budget. That is a sure way to keep them in the church instead of on the road.

STANDARD POSITION OF THE CHURCH PROPHET

When one serves as a church prophet, he or she stands watch in the realm of the spirit over the pastor and the church for their good. Offended or neglected prophets are not to become occupied with the church's demise or destruction. Should the church be involved in something dangerous, God expects the church prophet to pray and intercede for it to turn its heart and soul back to the Lord. He does not sanction the prophet's cursing the work to doom it to die because of the prophet's disappointment or disagreement with its direction or plans. Here is one more reason novice prophets should not be installed as church prophets. I have found that young and untrained prophetic people see only evil and doom in the beginning of their ministries. They discern who will die and what God should judge more than anything else. The fundamental nature of prophetic character inspires it until divine nurturing teaches otherwise.

An early predisposition to the flesh can motivate newcomers to the prophetic to confuse their soulish realm with the Spirit of God. Consequently, what they hear from God, although it comes pure, mixes with their immaturity, hurts, and anger, and makes them mistakenly deliver opinions, perspectives, and perceptions as prophecy. A tendency toward this reaction to church conflict threatens to make church prophets more psychic than prophetic. While it does not mean they are serving occultism, it does show that they are more attuned to the intelligence of their soul than the revelations of God's Spirit. At least initially, that is.

We have had new or unrefined prophets in our prayer groups and identified their immaturity and instability in the after-prayer visions and words they received. I remember remarking about one such seer that he received only negative words and visions from the Lord. It did not matter who the subject was; the word and revelations he received were consistently destructive. This seer's naturally negative personality had yet to be purged and so he hoped that anything he viewed was also wrong. Immaturity motivated this prophet to ask the Lord to shut down or destroy the work. It is not uncommon for people who have been abused or dominated by overbearing authority figures to see destruction and death as the only resolution of insurmountable problems. Therefore, when they come to God, they are immediately enraptured with His power to destroy all wrong and annihilate wrongdoers. Years of frustration and futility have bred in them the need for God to avenge them, even if they were permitted to witness a shortfall in another. These prophets' early years are fraught with the four Ds of damnation: doom, death, disease, and destruction. The redemptive and nurturing elements of the office come later. It takes a while for new prophets to see this as apparent misuse of their supernatural faculties and outright imposition of their personal criticism on the Spirit of God.

Seasoned prophetic servants, on the other hand, are on guard for potential harm and danger lurking to invade their flocks. Mature prophets recognize them as man-made tools of enlightenment, such as mysticism, occultism, secularism, humanism, and that most insidious seducer, tradition. Veteran prophets of the church recognize the signs and symptoms of adversarial invaders and combat them successfully while doing their best to keep the work intact and moving forward in God. They do not see demonic presence or infiltration as grounds for the destruction of the work as the novice prophet does. Education and training are how prophets avoid this, and so your church prophets must be learned in these and other prophetic subjects to expose them to the tricks the devil uses to get them to *prophesy* his will on their assigned churches. Training and education will equip them to know these groups by their death to the church campaign. Any injured prophet can fall into this trap.

Undeveloped wounded prophets make ready tools, or weapons, in the devil's arsenal. He only needs to study them briefly to note the doom and gloom that surround them. These prophets are unwilling for the Lord to forgive and redeem His works because they are full of unforgiveness. Such prophets remind you of Jonah the prophet in his disappointment at Nineveh's forgiveness by God.

When God wanted to forgive and spare the land, the prophet became angry and pouted because he wanted God's judgment to fall on it. To drive home the point, preventing this attitude calls for education and training. Without it, the untrained and slightly educated church prophet, stunted in ministry revelation and prophetic insight, tends to be doom- and gloom-minded. Such a minister can end up being no more than a megaphone in the congregation, amplifying doom's voice, or a busybody in the church's affairs, not impacting its people positively or appreciably.

Later we will discuss the necessary insights, abilities, and training a church prophet should receive. Still, the high- est capacity a church prophet needs is compassion for the flock. Church prophets are injurious if they are unmoved by the weaknesses, temptations, and trials of the flock. They are sorely wanting if they cannot have and show mercy on those who are not granted their same degree of wisdom and spiri- tual fortitude. I have seen some prophets so intent on being right that they are contemptuous of the sheep's suffering. It is good for all prophets to remain objective and responsibly detached, especially those of the local church. However, these professional safeguards should not overshadow basic Chris- tian compassion and empathetic ministerial consolation.

Chapter Summary

1. Hosea 12:13 indicates some of the duties and actions of the church prophet.

2. Church prophets served their leaders, mainly leaders of the kingdom and its institutions.

3. Prophets spiritually and spherically occupy the Lord's high places.

4. Two main features of church prophet submission are obedience and accountability with the church leadership.

5. Young prophets often make questionable prophets of churches.

6. Church prophets are not to divert congregant tithes to themselves.

7. Church leaders must allow church prophets to finance their lives. They, too, should receive salaries.

8. The standard position of church prophets means they are to fulfill their watchman duties as the church's perpetual lookouts.

Prophetic Action Items

1. Draw up a plan to show a group of pastors how having church prophets improves their world. Be specific, practical, and definitive in your response.

2. Outline an effective obedience path for a new church prophet.

Chapter 8

YOUR CHURCH PROPHET

In this chapter you will see how prophets best serve their institutions. It covers:

- Both sides of the pastor/prophet relationship
- How to explore conflict resolution options
- God's divine chastening of the prophet
- Veteran prophets' role in new prophet development
- The church prophet's roles
- The church prophet's chief resource
- Personal prophecy
- What prophecy is

CHURCH PROPHET INSTITUTION— LOCAL CHURCH PROPHETICS

Prophetics in the local church operate very differently from the free flow motions of the itinerant prophet. The fluidity of the prophetic in general usually has a difficult time molding to the necessary institutions of the church. Of all the reasons for this, the chief one is that the church prophet comes under the pastor, and this restricts the normal authority and latitude he or she enjoys. When it comes to the local church prophet, the assignment is not unlike the one between a contracted, howbeit respected, advisor and his or her assigned organization. If the prophet has not been broken and pruned by God, the arrangement may prove disastrous as the mainly ethereal mantle of the prophet clashes with the nurturing one pastors wear. Potential conflicts notwithstanding, there is much value to the arrangement. For it to work, though, prophets serving in a church must be aware that, for the good of the gospel, they are voluntarily surrendering great portions of their ordinary authority and privileges to fulfill another's mission and mandate. The decision is not unlike Christ's when He came to earth to carry out the Father's mission. According to Philippians 2:7, He deliberately made Himself of no reputation, knowing that what He had been before the assignment became irrelevant to the task at hand.

When a prophet comes into a local church because God has assigned him or her there, the object of his or her sojourn is to facilitate what the Lord wants the church to do. The challenge comes when prophets find it hard to do so without disrupting the church's culture and operations, or when they must discredit its present headship to succeed. The Lord expects the prophet to meld with the church's leadership and integrate his or her mantle into the customary life of the work as a support. Whatever authority the prophet on local church assignment wields is subject to that of the existing government of the church for the duration of the charge. *Charge* is a good word to use here because it includes the personal and professional costs of the duty, as well as the cost of its breadth of responsibility.

Prophets are errant (and arrant) if they see their call as being sent to wrest the sheep from under the pastor's covering.

When one meets prophets who are extracting sheep from the church and presuming to draw them unto themselves, these are prophets who are going against divine order. I recently heard someone say that he was leaving his church because a beloved friend intruded into the office of the prophet. I say *intruded* because, if the prophet were genuine and not a novice, he would be of a mind to spare the flock and therefore would discourage stable sheep from leaving their pastoral covering to personally serve the new prophet's calling. The reason the member gave for selecting his friend's position over his pastor is that he viewed his friend as his personal prophet. What a dangerous mentality. No one is meant to have a personal prophet to the exclusion of the rest of the body of Christ, and no prophet is ordained to strictly serve any one individual or small, isolated clique's will. Proverbs 18:1 says why, while Judges 17:1 gives us such an example in the Bible of this practice's detriment. When you read the account, you learn that only an idolatrous heart devoid of leadership wisdom resorts to such a spiritual order.

In an account in Judges, a man named Micah robbed his mother for his own objectives. He did not tell her he took her money, and she subsequently reacted by putting a curse on the thief. When he realized that his mother's curse could affect him, he confessed his crime, and she negated her curse. In a bizarre turn of events, she gave him some of the money back to fulfill his heart's desire to craft himself an idol. After he had done so, he invented an ancestral religion, and he installed his own priests. Of course, we know that during that era, the oldest males were considered heads of their houses, and so the authority to do so rested in Micah. However, this was not a pagan family but an Israelite one, and his deviations exacerbated the situation.

Meanwhile, a Levite (minister) was preparing to launch out on his own. Seeking a place to dwell, and presumably to offer his services, he happened upon Micah the idolater. The two men forged a covenant whereby the Levite would be the priest and officiate over Micah's new family religion. Judges 17:6 explains how Israel's spirituality so deteriorated: *"In those days there was no king in Israel, but every man did that which was right in his own eyes."* There was no kingship or headship, and so the people did whatever came into their hearts and minds. The Levite was supported by the idolater and lost sight of his initial calling. He ended up staying with Micah the idolater to serve as his personal priest. Read the last verse of the account.

God discourages prophets from seeing themselves as envoys of individuals rather than envoys of the cause of Christ, dispatched to His church. When the cause of Christ is intended, keeping sheep in their churches and serving the wider body of Christ become the prophet's primary objectives. If this is not so, it is safe to mark such a prophet as a wayward usurper of divine authority and to shun his or her divisive spirit.

I have had many conversations with prophets rising to the call from within a local church where they may have spent years. Suddenly, they legitimately sense the call to the office of the prophet. What happens next determines their credibility and God's long-term use of them in His service. Sadly, a great percentage of them respond to God's awakening crudely. They awkwardly manifest their gifts, abruptly sever ties, and callously crush loving pastors' hearts. In naive zeal, they recklessly disrupt the flow of the church where they grew up in the Lord so badly that they must be excommunicated.

In other cases, emerging prophets foster division by exercising their newfound ministries outside the confines of the church, refusing to be supervised by the pastors they now feel are beneath them. A distasteful struggle begins that can fragment the loyalties of the membership and wound many vulnerable sheep. Both extremes are infectious and should be avoided.

I remember talking to one church prophet who started a prophetic school outside of the church and declined to submit it to the pastor, even though the lion's share of the students came from the church's sizeable congregation. This is quite common, although somewhat unethical, by the way. As if starting prophetic education apart from the pastor's auspices were not damaging enough, the prophet shunned significant service in the church. He avoided prayer, never established a serviceable prophetic institute, and failed to identify and participate in grooming emerging prophets in the church. Those who were acknowledged were wooed away from the pastor's influence. There was nothing but chaos in the church, as a prophetic void was created by the prophet's disobedience. That disobedience released its seeds to flourish throughout the body and contaminated the faith of many of its members.

On the Positive Side

Of course, there are always two sides to every conflict, and the above is no exception. On too many occasions, prophets are suffocated in their churches by overprotective pastors who mean well but nonetheless sacrifice their prophetics to protect their flock. This happens regularly, often before the prophet has an opportunity to disrupt or subvert the work at all. Reacting to far too many horror stories and very little knowledge, normally tender and open-minded pastors can unintentionally slaughter a beginning prophet out of fear and overlook more positive options.

One positive option is to nurture young prophets and seek to establish the bounds of their ministries and establish prudent service parameters for your church. Require your prophets in the church to complete training, probationary trial, apprenticeship, mentoring, and the like before you trust them to serve in your church. Test the prophets' intentions by assigning them an important yet non-critical sphere of the ministry to manage and cultivate prophetically—perhaps the youngsters, new converts, or new members, if they have been with you long enough. If novices remain within the confines of the agreement, then you can increase their reach in the body and the weight of their responsibility. This process should take two to three years if the prophet is new. If the novices complete the process, you can move forward or identify a quality prophetic education program to which to refer them. Also, pastors, you do not have to wait two or three years for their formal education and training to commence. The two processes—your testing and their development—can go together.

Seeking the wisdom of other pastors who have successfully melded the prophetic in their churches is a good way to handle yours. Turning to reputable and seasoned itinerant prophets is yet another positive step. Besides following these suggestions, discuss your concerns honestly and objectively with the budding prophets in your church to elicit sound advice on how the office may be encouraged in the church. At the same time, have frank conversations with trusted colleagues about your fears to defuse tensions and enable you to take on a very important and far-reaching part of shepherding, that of nurturing, guiding, and facilitating a new officer's promotion in the Lord's kingdom. It is a great call, but unfortunately, many dutiful pastors overlook or shun it.

Pastors who boldly and competently take on the development of the prophetic not only facilitate its positive initiation in their churches, but also will reduce new prophets' potential to seduce the membership with mesmerizing prophetics. Pastors, be sure your new prophets understand that causing a church member to turn on his or her pastor is a deadly proposition, and according to Ezekiel 13:1–16, courts the Lord's wrath and can cost the prophet his or her place in God's eternal assembly.

WHEN ALL OPTIONS ARE EXHAUSTED

Conversely, prophets who find their pastors resistant to their call to the office and/or its operations, beware. If a pastor is truly dead set against your prophetic growth and manifestation in the church, seek a release from God to leave. Situations this dire can get tricky, however. Sometimes new prophets want to exercise their ministries so badly that they believe their brief encounters with God and the few early words He gives them to say are all that are needed to get going. They are unwilling to hear about grooming, training, seasoning, and proving, so they become difficult to handle. Impulsive and self-willed, they turn surly and unruly, becoming disrespectful and impudent. In young prophets' minds, God has spoken to them directly and that makes them just as knowledgeable of His ways as those who have gone before them. Talking sense, especially God's sense, to many of them at this point is impossible as they sit before you, arrogant and defiant.

In their minds, all you (pastors) want to do is sit on their ministries. Ironically, they feel you are holding them back because you are somehow jealous of their brand new gift and threatened by it. The leviathan spirit is all over them at this point as they reek with pride. Read Job 41 and pay particular attention to the last few verses. These neophytes are creating a case to turn on the pastor, penetrate the church with their untempered prophecies, and gain a sympathetic following to serve them in the bargain.

SHUNNING HUMAN INSTRUCTION COURTS DIVINE CHASTENING

After several attempts to reason with headstrong prophets, pastors finally conclude the best way for them to learn is the hard way. Either by mutual decision or outright rebellion, the new prophet commits the first of many spiritual blunders. Then God's fierce, pride-dissolving classes begin. Like Cain who committed a serious offense against God's divine ordinances, your young prophets too must be severed from the flock. If not, they may choose to leave and start their ministry unhindered by you—their way. Also like Cain, they are marked by the Holy Spirit as rebels, even though they continue to be well-loved by God and their pastors. Think about Mark when Paul and Barnabas traveled together. Although it took years, the young minister finally got the message and submitted to Paul after all. The unfortunate part of it was the path he took to do so. It was tough, no doubt, and he wasted years only to end up right where he started. It is the same way with today's hotheads.

God's invisible yet tangible mark mutes His favor on them for a time as they become fair game to the seductive and eventually brutalizing forces of darkness assigned by the Lord to facilitate their training. This spiritual analogy considers the Lord Jesus' work on the cross, which promises that the young offender, once trained and humbled, will be restored to God's useful service. The apostle Peter well understood this from what he said in 1 Peter 5:10. Hebrews 5 shows the Lord's pattern as set by Jesus Christ Himself. It says, *"Though he were a Son, yet learned he obedience by the things which he suffered"* (verse 8). It is no different for those the Lord saves and grooms for His service. Jesus suffered rejection, mockery, scorn, assault, and isolation. This He did as God's only begotten Son. How much more those who are truly stubborn.

VETERAN PROPHETS DISCERN DISSENTERS

As wayward novice prophets embark upon their humility, submission, and obedience training, they venture into the Lord's prophetic sphere and begin to circulate among the prophets. Seasoned prophets encountering such novices not only know these newcomers when they meet them, but they also discern the mark of the Lord on them. They understand why it is there. Having been on that route themselves, most of them are alert to the novices' victimized tones used to explain why they are all alone against the world and the church. They hear the undertone of stubbornness in them as they are determined to carry out the prophetic in their own way because everyone before them "got it wrong." Moreover, mature leaders sense independent prophets' subtle contempt for authority, resistance to accountability, and delight in assaulting the established church and its ministers.

Veterans have been there and are not easily fooled by the apparent anointing on the independent prophet's life or the amazing prophecies he or she utters. Veterans learned long ago that it takes more than a high-powered gift to accredit a prophet. It takes righteousness, the love of God, maturity, and submission. Senior prophets understand above all that the fundamental ministry law of God is respect for authority. Though they may be called from the ranks of the rebellious, if prophets are to excel in that calling, respect for authority is one reality they must prize. Jesus exemplified such respect in Matthew 23:1-3.

Experienced prophets who have been groomed by God's own hand recall the staggering submission lessons they learned from Him in their early years. Experienced prophets learned from God why the kingdom cannot withstand disrespect for authority. They will comprehend what makes rebellion the basis for the house divided. After a few moments with struggling, sullen prophets, stable prophets understand the learning path the King of kings has them on and how useful it will make them later on to pastors who want to install institutional prophets in their churches.

Those who have conquered what new prophets must confront and walked the well-paved road of the rebel know God's orders and are able to identify and redress those issues in others. If for no other reason than those just described, your prophetic superintendent must be comparably seasoned.

Once defiant prophets silently determine to walk away from the church, here is how to tell if they are leaving at the unction of God, or if it is their flesh reacting negatively to pastoral authority. Study the telltale signs below and ask yourself, *Is the prophet exhibiting the following signs as he or she considers leaving?* Answer the following questions to find out.

1. Did the prophet show that every effort was made to serve the Lord in the church and the pastor simply rejected it? If so, then the Lord could be reassigning this prophet to a more receptive and supportive leader.

2. Before the conflict, did the young prophet have a record of serving the church, obeying the pastor, and submitting to the church's rules? If not, then his or her motive for leaving is most likely selfish and not of God.

3. Is the young prophet leaving without sowing discord among the saints and without dragging his or her own little following behind? Then the call to leave could be of God. Otherwise, it definitely is not.

These three factors reflect the spirit in which a prophet or any minister leaves a church. They can help you identify any personal ambition that may have entered and spoiled the motives of the new messenger. When this happens, know that whatever comes from such prophets' mouths can be tainted with anger or jaded with personal bias. Before resistors leave, they criticize everything, refuse to participate in anything, and leave behind a trail of bitterness. Their anointing at this point mainly supports or explains their misconduct. They reek with self-justification, as well as pastor and church vilification. Organized churches and religion are the band of such an up-and-coming minister.

A good rule of thumb for assessing the prophetic motives of a potential or installed church prophet is to see how much the church at large voices its recognition of the prophet's positive influence in its vision, mission, and overall evolvement. If the prophet is not from outside the church, then the church congregation is the best judge of his or her potential. Good candidates for church prophet are actively involved in the members' lives, and the membership can attest to it. Generally speaking, the person with the most impact on the church overall appears everywhere, even if he or she is not in the forefront of the ministry. If a prospective church prophet is genuinely interested in the church, then that prophet's handprint, or mantle-print, will be as evident in the church's life as those of the pastors and its other leaders. Forefront ministers do not in themselves translate into the most effective servants. Often, it is the prophetic candidate whose work is seen long before a discovery that makes the best choice. This is because the historical fruits of his or her presence are more obviously present than the forefront prophet is, and the most credible church prophet signature. A chain of positivity and enduring fruit definitely has the greatest impact.

EXPLORING THE CHURCH PROPHET ROLES

The church prophet, in addition to what has been said so far, also serves as a divinely stationed sentinel. The mantle's prophecies sound the alarm that announces approaching danger to the pastor and the flock. A sentinel is a lookout, a demonstrator with a stake in the work he or she guards. Prophets see their call as ones who close the gaps in churches' coverings. As a sentinel, the prophet of the church scouts the supernatural regions surrounding the church to spot intruders (human or spiritual) from Satan and ward off impending seductive invasions. Through prayer, he or she patrols the spiritual terrain of the ministry as God's divine watcher. Agabus performed this function for the apostles in Acts 21. Study as well Paul's final public address to the Ephesians' presbytery in Acts 20:17–31. Both examples show the sentinel work of the stationary prophet.

Furthermore, during times of carnal relapse, the church prophet is the Holy Spirit's goaded objector, staunchly opposing the slackening of biblically moral lines. He or she can turn agitator and resister to hold back the flows of libertinism masking itself as New Creation liberty. Invariably, church prophets whose allegiance is to God cast the first dissenting votes against anything that threatens to jeopardize their churches' favorable status in the eyes of the Lord. In doing so, the *nabiim* institution of the local church can rally godly supporters for the pastor's aims or blockade in prayer whatever seeks to harm, hinder, or reverse the work. The very presence of church prophets can invisibly corral subtle or lurking sin and thereby close the borders of a church's sphere to protect its power link to Almighty God. The prophets' diligence assures that the stream of priceless yet invisible treasures, coveted by darkness, is not diverted from God's people.

Prophets, as part of God's spiritual surveillance networks, watch the landscape of the supernatural to report on and prevent demonic breakthroughs from occurring in their protective fences. They do on earth what the heavenly watchers of Daniel 4:23 and Zechariah 1:10 and 5:7 do in the spirit. Actually, the heavenly watcher reveals what church prophets must know to defend their posts, because mature prophets interact with God's angels. Therefore, every prophet's mantle is awakened by these supernatural counterparts. All bona fide prophets, without exception, are initiated by interactions with these powerful agents of God's invisible creation. No prophet can be genuine without an irrepressible awareness of the spiritual guard that surrounds him to supernaturally see to God's work and will on earth. The prophet's presence alone validates the minister as he or she unavoidably speaks in all God's worlds as casually as the one in which we dwell.

Consequently, church or staff prophets should be perceptive enough to discern good from evil and thereby detect invaders who steal from their flocks. Seasoned prophets have broad intelligence on such matters and are able to identify the forces with or against them. They skillfully cooperate with or counter their maneuvers accordingly.

For instance, church prophets spot and identify the problems with scripturally unfounded doctrine or nouveau worship forms that steer congregations away from God's holiness. They bring the balance between praise and worship and solid Bible teaching. The devil can take a church off its emphasis on Christ by pumping up praise and singing to the point that, week after week, all the church does is sing and dance. In the beginning the change may be good, but after a while it grows old, showing itself as a subtle trick to keep the Bible and biblical teaching out of the church, and thereby forestall the sanctifying process that is inherent in God's truth. I have attended services at churches whose congregations were proud of their praise being so powerful that they never had time for the Word of God. I reacted with concern, recognizing the remark as the stage-one tactic to making the church powerless. Prophets know that this is not God, as it is only by His Word that people grow and are grounded in His truth. Scripture shows that when Jesus could do nothing else, He taught God's Word. Being the Father's very truth Himself, it was impossible for Him not to do so. Over time, sensuality replaces spirituality in such churches, and the congregations never notice when it takes place. All they know is that they have become tired of singing and want to be fed the Word of God. It is an old tactic, but a highly effective one.

Another of Satan's popular tactics to keep the power that comes with God's Word out of the church is spiritual experiences. Satan does this by stressing meditating, basking or soaking, getting "drunk," or other physical actions that stimulate purely sensual responses. Such deviations are blamed on God's Spirit and are cunningly devised to replace teaching and study of the Lord's Word. The goal is to addict the congregation to sensuality by exclusively stressing what feels good. This serves to foster within it an intolerance for Scriptures and an irritation toward wise and intelligent Christianity.

Prophetic wisdom and knowledge enable prophets to inform, if not persuade, their churches of the inevitable outcomes and consequences of neotheology, pseudo spiritual antics, and risky ventures. Because they can easily detect wolves in sheep's clothing, prophets' service objectives should always be God's truth, holiness, and righteousness in the Holy Spirit. True prophets incessantly trumpet these words as divine commands. The wholesomeness of the Lord's purchased possession emerges as foremost in resident prophets' minds. For this to happen, church prophets must be well-versed in God's Holy Scriptures, and sadly, far too many often are not.

Bible knowledge skills, vital to credible prophetics, add reach and depth to the revelatory word of God when merged with other prophetic assignments. They also enhance prophetic accuracy. Otherwise *Scripture light* prophets just declare releases of the people's heart desires more than they unfurl divine revelation. Thus, their revelatory emphasis can be restricted to the congregation's most pressing temporal needs and fluctuating emotional states. The membership's spiritual state of well-being is generally ignored by church prophets under such circumstances and so becomes stagnant once its growth has been stifled.

The fruit of carnal church prophetics is perceivable because, like the Laodiceans, it *appears* a materially rich carbon copy of the world you thought you left behind. Material prophets are worldly in their views, fostering a totally *here and now* mentality. Prophets who share like perspectives will no doubt enjoy a prominent position in some churches. However, in the end, like the prophets of Jeremiah 23 and Micah 3:5-12, neither the sensual prophet, the material prophet, nor the carnal prophet will prosper each other sufficiently in the Lord.

THE CHURCH PROPHET'S CHIEF RESOURCE— GOD'S ETERNAL WORD

Many people enjoy hearing prophetic words of material possessions and supernatural deliverance from routine trials. However, there is a depth of the prophetic God wishes His prophets to bring into their houses that far exceeds the "bless you because you are blessed" words most have sought. There is a hallowed, priestly tinge to the prophetic word that springs from Scripture, because it uses it abundantly. The prophet who enfolds Scripture in prophecy unfolds the Lord's timeless connection between the hearers' call and redemption and the Creator's will for their lives on earth. To these types of prophets, securing your eternal life, maturity, and stability in your Savior, Jesus Christ, is all-important. They seek to separate you from sin and to present you holy to the Lord.

Furthermore, integrating Scripture in prophetic messages renews Christians to God. Life is difficult and the trials that bring out God's best in us are painful. Those who go through years of bitter trials can get weary as their fires wane. Their souls can get thirsty from the dry, parched existence they live as they barely hold on to God's Word. Such people then need prophets to reignite and revive their passion for God's service and sacrifice. That reviving, according to Psalm 119, can only come from the Lord's Word. Prophets who rely on Scriptures for their prophecies will find the Lord opening the pages of people's lives right before their eyes, manifesting a Psalm 139:11–18 moment where the Lord ignites His Word using ancient texts. Becoming relevant for today, both the prophet and the hearer get answers that each only wondered about until then. Such passages answer questions, release blessings, and bring healing and deliverance. True prophets should, above all, answer more questions with God's wisdom than they engender.

PERSONAL PROPHECY AND PEOPLE'S LIFE BOOK

Since the Bible tells us that God wrote a book for all of us, it comes as no surprise that behind every real prophetic encounter there is a Creator revelation. Nor should it be difficult for prophets of this era to accept that they do not have to manufacture the word of the Lord for His people. Psalm 139:16 emphatically states that God wrote down the days of our lives before they began. The psalmist, for example, understood how his life would turn out because what the Lord had written before his birth concerning him was revealed. It is accepted that David, because he was also a prophet, had the ability to discern the Lord's eternal writings and interpret them for his existence on earth. He was thus shown by the Lord that all the earth's past, present, and future inhabitants had inscribed destinies in His archives that orchestrated the days of their lives. David realized that the almighty God even wrote about those who would reject Christ before time began and penned this truth for our time. Psalm 37:13, 18 says this, and throughout the Bible it is recorded how the Lord wrote a book for this or that.

For instance, God wrote the book of life regarding earth and man, the book of the generations of Adam, and the book of the generation of Christ. There is the book of the wars of the Lord, the book of the law of God, and the books of blessings and curses. God has books on kings, kingdoms, nations, and judgments. The most common ones are the books of His prophets. He had His prophets write numerous books to chronicle His dealings with humanity and their diverse reactions to it throughout the years. The prophets' writings included God's reactions, as well as the detailed judgments that correspond to humanity's crimes against Him. When the priests of ancient Israel failed Him, the Lord wrote a book of remembrance to record the special deeds of those who courageously feared Him during His nation's reprobate times under the Mosaic dispensation. (See Malachi 3.)

The Bible mentions or refers to books nearly two hundred times. In the vast majority of those references, the books contained prophecies. Apparently, this amount of references to books and records says the Lord's respect for earthly as well as heavenly records is important to Him. In the New Testament, John's Apocalypse discusses books in relation to the activities of God at least twenty-five times. Overall, God's books contain the governmental guidelines His spiritual protocrats are using to administrate His will on earth as revealed to the prophets to be uttered to the earth at various times. Genres such as end-time prophecy and the second coming of Christ, the records of the living and the dead, the deeds of each group, and how the Creator disposes of the earth and its godly and godless inhabitants in the end comprise its subject matter.

Scripture's discussion of books is not just to show how important records are to the Lord, but also to reveal the prophets' source of information. The Lord's library provides the intelligence they need to prophesy His words to others at the appointed times. That is how and why personal prophecies are biblical.

Since the Lord wrote a book on every soul He ever created, there are eternal and temporal plans for each one of us. Those born on earth begin their journey, according to Scripture, in the book of Adam. (See Genesis 5:1.) Upon salvation, a person's life plan comes from the book of the generation of Christ. (See Matthew 1:1.) The writer of Hebrews understood this because he made reference to it in Hebrews 10:7. Psalm 22 and Psalm 110, in like manner, contain excerpts from the Creator's eternal books written about the Christ and His generation. Actually, that is what Isaiah meant when he asked the question about who will declare Christ's generation in Isaiah 53:8.

Long before Jesus' incarnation, Abraham saw the Christ and wrote his vision before His time. Jesus made reference to Abraham's pre-incarnate revelations of Himself as the Son of God when disputing with the religious leaders of His day in John 8:56. Not only was Abraham a recognized prophet of the Most High God (according to Genesis 20:7), he was privy to the Son of God's day. Genesis 15–18 records his viewing the entire plan of salvation for his seed when they had yet to be born. His revelation is referred to in Galatians 3:8, a New

Testament book. Even what Daniel received from the mouth of the angel Gabriel was from the eternal Scripture of God. Gabriel called it *"the Scripture of truth"* (Daniel 10:21). That is why the Apocalypse and all the other prophetic revelations of the Lord could be written in their times. They already existed and were waiting for their designated vessels to be born, live life, and be cultivated enough to pen the next body of revelation the Lord had for this world.

Scripture tells us each generation has a revelation to divulge because the Lord called His generations from the beginning and formed them for His various works and assignments in their times. Read Isaiah 41:4.

THE GENERATIONS OF ADAM

Adam's generations are many, as the Bible uses the plural form of the word in relation to his offspring. Apparently, Scripture's use of the word *generations* refers to his lineage because they keep dying out. Christ's offspring, in comparison, is one continuous world-without-end generation. It is singular because there is one Savior of mankind and only one way to live in Him, and He and His seed live forever. Eternal life requires an eternal plan to cover every inch of a person's everlasting existence. Therefore, the Lord precedes our destinies with His plan for how we will live to fulfill them.

Prophecies concerning Adam's generations are earthly and therefore soulish when they are not derived from God's Spirit's revelation of His eternal plan for them. At times, the Lord will release a futuristic word to His prophet on an unsaved life so that the forces assigned to seeing to his or her redemption are informed of the path God is taking with the person. Thus, a baby may be told that he will be this or that, or an unsaved person may hear from the prophet the reason why he was born, why the Lord wants to redeem him, and His plans for him after he receives Jesus Christ. However, in the absence of God's interjection, Adam's seeds rarely hear from the true and living God. What they get from the supernatural is chiefly soul-pleasing divination. That is why the psychics can *seem* to have as much knowledge about people as God's prophets, although they really do not. The difference is the source of information retrieved from the supernatural that they deliver.

Being lost themselves, psychics are limited to getting their readings from the soul realm and not God's Holy Spirit. Since He is not bearing His soul to them, they will never be able to divine what the Lord has hidden in Christ's book on a life, because that information must be spiritually discerned. Thus, the key difference between prophecy and divination is that, by the Lord's Spirit, the prophet speaks information that only the Creator can release to His redeemed. Psychic divinations comes from any spirit (divine being) that happens to be in the vicinity of the people who are uttering and receiving a psychic reading.

From all this, it is safe to conclude that what the prophets of God spoke, they received from the Lord's eternal record of world events and His Scripture on the generations of people's lives. What the occultists divine is another thing. It is what is contained in Adam's book, and so it is restricted to life on earth. Often it comes from dead spirits, demons that mask themselves as dearly departed relatives or generation ancestors. This is called *necromancy*. Now we shift our discussion to prophecy itself and what it is.

WHAT PROPHECY IS

As stated several times before, prophecy is God's divine communication medium, His means of making His inaudible self audible and his invisible self visible. Prophecy is not a vain imagination of the vocalizer, but a medium by which the earth can hear from and be guided by its Creator. As we have seen, prophecy is actually a prophet's ability to read the life book of the one standing before him. That is what the preceding section took great pains to stress.

Prophecy is really receiving information from God on a person's life or situations from eternity and manifesting His Word on it in our natural world. What's more, prophecy is encoded in everyday life and in all creation's existence. When the prophet speaks the word of the Lord, it comes to pass because it has been incubating in the spirit realm for years, waiting for the predetermined time and lineage to appear in natural form. Amos 3:7 is a popular verse of prophecy, but it is verse 8 that enlarges our understanding of its power. Both verses establish that the Lord speaks what He is about to do prophetically, somewhere to some prophet, to start the processes that materialize His word on earth. When He speaks, He impels His prophets to prophesy because that is the reason He permitted them to hear His thoughts in the first place. The word for the secrets the Lord reveals to His prophets in Amos 3:7 is *sod*.

Summarily, *sod* applies to the supernatural act of God in respect to His prophets, whereby He brings the spirits of every prophet into a private, usually midnight or twilight, meeting with Himself. *Sod* meetings are closed-chamber sessions where His prophets convene with His supernatural military, governmental, judicial, and punitive agents for a special move or work to take place on earth. As used in Amos 3:7, the word refers to private council deliberations between God and His prophets' spirits where He communicates His will and unveils His plans to them to declare at the proper time. The following chapter further discusses prophecy to give you insight into how it works and where it originates.

CHAPTER SUMMARY

1. Church prophetics operate differently.

2. Church prophets cannot benefit individually; they exist for the institution.

3. Pastors and their church prophets can clash but should be open to various options to work together.

4. Headstrong prophets will court the Lord's chastening.

5. Veteran prophets can help settle turbulent prophets.

6. Specific duties and actions justify the church prophet's roles.

7. Church prophets must stay connected to their spiritual roots.

8. Personal prophecy comes from a person's life book, written by God.

9. Prophecy is God's divine communication medium.

PROPHETIC ACTION ITEMS

1. Draw on your own and others' experiences with prophets in the local church, and detail the specific conflicts with prophets you (or they) encountered. Reflect on how:

   • they were addressed.

   • they could or should have been addressed.

   • they turned out.

   • they could have turned out and what this chapter's wisdom could have added to the situation.

   Be objective!

Chapter 9

PROPHECY CLASS 101

This chapter addresses the subject of personal prophecy. It covers:

- What exactly is prophecy
- The power of a prophetic mind-set
- Where prophecy originated
- Expanded prophetic abilities
- The anatomy of prophecy
- New Testament prophecy
- Prophetic preaching and teaching
- Basics of prophecy
- Prophetic prayer
- The source of prophetic power
- Professional prophetics

This chapter contains a brief prophecy basics class to help you appreciate what prophecy is and where it originates. Many people have had so much fun enjoying prophecy that they have given little thought to where it comes from and what makes it authoritative and reliable.

Oftentimes, the hearing of prophecy alone is sufficient enough for people to delight in it. Few people realize that prophecy is more than pleasant or inspiring words being said. Most Christians do not know that the pronouncement of prophecy sets in motion a host of powers and events that can initially shake up a person's life before the word comes to pass. The shake-up happens in order to materialize in its time what the word of the Lord as promised through the prophet's mouth. Hindering forces, misguided ideas and beliefs, and the presence of detrimental relationships and behavior in one's sphere of life can, and often do, delay the performance of God's words. There are several rational reasons for this.

God's spiritual diligence goes into action once the word of the Lord goes forth, to clear the way for its manifestation. Sometimes this can be very upsetting or excruciating to the hearer of the word. In addition, opposing forces who have sought to retain what they have withheld from the hearer for so long are aroused. In a knee-jerk reaction, these forces form invisible barricades that block the flow of spiritual resources the hearer needs to empower his or her faith enough to evidence the prophecy. These are not passive forces, mind you. They are aggressive, resolute, and vicious forces that seek to retain their hold on the hearer. Previously, they may have been silent as there was no contest for the hearer's faith, but once prophecy comes, they go into fierce action to see that the word does not come to pass or to ensure that the hearer is in the wrong place to receive it. Their goal is for the hearer to move out of the place where God's promises can or should come to pass, causing that person to miss it because he or she was never there at its fulfillment. Do you remember the earlier example of the little church on the corner? If this happens, another person enjoys your blessing, your children, your ministry offspring, etc., because you were out of the vicinity of the release. It is somewhat like what took place with the children of Israel.

The first generation that came out of Egypt did not receive the promise because they feared its conditions—attacking the giants in the land. On top of that, they made the mistake of following the wrong (usually counterfeit) prophetic voice. Even though Moses had led them for years and was the established voice of the Lord for them, they turned and listened to others who presumed to know better than Moses the Lord's plan for them. Today we see this happening often, as people hear the word of God and, fearing its cost and consequences, turn to another voice to get a prophecy they can live with, one that has fewer strings attached to it. Similar fears caused the apostle Paul to tell Timothy to wage spiritual warfare with (and over) his prophetic word to provoke its performance in his life. (See 1 Timothy 1:18.)

PROPHECY CLASS
WHAT EXACTLY IS PROPHECY?

How many times have you heard that question? The majority of the time, the answer is simply the word of the Lord. While that is true, it seems to come short of the answer most people look to receive. They want an explanation that fosters their understanding of the medium of prophecy so they can properly handle the prophetic words they get. For those people, a somewhat more intricate response is needed. When New Creation faith and godly reason mix, the result is spiritual intelligence in the supernatural ways and wisdom of God. Thus, prophecy is the Lord's word performed, achieved, and mobilized in the spirit, soul, and body of its believers. As the invisible, eternal word of God is spoken in the natural world, it operates what He deposited in creation to perform or fulfill something He wants to be.

Prophecy involves the past, present, and future interchangeably. It takes spiritual faculties to hear, see, dream, and otherwise receive it from Creator God's spiritual creation. A special attunement of the normal human faculties is needed for prophetic types to receive their messages. To affirm that what one receives from the spirit realm is prophetic and not merely psychic takes a very highly constructed spiritual apparatus. It takes the uniqueness of the prophet's spirit upgraded by the new birth. Review the section on the seventh sense to better understand this.

Prophecy is normally spontaneous and can be predictive, revelatory, didactic, literary, or oracular. That means the prophetic can manifest itself through *foretelling, forthtelling, teaching, writings, or verbal utterances under the inspiration of the Spirit of God.*

As a medium, prophecy's purpose is to reveal the invisible mind and dispense the material provisions of God to His visible world. As a tool, it is the vehicle by which the Lord enables humans to access His invisible form, services, wisdom, and products. Once someone has gained access to heaven's hidden treasuries, prayer and belief in prophetic utterances shape and conform his request to transform them into divine purpose. Sustained, these ultimately attract and adorn the petition's natural physique and appearance in our world so that it takes on the substance and appearance of prophecy fulfilled. Here is what Paul meant by his counsel to Timothy in 1:18 and 1:14. It is what happened when Christ cursed the fig tree, when Elisha summoned a child for the Shunammite woman, and when Jesus multiplied the fishes and the loaves. Based on His covenant and comprehension of His Father's ways, they were already in existence, awaiting His command to manifest.

The Power of a Prophetic Mind-set

The key to accomplishing such great feats as those mentioned above is a prophetic mind-set. That is an ongoing realization that what you want and need from God already exists in your kingdom account and all you need to do is withdraw it from the supernatural and embody it in the natural realm. Many things go into making this happen on purpose and on command. Mark 11:24 hints at it, saying that if you believe what you ask for, you will have it. The Greek word for "will have it" is *esomai*, and it literally means "will be." The term implies that your belief will cause the object or events of your belief to be—that is, it to exist. While there is much more to say on this subject, for now it will suffice to say that this is what Christ was talking about when He said, "Whatever you ask in My name I will do." (See John 14:13.) The word for "will do" is *poieo*, and it actually has Jesus saying He will prepare, construct, acquire, fashion, and author it at your word, according to your faith, cause your desire to be.

As the Logos—the word, intelligence, and power that created all things—He gave us a clue about how to bring what He and His Father prepared for us from the foundation of the world into view and use. That clue is proclamation of His Word and declaration of one's desires. Read Job 28:27, which is based on Job 22:28. It is easy to see from this why Satan works feverishly to divert Christ's churches from His Word and His truth from its authentic spiritual manifestations. You, as a church prophet, must be on guard against this in the church you are assigned.

To continue, a special collaborative arrangement between the Lord and His prophets, accomplished through their uniquely empowered spirits, enables their commands to cause their words to appear in natural form. You only need to read 2 Chronicles 20:20 and Isaiah 44:26 to be persuaded by this truth. God declares that He reveals His works and plans to and through His prophets. What a tremendous statement. The Maker of all things binds His powers to the words of His messengers to produce on demand what they utter as prophecy. This promise on God's part makes true prophets more than merely His voice boxes; they are His implements and instruments as well. Review Hosea 6:5 and Zechariah 1:6. Below are some of the functions and objectives for prophecy and God's uses of it.

- Destiny
- Ministry
- Correction
- Blessing
- Admonishment
- Change
- Creation
- Healing
- Power
- Possession and dispossession
- Instruction
- Counsel
- Impartation
- Empowerment

WHERE PROPHECY ORIGINATED

As I explained previously, prophecy comes from the Creator. What makes it prophecy according to definition is its sphere of formation, which is eternity. Anything God says is prophetic because He spoke it outside of our time to be manifested in our era. This is why prophecy relies much on dreams and visions. These mechanisms of divine communication are not time-bound, even if the dreamer receives them on a given day or night. When they come as images depicting what God is doing or wants to do, they are prophetic. Since the messages emanate from eternity, they originate outside of time and are made alive in the dreamer's mind. It is like the sperm and egg that make a baby. They always existed as potential people in the man and woman's bodies, but are not time-relevant until they are first conceived. After gestation and birth into the world, the child is subject to its tempo. As long as a baby is in the womb, it is exempt from time and its ordinances as we know them. It lives, is alive, and is a person, but it is not on life's clock—the timepiece of earthly life, that is. Once the baby in the womb is born, it receives a birth date and becomes subject to the laws and processes of the earth. So it is with prophecy.

By definition prophecy is *pro*—"beforehand" or "time"—and *phemi* (or *phani*)—"saying"—that which is said before it happens. Inasmuch as the Lord created and formed all we see, feel, hear, and touch outside time, every element of human existence may be seen as prophetic or as a manifestation of prophecy. The Genesis account of creation supports this. Before the world was, God said, *"Let there be...."* The Bible goes on to tell us that what He declared to be came forth, because the record says, *"and it was so."* This truth is upheld in 2 Peter 3:5, a reiteration of Psalm 33:6 and Hebrews 11:3.

Once the Lord God spoke what He wanted to make appear, He observed its formation and outworking from eternity as it moved from there to here. In eternity, things manifest at the speed of God, not man. With His word not being confined to our time clock and calendar, it was not a problem for Him to create His world in a week. Afterward, He assigned everything its time, season, purpose, vessel, genealogy, and history, and spoke its physicality into manifestation. They had always existed resident in Him, like the sperm and egg of a future baby. Once full gestation was complete, the Lord merely spoke His physical creation out of His being and into the world's space He had created for it. It appeared whole at His word because He had carried the whole thing around within Himself until it could stand on its own and serve His purposes. Still working from heaven and earth at once, the Lord then recorded in eternity the events that unfolded in His earthly chronicles. From then it was all set in motion (albeit a drastically slowed-down motion) to be lived out in the flesh over time.

The Lord has given us this same formula to repeat what He did in our own world and lives. Thus, prophecy mirrors God's beforehand record of what took place at the speed of eternity, now unfolding in us in time, age to age, before it appeared on earth. Even the variables of human free will are known by God because, for the most part, what we do at a snail's pace compared to eternity's speed done under His observation before He placed us in our clay vessels on this planet. Prophets then get their information from the spirit realm. It comes from the Holy Spirit who communicates select portions and pieces of the Creator's divine record to them at prescribed periods in history.

Prophetic revelations come from the pages of human lives in Adam and those in Christ. They divulge the Lord's purposes for our existence as only He can know it. At any given stage in human, earthly, and individual histories, the Lord can open a page of a person's book and reveal it to His prophet. This is in addition to, but aside from, the normal operation of prophetic faculties that give prophets the ability to pierce the veil of the flesh and detect what is happening in the future. Prophets do this routinely as part of their occupational duties to the Lord.

EXPANDED PROPHETIC ABILITIES

Extended prophetic information comes from the overt and direct actions of the citizens of the supernatural world. The Bible identifies these beings as the angels of the Lord. In ancient times, for example, it was accepted that a dream angel caused all prophetic dreams. The expansion of a prophet's mantle determines the spherical range of his or her prophetic reach and aptitude. The mantle as it appears to the invisible world says whether the prophet's supernatural faculties can operate on a local, national, international, or even stratospheric level.

Many new prophets are limited in their prophecy scope and range. They can only receive tiny fragments of what a seasoned prophet can retrieve from the spirit realms of God. God purposely restricts the breadth and level of prophetic information the prophet either receives or comprehends. He does this by contracting a prophet's prophetic orb to minimize the messenger's access to His spirituality and thereby controlling the breadth of his prophecies. The reason the Lord does this most of the time is developmental. It helps Him refine the prophet's skill, fine-tune his or her prophetic receptors, and qualify (and certify) the new messenger's prophetic motivations. At other times it is punitive. When prophets have a constant track record of ignoring God or perverting His words, He shuts their lights off. Micah 3:6–7 describes it as follows:

> *Therefore night shall be unto you, that ye shall not have a vision; and it shall be dark unto you, that ye shall not divine; and the sun shall go down over the prophets, and the day shall be dark over them. Then shall the seers be ashamed, and the diviners confounded: yea, they shall all cover their lips; for there is no answer of God.*

The Lord can curtail or cut off entirely a prophet's ability so that his or her prophetics have to resort to demons to operate. Micah also explains:

> *Her heads judge for a bribe, her priests teach for pay, and her prophets divine for money. Yet they lean on the LORD, and say, "Is not the LORD among us? No harm can come upon us."* (Micah 3:11 NIV)

ANATOMY OF PROPHECY

TECHNICAL PROPHETIC INFORMATION

In an effort to provide a solid biblical basis for prophecy, here is a lecture that anatomizes it for the prophet who wants to thoroughly grasp the mind of God on prophetics.

To begin, one word for prophecy helps us understand its meaning, the purpose it serves, and its aim. Found in 1 Chronicles 9:25, it is the word *nebuwah*, which means "a prediction given orally or in writing." It defines a specific prophetic word, whether true or false. Another prophecy term employed in the Old Testament is *naba*. You may also see it spelled *nava*. This word is a verb, "to prophesy." As a root term it identifies prophesying in song. *Naba* can apply to psalmism or a predictive discourse, lyrical or not, through a genuine or false prophet. Whatever is the case, the gist is that the message delivered is unquestionably under the direct influence of a divine spirit. (See 1 Chronicles 15:8 and Nehemiah 6:12.)

For the *nabi* prophet, which we discussed at length elsewhere, Daniel 9:24 is a good scriptural reference. It defines *nabi* as "a prophet, a person who is an inspired messenger." The word includes "the specifically declared prophecy that comes from the official prophet as the spokesperson of a deity, true or false." When the *nabi* pertains to prophesying, it stresses the prophetic message that specifically comes from the one in the prophet's office that, when uttered, establishes the messenger as an authentic prophet.

There is another helpful word for prophecy that is especially significant answers the experience of the weight of the prophetic word from the Lord. It is identified in Scripture as a prophetic burden. The word is *massa,* and Proverbs 30:1 and 31:1 passages both distinguish it as "prophecy that is carried as a burden." *Massa* transmits the essence of what we would call a prophetic burden as a weighty word from the Lord. Such prophecy flows from an accompanying spiritual charge from the Lord that is felt with the natural senses. It is recognized by utterances in definitive, concrete, or symbolic terms. Generally, *massa* prophecy is likely to use figurative (parabolic) language that expresses God's intellectual desires or reflects the prophet's intelligent cognition of a cause that is ultimately translating to an effect or consequence. In the message, the prophet is moved by spiritual and godly aspirations to see that God's justice and righteousness correct the situation to restore the scales of balance and equity in the person's life. For this reason, a *massa* burden is often characterized by a message of doom, although not exclusively.

NEW TESTAMENT PROPHECY

In the New Testament only two words are used for prophecy. One of them is used three times. It is the word *prophetikos*, which defines "what proceeds from a prophet as prophetic." The ending, *ikos*, sets the word's meaning in the arena of technique or systemized mechanical performance. It covers more than the prophet's prophesying and encompasses the full range of supernatural and revelatory activities that identify the office. *Prophetikos* not only constitutes prophecy as known and recognized by the people of God, but encapsulates the behind-the-scenes outworking of the prophet's word that manifests a prophecy in its literal form.

Prophetikos also refers to foretelling prophecy and the corresponding operations that cement its prediction or unveil its revelation. Demonstrative prophetic techniques are likely to follow the word, such as dance, imagery, drama, poetry, or rhyme, to depict its symbolism and certify that it will come to pass in its time. Gabriel's rendering skeptical Zacharias mute under these circumstances is one example of this. (See Luke 1.) See also Romans 16:26, where the term is used twice in one verse. The last usage comes from 2 Peter 1:19.

Every other term the New Testament uses for prophecy falls under the meaning of the word *propheteia*. Basically this word defines a prophecy whether it comes from mere recitation of Scripture or from an outright spontaneous utterance from the present mind of God. The *propheteia* word declares God's thoughts, feelings, reactions, and emotional responses to earthly affairs and human matters.

Prophecy of this kind typically links to some future event where the matters or affairs divulged are complemented with some corresponding or subsequent divine action on God's part. Signs appear shortly before or after the word leaves the prophet's mouth. Since the words are God's, He is the one who releases the prophetic sign that seals its certain performance spoken by His prophets. The sign may be displayed by the prophet, but more often it is a sign the Lord Himself gives to quicken to the mind of the hearer to the prophecy's authenticity to assure that it will surely come to pass. The sign also doubles as a foretoken that reasserts itself when the prophecy comes to pass to remind the hearer that it was what the Lord had in mind when He sent His prophet with the word.

One example of signature prophecy is the occurrence of an event that seems unrelated to anything in the person's life or experience triggered by and related to a prophecy. Prophetic signature is totally consistent with the Old Testament prophet's words that brought us to the New. Isaiah 7:14 orients us to the reality that prophetic signs confirm the Lord's words as in the coming crucifixion and resurrection of our Lord Jesus Christ. The birth of the church and the redemption of the Gentiles are other examples.

Propheteia includes the Creator's appropriation of the prophet's spirit, the source of the messenger's predictive ability, and revelatory sight. It contemporaneously pertains to didactic prophetics, where teaching permeates the prophet's discourse to combine the wisdom of the now in Christ with the insightful predictions of ancient prophets to reveal Him. Predictive and didactic prophecy join instruction to unfold the existence, purposes, and work of His church on earth. Didactic prophetic predictions foretell how and where the church, its ministers, and its operations, empowered by the Holy Spirit, are to manifest their reach and demonstrate the powers of the Living God as Christ's representative. Luke 24:44–49 is an example, as is Matthew 10's record of the training and commissioning of the apostles, seen also in Luke 10, where the seventy were likewise dispatched.

PROPHETIC TEACHING AND PREACHING

Aside from bringing the word of the Lord, one of the most intriguing things about prophetic ministry is its distinct style of sermonic delivery. According to Romans 12, which mentions the gift of prophecy, revelatory and predictive influences are typical of the mantle. The prophet's style of sermonizing incorporates several spiritual and supernatural features that help stimulate hearers' understanding. With their sometimes humorous and pragmatic way of speaking, prophets frequently integrate symbolism, parables, and similitudes in their messages to instruct and invigorate their audiences. The prophet's spirit, combined with its inherent actuating force, amplifies this fundamental gift. The capability enables the prophet to rotate perceptively between teaching and prophesying as the tenor and mix of the audience requires. Prophets can slip into predicting something to come to pass or casually revealing something otherwise concealed in God while preaching. Our Savior often used this technique to communicate the fullness of the gospel message His Father sent Him to preach. Luke 4:23 and 13:4 are good examples of such sermonizing.

Prophets also take God's ancient Word and apply it with ease to modern situations. Here is another capacity of their unique teaching and preaching ability. What may seem old and outdated to the typical Bible reader is not so with the prophet. This unusual minister sees past, present, and future in one sweep, looking at life through the Word of the Lord. He or she compares it to what is observed in the world around him or her to isolate the prophetic from the mundane and apply to a Bible prophecy's fulfillment in time. To the prophet, the chariot is not merely outmoded transportation; it is a vehicle regardless of its shape and engine. Prophets can see how the ancient chariot that was used in transport or battle symbolizes today's modern tank. Likewise the bow and arrow represent missiles to the prophet. Rigid thinkers can easily overlook the fact that they are nonetheless weapons of war and miss their use as missiles aimed at another. So when the typical saint reads Scripture, he or she gets locked into the era in which the Word is reporting, but not so the prophet. He or she sees the events that led up to the war in question, or other event, as an example for us today. Prophets identify the attitudes and conduct of the war and the way the weapons were fired, whether powered by humans or nuclear energy. For instance, it has been said that David's stone that slew Goliath was a guided missile. David threw it, but God's hand guided it to its target.

Prophets can also take the practical and spiritual doctrines of the Lord's Word and update them using contemporary imagery and metaphors without altering His word of truth one bit. Anointed prophetic wisdom makes hearers see how what prophets say and teach really does fit their modern situations. To the prophet, sophistication is but a remaking of the archaic. They echo Solomon's sentiment: *"That which has been is what will be, that which is done is what will be done, and there is nothing new under the sun"* (Ecclesiastes 1:9).

FINAL NOTES ON THE BASICS OF PROPHECY

1. **Amos 3:7**—*Emphasis:* The meaning of the word *sod*.

   - The word for the secrets God reveals to His servants the prophets.

   - *Sod* distinguishes prophetic hearing from the range of spiritual hearing the Holy Spirit allows.

   - *Sod* designates the official character of the prophetic message's delivery system as what God uses exclusively with prophets.

   - *Sod* centers on the deliberations that take place among high officials in closed-chamber sessions.

   - *Sod* relates the distinctions of the prophet's means of revelation and grounds for perceptions to the sphere of prophetics in which he operates.

2. **2 Chronicles 20:20**—*Emphasis:* The powerful prosperity anointing inherent to the prophet's mantle.

   - This Scripture establishes how and why the prophet's power extends to the sphere of prosperity.

   - Prophecy is prosperity's tool in the world of prophetics.

   - The benefit and basis of the prosperity link prophesying at God's will to money and triumph.

   - It says how and why prophets are instrumental in the Lord's triumphs in a life.

- It answers how the previous statement relates to Amos 3:7.

- The word *prosperity* actually means "good fortune, fortunately provided for due to encountering favorable conditions."

3. **Psalm 139:15–16**—*Emphasis:* The eternal writings of Creator God.

    - God wrote it all down in advance.

    - Foreknowledge means that the Lord wrote everything down in eternity to manifest as prophecy in due time.

    - God's writings translate to prophecy.

    - What the Lord wrote in advance affects the events of the lives of those He recorded in His prophetic ordinations.

    - Hebrews 10:7 exemplifies how a volume of the book in which each of our lives are recorded exists. Its variables are accounted for and yet remain immutable for prophets to declare.

4. **Numbers 12:6**—*Emphasis:* The visions and dreams used to induct prophets into office.

    - Visions and dreams are the primary media of prophetic induction.

    - Dreams and visions are decidedly the best ways to awaken the prophet's spirit.

    - What makes prophets inherently susceptible to God's spiritual activation is their prophet's spirit.

- The passage contributes to, complements, and supports the prophetic's reception and transmission.

5. **Acts 15:18**—*Emphasis:* Eternity and time are known to God.

- This links to Hebrews 10:7 and Psalm 139:15–16.

PROPHETIC PRAYER

Needless to say, more than with most other ministers in the New Testament church, the prophet's chief responsibility is prayer. Prayer for the prophet is above prophesying, for without prayer, the prophecies the prophet gives may not be totally accurate, relevant, or timely. Prayer synchronizes the prophet's clock and perspectives with God's. It unites his or her supernatural self with the supernatural forces assigned to the work on earth. Prayer opens the heavens, removes the darkness, and sheds God's light on the matters prophets handle. A shabby prayer life eventually renders prophets feeble in their ministries and hinders the execution of their prophetic duties.

Another reason prayer is so vital to this mantle has to do with the weighty intercessory obligation of the messenger. The prophet's primary charge, if you recall, is to stand in the gap and make up the hedge for God's people on earth. This responsibility is where Israel's prophets failed in Ezekiel 13:5. But what is it for the prophet to pray?

According to the Bible, there is no more effective prayer group than that of prophets and apostles, collectively and respectively. I used to wonder about this until I had the opportunity to observe and experience the difference. When prophets pray with others, they may have a productive prayer time. However, when they pray with their peers of like spirit, the results are explosive. Their respective mantles collaborate, and each one's anointing and power are magnified a thousandfold. When this group assembles, the time it takes to transcend the world and flesh is milliseconds in comparison to other prayer groups.

Prophets do not need the long spiritual prologues, extensive meditation, or empty praise-fillers that are normally required by others before they transition from the human to the heavenly. In an instant, prophets' seasoned spirits leap onto God's plane, ready to do business as He requires. Prophets further understand what to expect from their prayer vigils and approach them with a confident determination to plow through everything in their way. With other prayer groups it is different. Their spiritual immaturity or weakness can lag behind in the spirit as they are unskilled or unable to shake off the flesh that holds down their spiritual power. Many believers frequently lack the fortitude to push in the spirit and are easily driven back to carnality by any hint of demonic resistance or fatigue.

Prophetic prayer groups, on the other hand, are able to confront and conquer the spiritual bullies the devil assigns to their gatherings. They enter prayer with a sense of assignment, duty, and invincibility. Prophets are not quickly or easily cowered in prayer, and over time, they resolve to outgrow the weaknesses that make them vulnerable to such tactics in the future.

Once on God's plane, prophets are attuned to His most intimate thoughts, being experienced in conceiving what the Lord wants to deposit in them. Prophets' prayer companies immediately transform their environments into a battlefield, a revelation hub, a military camp, and a worship and praise center. Throughout the prayer, the group travels through all these stages to make happen on earth what the Lord has shown them to be His will in heaven. Before tackling other issues, responsible prophets come to God to be healed, cleansed, empowered, and impregnated. They are conditioned to conceive His thoughts, commune with His Word, and be further transformed into His image and likeness. Prophets not only seek this from their prayer times; they expect and insist that the Lord grants them this fruit as a result of it. When the prayer ends, the room is changed to a sanctuary. The glory is present and the word of the Lord flows abundantly.

It is sad that the least communal prayer group in the body of Christ tends to be the leaders, prophets, and apostles, most importantly. I have witnessed how pastors and church leaders rise to fame and begin to see prayer as beneath them. They know how to reach God, but they assign special groups to do it for them. Unless there is a crisis, far too many in leadership of churches of the Lord Jesus replace valuable prayer time with works while still relying on the Lord's Spirit to support them in their ventures.

Biblical prophetic prayer models, Samuel, Moses, David, Daniel, Job, and Abraham, to name a few, would never cast off this privileged duty. What they all shared was their conviction for intercession. Many times active prophetic prayer can halt or derail an attack of the enemy meant to overthrow God's plans and purposes. When prophets enter active prayer, visions flood their minds. The Lord's thoughts stream at them at accelerated rates as their spirits overwhelm their natural selves. At this time, the Lord's broadest and most finite matters are divulged and the *sod* meeting discussed earlier begins. The messengers hear God's plan, understand the strategy, and are enlightened on the objects of their next prophetic assignment. From all this, you can see how important prophets' prayer lives are to their accuracy and effectiveness.

Another unique feature of prophetic prayer groups is recognizing that fault and failure for life's crises lie with humans and not with the Lord. Prophets differ from other groups because they never assign blame to the Lord or wrangle His Word to excuse human behavior or rationalize their retaliation against God for their suffering. Rather, prophets are aware that problems of sin reside with humans. Therefore they include in their intercessory sessions vicarious repentance for the sins of the people of the lands they pray for and then proceed to use their authority to release their blessings. Daniel's intercession in chapters 9 and 10 shows this practice in action. Praying prophets are a most valuable tool in public ministry. Without prophetic prayer, the institution of prophecy is only marginally effective. Read about pastors' prayer lives in Acts 2.

THE PROPHECY ANOINTING

It might be helpful to church prophets and their pastors to know about the prophecy anointing as it streams from the baptism of the Holy Spirit. The name of the anointing that empowers Christ's ministers for their service to the Lord is *chrio*. As an aspect of the Lord's many anointings, this one is distinct in that it may also be called the ministry power anointing. *Chrio* describes the outpouring of the Holy Spirit that specifically rests on His officers and ministers in active service. *Chrio* furnishes what is needed to perform the duties and exploits of one's call.

According to *Strong's Concordance,* the word *chrio* is used four times in the New Testament. Only one of those times is it applied outside of Christ, which is not to say that it does not apply to human ministers, because that is inaccurate. What it is to say, though, is that the *chrio* anointing specifically empowers divine service. The single time the word *chrio* is used for anointing for human ministers is in 2 Corinthians 1:21 in relation to the apostles. What makes it relevant to us today, however, is that Jesus was sent to earth as the first Minister of the New Covenant. He came as the Prophet who was to come and the Great Apostle. All this states that the *chrio* anointing to minister is more than the *chrisma* all believers get. It goes along with Acts 1:8, where the Lord instructs His followers to remain in Jerusalem until they are endued with power from on high in Luke 24:49. Otherwise, it is only used in the New Testament one other time.

Without *chrio,* ministers rely entirely on their human talents and have a lesser degree of potency and consequently less ministry success. *Chrio* is a power anointing, period. It comes upon the Lord's servants for one reason, and one reason only: to empower them as effective witnesses of God's Word, truth, and power. Because of this goal, *chrio* also supplies what it takes to yield to the moves and waves of the Holy Spirit. Without it, Christ's ministers cannot quite submit to God's will, be used by His power, or execute what cannot ordinarily be done by mortal humans. The anointing, when manifested in this context, uses the vessel rather than the normal course of affairs where the vessel uses the anointing in ministry. To clarify the distinctions between the *chrio* anointing and the others, in matters and tasks of a routine nature the vessel, God's minister uses the anointing, or employs it, which is a better way of saying it. *Chrio,* on the other hand, uses the vessel.

The connection between the Lord and His ministers under these circumstances is rigid and distinct. Enormous latitude and trust are accorded those whom Jesus baptizes with His *chrio* anointing. Their obedience must be firmly established and their motives and agenda beyond suspicion. These being confirmed, the Lord imparts *chrio's* powerful authority and potency, because without them those called to His service would fail in the face of the severe trials and contests associated with ministry.

THE PROPHETIC AND *CHRIO*

With the prophetic, the *chrio* anointing is centered primarily in the dispensation of prophecy, although not exclusively. Several noticeable sensations can accompany the onset of the prophecy anointing. Jeremiah spoke of quaking, burning, weakness, or loss of strength. In relation to the prophecy anointing, Daniel spoke of a heaviness that weighed him down and something akin to passing out—what we call today being slain in the Spirit. Some prophets voiced a distinct weight placed upon them that they identified as the hand of the Lord upon them to prophesy. Usually they felt this in the shoulder, neck, and back area, as the term *yoke* is synonymous with mantle. Others identified the *massa* prophetic burden for the oracle. While such sensations are not essential to prophecy, the Bible often mentions the weight of prophetic oracle being felt by the prophet. It seemed to be its heaviest when the message was being deposited in the prophet for later utterance.

THE SOURCE OF PROPHETIC POWER

People invariably ask what makes a prophet's words come to pass. Although much discussion has alluded to the answer, below are some concrete factors that ensure a prophet's word will come to pass.

The source of prophetic power is summed up as follows:

- **The prophetic word itself.** The Lord's empowerment of the prophet's spirit gives weight to his or her prophecy. The weight, though imperceptible, gives off an aura detected by the invisible forces of creation to cause them to take what the messenger says seriously and do it.

- **The angelic guard.** The team of angelic forces God deploys to the prophet's sphere at the time of the messenger's installation to guard the work and enforce the prophet's word. This force powerfully imposes the Lord's will on the devil.

- **Divine license to act legitimately.** The spiritual certification and validation the Lord confers upon the prophet that authorizes him or her to act in supernatural matters within an assigned sphere. The license may not be discernible to humans, but it is recognized and respected by the forces of darkness. Divine license is generally uttered aloud from the mouth of the prophet while it is at the same time declared by God to His hosts. Jesus' instructions to the apostles in Matthew 10, along with His response to the return of the seventy's joy over their authority, are two examples.

- **Divine appointment to prophetic service.** God may induct a prophet into His service privately, but He will cause that appointment to be recognized and honored by His leaders. More than once He will have it voiced in His seen and unseen worlds by their authorities.

- **An approved prophetic station.** This is what Habakkuk referred to when he waited for God to answer him after his frustrated outburst over Israel's sin. He knew that he perhaps even deserved to be reproved because of it and a reproof from the Lord could be painful. Therefore, the prophet sought refuge in his prophetic ward, or watch station. (See Habakkuk 2:1.)

- **Approved prophetic assignment**. The Lord's dispatch of the messenger with a message. The fact that the charge is given by God means that He will uphold it. What Moses received from his burning bush encounter with the Lord was a prophetic assignment.

These are some of the most concrete reasons why the Lord upholds and performs, or ignores, a particular prophet's word. Share your receipt of these confirmations with your study group or prophetic company. Compare notes to see how they line up.

PROFESSIONAL PROPHETICS

Professional prophets were once a respectable guild of ministers in earlier times. Look at some of the standards professional prophets of the Bible's day were held to in the ancient world.

- Professional prophetics never undertaken by the novice or the unproved.

- Professional prophetics were balanced by others in community groups of prophets.

- Professional prophetics generally had secluded quarters

where group (and individual) encounters with the deity occurred.

- Professional prophetic men and women were tried and proven for their positions.

- Prophetic women were often seen as more visionary, men more vocal.

- Various forms of prophetic reception were employed.

- Prophetic reception required diverse actions for preparation.

- Various forms and styles of readiness were used to equip one for the prophetic.

- Numerous aspects of prophetic functions were dedicated to special prophetic vessels exhibiting exceptional prophetic aptitude.

Different vessels in the prophetic company were often employed by the deity in unique ways, to dispense distinct technical manifestations that expressed its sentiment and will in matters. For instance, a comprehensive company of prophets may demonstrate their office in numerous ways. In official service, for example:

- Some only sang.

- Others only wailed.

- A few cried and wept in travail or as wailing vessels of the deity's sorrow or injury.

- Others ranted and raved as in spiritual warfare.

- Some decried and declared prophetic statements to illustrate what the deity was doing with their petitions.

- Some entered into, acted out, or incited military strategy.
- Some simply peered into the supernatural and uttered what was seen.
- Some summoned and actuated the supernatural with prayers, descriptive utterances, or authoritative commands.
- Some ecstatically worshipped until spiritual manifestations appeared.
- Some sacrificed animals to coax spiritual activity. (Our Lamb has been sacrificed.)
- Others imbibed various concoctions, narcotics, or hallucinogens to stimulate and awaken their spiritual receptors to identify and define what the deity's spiritual hosts were doing. (We are drunk with the Holy Spirit.)
- Many simply offered prayers and fell asleep to receive instructions in the form of a vision or a dream. Numbers 24 shows Balaam using this method. He always went off to sleep in order to hear from God. That is how he received his famous "I see Him but not now" prophecy for Israel.

Specific spiritual maneuvers were delegated to each person to operate by a prophetic leader whose job it was to assure the prophetics of the group met with deity's approval.

The Psalmist and the Seer

Since not everyone exhibiting prophetic signs or uttering prophecy is an official prophet, the question becomes, what other type of prophetic calling does someone have on his or her life? The answer may be psalmist, if he sings his revelations and predictions frequently or rhymes them and exhibits no further prophetic conduct. Or, another type of prophet may be a seer. This is likely if he or she regularly peers into the other world, whether or not his or her observations are translated, enforced, or interpreted. Here are some action features of each of these types of prophet:

THE PSALMIST

- Is a singing prophet
- Is prone to poetry
- Uses lyrical delivery
- Is included to drama
- Is innately musical
- Is impressively creative
- Is effective at rhyming
- Possesses a literary talent
- Performs best with musical stimuli
- Is potent in praise

THE SEER

- Is a dreamer, visionary
- Possesses supernatural sight
- Is a discerning detective in spirit
- Is likely to have strong interpretations
- May translate spiritual happenings
- Can often see and not be able to say, or sometimes only describe, what is seen

- Shares visions that often rely on recipient application of pictures to situations
- Uses symbolism and imagery interpretations that may accompany spiritual sight faculty
- Exhibits a definitive delivery style
- Confirms members of prophetic team

QUICK STUDY CHART
Basics of the Prophet Personality and Temperament

Prophets are characterized by consistent traits, attitudes, and behaviors that all prophets share to some degree. The chart below describes some commonalities that may help emerging prophets, pastors, and their flocks recognize a prophetic personality and better understand his or her unique temperament. Prophetic types across the board are:

- Prone to exhibit a strong authoritative presence
- Predisposed to the prophetic's messenger office
- Easily motivated by the visions and dreams that induct the prophet into the ministry
- Compatible with the typically itinerant minister calling
- Relatively godly and spiritual minded
- Incisive and judicial in nature for prophet's leadership role
- Potent and provocative worshippers who inspire the same traits in others
- Suitable to serve as divine functionaries via visions and dreams
- Naturally disposed to inordinate divine communications

- Inclined to *nabiim* authority
- Unavoidably detached loners
- Naturally discerning and probing
- Naturally oriented to the prophet's odd office require-ments
- Daring, bold, and outspoken
- Practical, piercing and confrontational
- Scrupulously obedient to spiritual ways
- Articulate and ambassadorial in spirit
- Preaching teachers
- Compelling, corrective, and chastening
- Impressed by God's divine order
- Inherently provocative in office
- Highly intelligent, inquisitive, and driven
- Analytical, probing, and astute

Portrait of Church Prophet Distinctives

What is very important in selecting a prophet of the church is an understanding of the qualities and traits that do not make for a compatible church prophet. As with any other organization's staff or departments, God's prophets come in an array of different designations. Some are designated to one level and others to a higher or lower one. Those levels may be national, community, global, or local. When it comes to the church prophet in the local church, it is best to install a prophet who is more home-base-minded than one with a national or international passion. A basic homebody character in a person translates to a homebody prophet. Your church prophet should not be elsewhere more than he or she is with you. The church prophet also should not resent having to be in church or actively involved in the spiritual life of your congregation, favoring instead his or her field ministry trips above all else.

You will know the home-based prophet by his or her conversation. It is usually centered around the house of God, the condition of a specific congregation, and the importance of a prophetic presence in the church as a watch force for the Lord on the pastor's behalf. If a prophet's sights are more field-minded than church-minded, chances are that he or she will not do well confined to your church. Listen to a potent church prophet's conversation and explore his or her ministry vision a bit before deciding to set him or her over your membership. While it might be glamorous to have a world prophet on staff, sound judgment indicates that global and national prophets are best used as advisers. They can make poor local church prophets. Their messages can be too high above the people's heads far too often, and their visions for your church more for the corporate body of Christ. That means what God is issuing to the worldwide body could be dumped on your church, though it may not be applicable to it.

Besides this, the global or national prophet may be great for fortifying missions outreach from time to time, but when it comes to succoring the individual needs of the flock, its issues may appear petty to the prophet in comparison. Such a prophet of the church could react callously, unintentionally or not, to the perceived childish needs and plights of the local body. Lastly, the world-class prophet may also come off unwittingly as superior to the local pastor, deeming his vision and methods trite in contrast to the needs of the world front.

Following are some clues you may use to detect who is or is not a good church prophet candidate.

QUICK STUDY CHART
CHARACTER TRAITS THAT INDICATE A POTENTIAL CHURCH PROPHET

A most suitable candidate for a church prophet conforms to the following:

- Is stationary or demonstrates a capacity for staying and functioning productively in one place
- Is interested in the church, its members, and church vision
- Interacts positively and closely in a supportive role with the church's headship
- Supports leadership actions and initiatives that are clearly the will of the Lord for the church
- Is able and desires to guard and supernaturally intercede on the church's behalf
- Is interested in superintending the spiritual activities of local church and diligently screening and upgrading its prophetic operations
- Demonstrates an ability to function in full *nabiim* capacity
- Is able to oversee prophetics, psalmism, intercessory prayer, and membership prophetic development
- Is comfortable in collaborations with pastor in subordinate role on the welfare and prophetic benefits of the mantle and ministry in church

- Is open enough to introduce and promote new prophetic inflows and accurately screen manifesting prophets arising from local church midst
- Is knowledgeable enough to evaluate active prophetics, confirm emerging prophets, and train prophets for in-house use and/or church dispatch to other areas
- Is experienced enough to validate actuating prophetics and certify their authenticity
- Shows leadership potential that is harmonious with the existing and emerging church leadership and government
- Is able to diplomatically suggest prudent changes that better align the church with the kingdom of God
- Is able to provide safe and reliable counsel to pastor confidentially
- Is skillful and productive when interacting with and serving the membership without undue familiarity that could bias later prophetics
- Demonstrates an ability to be objective and to detach easily from the body to seek the Lord and remain credible with leadership

To talk about the prophet in the church and neglect the officer's number-one opposition, the occult, is derelict. The main reason why people find it difficult to reconcile God's need for the minister in contemporary times, and especially in the New Testament church, is because the reason God ordained prophets seems vague. As we have proven throughout this text, people often see prophets as mere vocalizers of future events. They see prophets as those who just speak God's words for no apparent reason. Herein lies the church's difficulty with prophets, a difficulty the Word and the spirits of darkness do not share.

When thinking about the Lord's use of the prophet, one must consider the backdrop against which the Lord presents the officer to His people. That is the first clue to why the Lord needs the prophet. Beginning with Abraham, also called a prophet in Scripture, God initiates His method of getting His Word and will into the earth and people's hearts. He spoke to a prophet. God's words empowered the man to do amazing things. In an unprecedented battle against the kings of the land, Abraham accomplished a monumental feat with the help of his God. He slaughtered the five kings, recaptured his family and treasures, and discovered the Almighty truly is the greatest of all gods. This awesome being became his covenant God forever as a result. Following this came Joseph, another Scripture-declared prophet. His prophetic ability succeeded in placing him as the third leader in Egypt, where he became the savior of his nation Israel through the use of his prophetic acumen. Joseph's position turned out to be providential as his status ended up being redemptive for his family and later all of Israel. Dreams and visions were used by God to set Joseph's course.

We see this method in operation again with Moses, whom God sent to deliver the people of Israel. The Lord brings us into the world of the prophetic by speaking through fires. God talked to Moses from a burning bush and told him what he was called to do. He was to display the Most High's power to Pharaoh of Egypt and systematically dismantle the powers of one of the oldest and most menacing kingdoms in history. Moses was to do so with only two resources: a wooden stick that he used to handle the flocks of Midian, where he fled after killing an Egyptian officer many years earlier, and a prophet. God told Moses that his brother Aaron would accompany him into Egypt and serve as Moses' prophet (spokesman for a deity). Moses would be a god to Pharaoh by virtue of the calamitous events that befell the nation at his words. With only two implements that transformed themselves into weapons of a cosmic war, the Lord toppled the entire Egyptian nation, bringing one disaster after another on them in a clash with every one of Egypt's gods (see Numbers 12:12), by merely speaking. What is scarcely known by the Lord's church is that God Almighty through His prophet engaged the entire Egyptian pantheon in a divine contest and won a decisive victory for them. The history of the prophetic goes on as God continues His pattern with Joshua, Moses' successor.

Again, enlisting a supernatural agent to complete His project, God used His militaristic prophet, Joshua, to conquer the territory Israel had been gathering. Joshua's prophetic mantle continued the legacy and was passed on after a few generations to Samuel, the prophet who instituted Israel's judgeship. Samuel blended judgeship into his prophet's mantle as commander in chief and high priest. His fourfold gifting emerged as a developing model of diverse prophetic service. Samuel went to war with the Philistines, called the nation back to true worship, and restored devoted worship of Yahweh. Lastly, he organized and formalized prophetic education and ministry and propelled the nation forward in its destiny.

God's prophetic mold continued as yet one other office merged with the prophetic—that of king. After Saul's demise, his replacement, David, assumed the role of prophet and priest (not unusual for monarchs of that day) along with roles previously anchored in the mantle by Samuel. David, a born warrior, exhibited a wholehearted working relationship between the Lord and His prophet. He inquired of God and received answers to what he asked by consulting the *ephod*, a kind of interrogatory vestment normally restricted to priests. Revelation became commonplace to this king as he portrayed powerful and amazing relations with Israel's God. Once more, the prophetic surfaced as the common denominator, the indispensable implement of God's activities.

By the time David's reign was in full swing, the connection between God and His prophets was permanently forged. History had been made, and Lord's archetype was forever set. From here on it was official: surely the Lord does nothing without first revealing His secret to His servants the prophets. (See Amos 3:7.) Throughout Scripture the prophets show up as the voice of God, the power of God exerted, His implements and weaponry. The most striking and telling account of this organization was that of the prophetic institution of Jezebel, the Phoenician witch King Ahab made queen of Israel. Her staff consisted of nearly one thousand prophets whom she used to seduce, manipulate, and tyrannize the nation. She utterly usurped the Lord's messengers with her own and had the majority of Yahweh's prophets killed to stop their influence over her own institution.

Solomon, years earlier, did likewise. His prophetic perversions show themselves in his receiving three personal visitations from God and still ending up giving the Lord's spiritual and governmental domains to other gods. His treason inseminated the nation's consciousness so that it was well-accustomed to the idolatry by the time Jezebel came along. Over time, things shifted a bit as the kings were assigned prophets to serve their reigns. Eventually the institutional arrangement took hold and the custom became professional policy. Jeremiah, Elijah, and the other major and minor prophets all continued its protocols up to and including the Lord Jesus Christ.

What all this says is that the occult, the supernatural, and witchcraft are all reasons why God maintains a prophetic staff. Elijah proved this point in his Mount Carmel clash with Jezebel's staff. The Lord showed apostate Israel that indeed her God really is the God of all gods, even though Elijah's contest showed itself as too little, too late. Nonetheless, our point is made. That is the prophet is God's arm, mouth, thoughts, and will. The reason is simple: the occult as we know it demands for the God of all humanity and the sake of the Most High's dominion over the works of His hands, an indomitable counterbalance to Satan's terrorism.

The word *occult* means "secret or mystical knowledge." It is a term embraced by witches, psychics, wizards, and sorcerers to identify the body of knowledge from which they gain their wisdom to exercise supernatural powers. Its relationship to the prophetic is obvious. It rivals the Lord and His people with opposing sensual and worldly wisdom. Branches of the occult in addition to those stated above are divination, necromancy, astrology, magic, witchery, and sorcery. All are elements of the New Age religion that subscribes to polytheism, ancient mystical religions, and funerary death cults from the ancient Near East. These have always been condemned by Creator God.

As a supernatural, spiritual, and political empire, the only godly counter to such powers and their forces are God's prophets. Church prophets need to know this, because these agents are insidious in their infiltration of the modern church. For instance, yoga, a prime entree to the occult, is pushed daily by the media and entertainment industry. Now, even education and psychotherapy tout it as the rediscovered answer to the stresses of the world. Public schools peddle its ancient teachings under the guise of holistic wisdom, ignoring their religious and pagan roots. More than a few churches today subscribe to portions of this practice, overlooking its original aim to condition meditators to receive and embody the spirits of other gods. Much of the introspective worship forms utilize "soaking"—sitting still to let whatever ethereally happens to a worshipper to do so unimpeded. Such theologized widespread practices smack of eastern yoga and mirror the principles of transcendental meditation. Many such New Age practices are supposedly helpful, healthy, and wholesome for today's frenzied world. Presented apart from the ritualistic and religious roots, they mask the detrimental results of these teachings. A church world devoid of insightful revelation is ready prey for these seductions.

Of all the elements of the occult, divination is the most pervasive. It behooves prophets of the local church to understand it. Divination's most pronounced treatment in Scripture is Acts 16:16. It is simply speaking by the power of a fallen angel, devil, or demon. The definition alone tells why God has a problem with it. The "divine" in the word identifies the source of divinatory words; psychics call them "readings." In ancient times, spirits were called divine beings because, when they represented themselves to people, they sought to enlist worshippers in their service and worship as gods, or divine ones. Thus, over time they were dubbed "divine ones," and their words to humans as "divining." Eventually, a supernatural institution developed around their visitations and communications that relied upon the hearer's performance of certain rituals. The collection of practices and rituals required to receive their words of wisdom and mystical knowledge from divine beings became known as divination. It rested on animal sacrifices, severed body parts, nature worship, and the handling of objects believed to possess magical powers. Supposedly embodiments of the divine one, various objects were ritualized in area revered as magical sites. Inquiring worshippers resorted to them to answer their questions. Such sites were seen as sources of supernatural deposits that were designated by the interrogated deity as the exclusive mode of approaching and appealing to it for information. The information routinely retrieved includes astrology, tarot and palm readings, crystal gazing, and necromancy, to name a few. Baal, Ashtorath, and Molech of the Bible, along with Diana (Artemis), Apollo, and Zeus, all had such sites, usually in forests or groves that they centralized for worshippers' sacrifices and petitions. Nature and astro worship exemplify the Lord's objection to their religious forms. As Deuteronomy 4:19 indicates, they worship the creature over the Creator. (See also Deuteronomy 17:3 and Romans 1:25.) Today, these are often popularized as entertainment to hide their true aims.

Countless Christians call psychic hotlines to learn about their futures and to get advice from the supernatural about their life affairs. More than a few engage in talking to the dead to ease the grief over a lost loved one. Millions follow their astrological signs and have their palms read. Psychic networks are a multi-billion-dollar industry that refuses to be curtailed no matter how many of its front-runners are found to be charlatans. The hunger or need for answers about tomorrow drives people to do anything and to pay any price to get even a tidbit of information.

Such information for the Christian, on the other hand, is locked up in the house of God. By His Spirit in the prophets, the Lord ordained the performance of this function to be by His people. That is the whole goal of Pentecost. The entirety of creation's spiritual activity and its authorities, once distributed to all invisible powers and beings, is now gathered and localized in the church of Jesus Christ. (See Acts 2.) Having a prophetic staff in every church regulates its releases to thereby discourage the Christian's temptation to seek the darkness for the light. (See Isaiah 8:19–20.)

Chapter Summary

1. Giving a prophecy of any kind triggers a chain of events that affect the hearer.

2. Prophecy articulates the Lord's past, present, and future mind on a given issue.

3. Prophesying takes spiritual faculties to work.

4. Powerful prophets have a resolute prophetic mind-set.

5. Prophecy has an origin that predetermines its validity and accuracy.

6. Understanding prophecy's anatomy is important.

7. Prophetic prayer, preaching, and teaching all emerge from different anointing.

8. Other powers facilitate and perform prophecy.

Prophetic Action Items

1. Use the words of another prophet (make sure he or she is an official prophet), and study their composition, terminology, implications, etc. From your analysis, determine how valid and potent they are.

2. Draft a service description for the types of prophets named in this chapter.

Chapter 10

THE PROPHET'S JOB DESCRIPTION

This chapter discusses in detail the job the prophet is to do. It covers:

- Sixteen key questions for the local church to consider
- How to staff a prophetic institution
- The pastor and the awakening prophet
- Mentorship
- When to call in a prophet

ROUTINE ACTIVITIES OF CHURCH PROPHETS

This chapter of the book deals mainly with the local church's prophetic institution. It gives further occupational details on the role and work of the church prophet. I have clearly established why the prophetic should be a functioning institution in the local church. Now that yours has been decided upon, here are some of its areas of operation.

THE PROPHETIC IN THE LOCAL CHURCH...

- Should be a full, functioning institution.
- Should be under a prophetic superintendent.
- Should be a graduated appointment.
- Should ensure that training and proving precede placement on the team.
- Should have standardized qualifications and a formal means of screening and selection.
- Should have a uniform criterion-based means of evaluation, assessment, and verification before placement.
- Should only receive eligible appointees after a trial period.
- Should have regular worship and congregational outlets.
- Should be assigned to various aspects of ministry for prayer coverage, insight, and spiritual watch care.
- Should be visibly represented in the local assembly.
- Should be replicating and outreach-minded.
- Should have certified trainers and supervisors.
- Should require training and apprenticeship.
- Should encompass all spiritual activity.
- Should collaborate with the church's school or learning department.
- Should develop and refine prophetic outlets in the community for its ministers.
- Should arrange prophetic interaction and collaboration with other church's prophets.

- Should be active in church's prayer, especially in its congregational prayer.
- Should structure uniform corrective, disciplinary, and advice and appeals process.

PROPHETIC INSTITUTION STAFF SHOULD CONSIST OF THE FOLLOWING:

- Prophetic types and prophets
- Intercessors and prayer warriors
- Special prophetic musical ensemble for psalmist
- Seers and church visionaries
- Prophetic trainers
- Prophetic mentors who are answerable to a prophetic superintendent
- Staff prophets—*well-trained senior and junior ministers*
- Supervisory personnel over small units immediately answerable to superintendent and pastorate
- Superintendent of church prophetics answerable to senior pastor(s), chief prophets, or apostles
- A well-trained force of competent prophetic voices

DESCRIPTION OF CHURCH PROPHET ACTIVITIES

With their prophetic faculties, resident or church prophets teach the flock about God's ordained prophetics and help them determine the true from the false. They train the church to be responsive to the Lord and receptive to His Holy Spirit, paving the way for the pastor's actions, sermons, or announcements. It is through church prophets that God expects to ensure the church's accurate divine revelation in both spiritual and natural matters. The prophets then become the seasoned ears that try prophetic outbursts and the discerning eyes that sift the false from the true. They are always alert to recognize emerging and awakening prophetic vessels in the congregation and prepared with a proven screening and training program to develop them.

Once budding prophets have been spotted, as with their ancient predecessors, church prophets should be set to responsibly equip newcomers to the office, and later qualify their readiness to serve. Church prophets' superintending and training goals, considering this requirement, should be positioned to educate and supply prophets-in-training (PITs for short) to answer God's call. More than the ability to see something spiritually with their mind's eye and utter it should be required as mandatory training should prove. The ideal superintendent of the church's prophetics is interested in what smoothly integrates the new prophet into the cultural life of the church. Master or chief prophets should then gear their PITs to serve competently when the time comes for them to be inducted into God's service. Their learning programs should implement every pedagogical method available to ensure their success. Structural schooling then figures prominently in the constant ministry of the church prophet, or at least it should.

The work of a prophet in the local church, as you can see, is infinitely more involved than standing up in church and yelling, "Thus says the Lord" or "I see a car, money, or home for you." Any psychic can do that. It is these other powers and functions, which many prophets know little about, that distinguish the two. They must be tried, purged, proven, and then authenticated to separate the prophesier from the official prophet, or even the intercessor.

Resident or staff prophets identify the lively stones, that is, potential workers, leaders, and ministers in the work, and collaborate with the pastor on their development and installation. Staff prophets participate in the church's government as subordinates or compeers, ideally helping to shepherd, order, structure, and maintain the house of God. Church prophets are key to their churches' overall training aims and activities and are instrumental in the success of their holistic spiritual stature in Christ. Staff prophets are also to be the sage counsel and the divine flow of wisdom pastors can look to for assistance in every godly way. They each serve as one of their church's significant visionary pillars to validate and expedite the pastor's vision and the church's mission. This is important when the membership falls into skepticism or cynicism over a proposed venture or project the Lord wants the church to undertake. Old Testament prophets Zechariah and Haggai were prophets of old who performed this function. (See Haggai 1 and Zechariah 1.) Here is how they relate.

When the word came down from God to start rebuilding the temple and the wall of Jerusalem, the people were not at all motivated to do so. These two prophets stepped up and called on the people to obey God's decree. They confirmed the word was of the Lord and supported the leaders practically, spiritually, and supernaturally in the project. Ezra 5:1–3 is one example of this. Prophet involvement guarded the work and backed it supernaturally to see that the vision of God did not veer off His designated course. So effective was the prophets' involvement that one wonders, considering Ezra and Nehemiah's conflicts during this work, if the task could ever have been done at all without them. A study of Ezra 6:14 shows how the passage strongly supports the exhortation in 2 Chronicles 20:20 concerning the ministry of the prophets. Nehemiah 6:7

enhances this phenomenon by underscoring God's use of His prophets to spiritually achieve anything significant He wants done.

A brief warning is needed at this point. Do not forget that these abilities are available to all prophets. Satanic prophets of the world do the same thing: they rely on their powerful prophet's spirit (see Nehemiah 9:30) and divine covenants to achieve their diabolical ends. Nehemiah 6:14 alluded to this when he spoke of the prophetess Noadiah and the rest of the prophets sent against his effort to make him afraid and quit the task the Lord had assigned him. A name for the tactic is mercenary prophetics. Because they were paid to do so, Nehemiah's contemporaries repeated Balaam's error. They sold their gifts to the highest bidder and sought to exercise their authority to destroy a new work of the Lord.

Considering this, a most logical question is: How can these extensive duties and functions of the church prophet be settled and employed by the pastor? The answer is: They can when prophets are thoroughly oriented to what the church needs and diligent in their spiritual watch. However, it must not be overlooked that great responsibilities carry with them corresponding privileges and consequences. To ensure both are balanced, pastors and church leaders must set limits on their church prophets' service and conduct regular evaluations and brainstorming sessions to make sure the ministry remains viable in the church. Here is another place where the mutuality of the two, the prophet and the pastor, can suffer. The pastor's interests in sparing the flock must not erode the prophet's value to the Lord and the church. Restraints placed on the prophets should not silence the Lord's voice to His people or tie His hands. Healthy restraints should favor

God's wholesome use of His most reliable prophets, while safeguarding the church overall from the most ill-equipped or unreliable ones. As with any good team, the pastor and the chief prophet should confer on the guidelines to set for the church's prophetic institutions. These should spring from wisdom and knowledge, not just sentiment.

CHURCH PROPHET LIMITS

As said earlier, the prophet's authority in a pastor's church is strictly influential as delegated by the pastor. Church prophet limits, largely set by the pastor, are subject to his or her revocation at any time. The resident prophet is not to displace the shepherd as head of the church in the eyes of the sheep. When there is a conflict that could harm or spoil the flock, the pastor has the final say (right or wrong). Prophets are to acquiesce to the pastor to spare the flock. If there is an irreconcilable difference between them, the prophet should move on, leaving the church and its headship intact. The prophet's anointing being the higher of the two means he or she can quickly overturn devilish attacks (should that be the case) and pray the Lord move upon the pastor's heart. If God does not do so then, it could be a sign that the Lord is removing the church's spiritual covering.

IDENTIFYING AND SELECTING CHURCH PROPHETS

When it comes to recognizing and ordaining church prophets, as has been said, pastors must take great care. By now you understand that the person placed in the post should be a confirmed prophet and not a novice, an intercessor, or a prophesier aspiring to the official post. Requiring church prophets to train for their posts, especially if they rose up from the pastor's flock, is wise. If a candidate for the position did not rise up from the pastor's flock, he or she should be ready to present reputable credentials to the pastor before being assigned to duty, and even then the assignment should be subject to an orientation period to make sure the incoming prophet is a good fit. Even so, until the quality of the prophet's service is confirmed, his or her appointment should be temporary until the prophet's credibility is verified.

Submitted prophetic credentials should supply the pastor with the candidate's experience, background, years in prophetic ministry, and degree of training. The prophet's level of competence and skill for church prophet service should be stated in specific achievement and accomplishment terms. Also, a service record and references for the pastor to check before installing someone as official church prophet should be made available. (This *need not* apply to prophets called in as guest ministers, but it is still good policy.)

For church prophets there should be a trial period set to determine if they are compatible with the flock and its vision, mission, and perspectives. This requirement should become policy regardless of the number of years a candidate for the position of church prophet has been in prophetic ministry. It is common sense that protects the flock from prolonged discomfort or harm if the arrangement turns sour, and moreover, the Bible encourages it. For pastors considering authorizing prophets in their churches, guidelines of this sort are more than practical; they are critical.

Requesting references may seem unpleasant or worldly to pastors, but they can prevent years of trouble. It is not secular to want to confirm the credibility and reputation of your incoming guest or candidate prophets as a precautionary measure; it is actually quite spiritual. The Lord exhorts us to know those who labor among us. (See 1 Thessalonians 5:12.) As a matter of course, investigate more closely candidates who balk at this requirement to confirm their qualifications for the post. Sometimes negative reactions mean such prophets have something to hide.

Further, there is nothing wrong with asking for a background of the proposed church prophet's ministry covering and past engagements. Listen to a series of the prophet's messages on random dates before deciding if his or her teaching is sound. If he or she is published, review his or her works and readers' critiques. As a pastor responsibly employing, endorsing, or assimilating the prophetic into your church, you are looking for consistency in every professional area of the ministry.

Qualifying potential church prophets should include a thorough screening process. This is recommended for verifying an incoming prophet's overall potential and for identifying the true prophet and the prophet's truth. The screening process should consist of pointed questions that draw out informative answers about the prophet that pastors can use to base their decision upon. Such answers should provide insight into the candidate's prophetic vision for the church's covering and the means by which he or she proposes to implement it. The questions posed should reveal the heart of the minister, his or her outlook on church prophetics, and his or her perceived place in it. Naturally, doctrinal compatibility is crucial. The questionnaire you draft should tell you the proposed church prophet's spiritual and practical knowledge, since teaching is likely to be a large part of his duties. How the prophet measures up as a potential leader, as well as matters of confidentiality and loyalty, should be addressed. A good standardized assessment could do much of this work for you. I developed one that has proven to be quite effective.

THE PASTOR AND THE AWAKENING PROPHET

Should a pastor discover an awakening prophet in the congregation, the discovery should not automatically consti- tute an ordination, installation, or appointment to the church's prophetics. The most it should do is identify young proph- ets' calls and inspire novices to become trained and seasoned. Awakening does not in itself guarantee anointing, nor does it guarantee the quality of the awakening prophet's mantle or its compatibility with the church and its vision. Prolonged obser- vation of the novice's development is in order. For an exhaus- tive description of the traits and attributes that indicate the possible presence of a prophet's spirit, review previous chap- ters that profile prophetic character, abilities, and the like. To confirm the one you suspect may be prophetic or a prophet, assign a few inconsequential ministry-related tasks. Observe the person's handling of the tasks or resolution of assigned problems to be sure. This approach may be used by pastors to prove those who claim to be prophets and to sift the mature from the marginal, and to successfully weed out more aspi- rants to the office. Again, it will also distinguish the interces- sor and prophesier from the office-qualified prophet.

A critical factor to consider when dealing with an awak- ening prophet is the radical alteration it causes in the relation- ship between the prophet and the pastor. When this occurs, many dynamic factors come into play that did not exist before. Relations between pastor and the member-turned-prophet may become strained now in ways previously unknown. The mandate given them both may clash. This could signal the prophet's call to another church when the reasons are not merely contention or resistance to change on both sides. All these considerations should be weighed carefully by the shepherd seeking to use a sheep-turned-prophet as the resident church prophet.

When the office of prophet is installed in the church, the same safeguards and precautions used for other staff members should prevail with the church prophet. These precautionary measures should be clear before the ordination ceremony. I cannot stress this enough. Pastors do not have to submit their flocks to untrained, inexperienced, or unverified prophets, nor should they be hesitant about requiring a proven track record from them. It is responsible shepherding to release to the congregation well-trained and stable prophets. As a pastor, you should do all you can to ensure your church and its prophets are compatible. Another suggestion to foster this is to take time to acquaint your church with biblical prophetics while you ready your prophets to serve them. Teach your people how prophets think, minister, and handle the Lord's word. Tell them why it is different from the pastorate. Explain and bring in seasoned prophets to explain how the prophets benefit them. Begin your process with your leaders so they can support your shift.

Special Precaution

Pastors, be wary of lone prophets who have neither church accountability for their ministries nor a reputable company of their peers to whom they voluntarily answer. Pastors, if prophets have not come up under your ministry, someone somewhere should be able to tell you about their prophetics and ministry before you even meet with them. Press for details of their ministry experiences prior to releasing them in your church. Rigid reliance upon the Holy Spirit for revelatory confirmation of those you trust for prophetic ministry is acceptable. Nevertheless, it should be infrequent and not a routine substitute for reliable screening practices. Even spiritual decisions require practical due diligence. The wisdom of God's Word dictates this for the protection of the pastor and the church. I have learned over the years that when brothers and sisters in the Lord first meet each other, their introduction is likely to be primarily spirit to spirit, and this is good. However, not all working relationships stay on that plane all the time. Therefore, pastor and prophet should want to get to know each other flesh to flesh; that is, the two of you may want to take time to get acquainted with one another's human sides.

The Church Prophet

Do you recall how I said God awakens young prophets? It is often in private, which lends itself to immature prophets' resistance to established church authority. We talked much about this elsewhere. In this section we overview the chain of events that occurs when God alerts a person that he or she is a prophet. The information to follow is not given to show that the Lord's methods are wrong, but rather to show that the darkness in humanity can yield the early results that can usually make new prophets surly and unpleasant. Pride is always at the root of the human heart, and the call to the prophetic surfaces it quickly. That is what happens with new prophets.

Since young prophetic messengers get their start from God in secret, they feel such a start means they are never to submit to anyone but God. This attitude makes for turbulent times, as we have shown, and all too often ends with the novice prophet leaving the church and the frustrated pastor being left to deal with the wake of disaster the neophyte may have left behind. Meanwhile, the young prophet is most likely outside the camp of the Lord and away from the safety of the ark, embittered, embattled, and now wary of prophetics in the future. If there had been a medium between the two—the budding prophet and the busy and protective pastor—maybe things could have turned out differently. Perhaps the struggle that ended so badly could have been avoided. What would have happened if there were better ways for pastors to bring their new prophets up in the Lord?

One way to reduce the customary struggles between new prophets and their pastors is to direct awakening prophets to seasoned messengers who understand what they are going through that can help them learn their callings, their mantle, their ministry, and their place in the church. Here is where prophetic mentorship comes in.

The first thing all upset parties in a chaotic prophetic awakening should do is not throw out the baby with the bath water. Frequently, out of sheer frustration, that is the response of the typical church pastor. The prophetic on its own is a weighty institution. Typically, those called to it are headstrong, strong-willed, and independent—qualities that make them good candidates for the calling in the first place. These traits fuse well with the underlying prophetic nature and enable messengers to endure the often negative experiences associated with the ministry. Getting them off to a good prophetic start can be precarious. You see, prophetic types survive because difficult lives accustom them to resistance. Potential prophets are usually seasoned fighters, able to isolate themselves and thrive in isolation. They adapt easily to the mood of their surroundings and deftly counterattack anything that threatens them. Prophets in general find it quite convenient to walk away from the crowd and to go against the grain of the masses. All these powerful tendencies, when sanctified, will make them good vessels of the Lord in prophetic ministry, but at the outset they are nerve-racking and quite destructive.

Seasoned prophets know this well. That is why they should be available for prophetic mentorship and established in the church as such. Churches that are committed to hosting and endorsing Christ's prophetics should have a number of prophetic partners and peers on hand to help them with their new prophets over and above their inhouse institution. These people should help mentor the church's entire prophetic ministry. Outside prophetic mentorship means the burden of coping with a budding prophet is handed over to someone else, even if the pastor is a prophet.

The work of training, pruning, restraining, and trying the sincere novice prophet is left on the mentor's shoulders. Once assigned, the prophetic mentor should make himself available to his juniors for long talks, questions and answers, and other requirements of tutelage and training. A structured curriculum with teaching tapes and good books on the subject helps also.

The person usually assigned the prophetic mentor's function in the church is the church prophet superintendent. In a small church, this person generally doubles as the prophetic superintendent of the church. In either case, an outside veteran prophet would be a good addition to the team. This person can bring the objectivity that detachment from the church's issues requires. In large churches, the function may be delegated by the prophetic superintendent to a subordinate, but the outside mentor is still strongly recommended. Large churches are likely to have a staff of prophetic trainers assigned to this detail in the church. Whatever your structure, anyone in the church feeling the call to the prophetic or the awakening flames of the office of the prophet should be directed to the prophetic superintendent promptly.

THE PROPHETIC SUPERINTENDENT

The prophetic superintendent should have an established training program of coaching, counseling, and grooming methods to help novices serve responsibly and harmoniously in the church. This position should be publicized so church members know where to turn when they think their prophetics are being aroused. When they turn to the church's prophetic superintendent, they should be prepared to engage in a structured screening and preparation process. There should be initial discovery tests: skills-based activities and exercises, as well as extensive evaluative systems that gauge their prophetic potential. After that, placement becomes the issue as the prophetic trainer administers programs to foster learners' growth systematically, qualifying and strengthening their skills along the way. All efforts should be aimed at progressively fortifying their prophetic reliability. The goal of all teaching tools is the novice's maturity as a prophet. All prophetic learning and teaching processes should be well-defined and instructors should observe the students. Prophetic teachers should consistently adjust and confirm their students' progress and record it for later pastoral and church leadership use. A routine training record should accompany the trainee prophet's record of service. The umbrella under which this prelude to prophetic readiness falls is called readiness. It entails tutelage, orientation skills and drills, course apprenticeship, and mentorship.

MENTORSHIP IS AN OFFICE

Mentorship of any kind in the Old World was understood as an official function. What made it so was the fact that parents, guardians, or other authority figures engaged mentors in a learner's life. In addition, mentorship was initiated because the learner was gifted and/or highly called and so thus needed specialized training to succeed in that call. Mentorship assignments were given to knowledgeable representatives of the professional class or field to which the learner was called and were identified by their skill and proficiency in their occupation. Not just anyone would dare to undertake the task of hanging out his or her shingle a as mentor and enrolling students. Mentors were highly respected as experienced and learned professionals in their fields—experts.

Mentors differed vastly from typical educators. What mentors gave their students far exceeded mere academic knowledge. They distinguished themselves by the performance edge, skill advantage, and professional head start they gave their learners. The very things that qualified them as mentors are what benefited their students the most. As seasoned and successful professionals, mentors are identified as being well-informed, well-trained, and thoroughly experienced in their fields. Their well-documented skills and overall knowledge far surpass the majority of their contemporaries' because of a proven track record. Mentors' expertise makes them able teachers and trainers because they effectively and profitably demonstrate their field of knowledge through competent instruction in the theoretical and technical aspects of their industry. Mentors foster their learners' development with instruction and activities that go to the heart and soul of their students' potential and performance, as well as that of the profession to which they are called. Mentors inform, transform, and enable their learners to conform to the conduct, attitudes, and behaviors of their fields. Besides academic knowledge, training, and skill development, mentors counsel, guide, and coach. They provide as much affective readiness to improve their mentorees' emotional intelligence as they do to sharpen their cognition for God's service.

AIMS OF MENTORSHIP

With any nurturing endeavor, there are concrete aims that regulate its activities and verify its success. Mentorship is no different. Mentors initiate their services with specific ends in mind. Serious mentors are mindful of not allowing the agreement to become merely a social or servile arrangement. The following are some of the aims of a productive mentorship.

QUICK STUDY CHART
AIMS OF A PRODUCTIVE MENTORSHIP

- Protect
- Prepare
- Instill valuable wisdom
- Fix perspective of the field
- Create instincts internally
- Allow manifestation of skills
- Impart confidence
- Apply lessons practically

- Cultivate wisdom

- Develop skill

- Provide mantle treatment

- Educate

- Work toward mentorship outcome

WHAT TO EXPECT FROM MENTORSHIP

When you enter a mentorship, you should expect to be represented in and presented to your field to showcase your mantle and be promoted to your official calling. After basic readiness activities in the rudiments of your calling, there should be some preliminary opportunities to work in the position you plan to occupy. Below is a series of Quick Study Charts to help you appreciate the parameters, guidelines, and benefits of mentorship from a professional and productive vantage point.

QUICK STUDY CHART
IMPORTANT MENTORSHIP FACTS

- Mentorship is integral to all creation.

- Mentorship is an official function.

- Mentors should be educated in the field of ministry to which their mentorees are called.

- Prophets especially need to be mentored.

- Mentorships are to be mutually rewarding and mutually cooperative arrangements.

- Mentorship involves more than servitude, while not excluding the attendant services that qualify them to lead one day.

- Mentorees should expect to have scheduled training, lectures, and development and be required to attend them.
- Mentor assignments should look to practical ministry functions and outlets.
- Mentorship relies on integrity, devotion, diligence, and loyalty.
- Mentorship must be formed with clean, honest motives and well-defined objectives.
- Undeclared objectives and outcomes endanger the success of any mentorship.

Quick Study Chart
What Is Involved in Prophetic Mentorship?

- Professional tutorials
- Pneuma academics and teaching in the pragmatism of the Lord's spiritualities
- Biblical scholarship and applied learning
- Ministry business administration
- Occupational equipping
- Minister character development
- Mantle skills development
- Office competency training
- Supernatural prayer and spiritual warfare training
- Prophetic fluency coaching
- Kingdom and Christian communications
- People skills and people management training, interpersonal skills, and ministry relationships

- Problem-solving, critical thinking, conflict management, situation assessment and relevant response, sound judgment, and discretion
- Crises management and intervention
- Staff, worker, and volunteer management
- Fund-raising, fund management, organization building, and solvency
- Counseling and ministry execution

QUICK STUDY CHART
THE UNIQUENESS OF PROPHETIC MENTORSHIP

- Prophetic mentorship is unique compared to most mentorship agreements in that it is, of necessity, two-dimensional.
- Prophetic mentorship involves two-tiered treatment of the mantle: heaven and earth, eternity and time, spiritual and natural.
- Prophetic mentorship is an immutable standard for the Lord's true messengers.
- Prophets must be escorted to the realm of the spirit by a senior messenger if they are to be recognized and accepted as an authority in that sphere.
- New Testament prophets must be mentored as well, even though the Lord Jesus' testimony constitutes the Spirit of prophecy for them.

New prophets tend to be eager, somewhat overzealous, and overly reliant upon purely spiritual inflows and outlets for their early prophetic words. The ecstasy of the Holy Spirit becomes quite addictive to them as they seek to merely enjoy

His sensations rather than His good sense. In the beginning, the idea of having a mentor is exciting. People seek it in much the same way as they look for a guru or a casual advisor. After they get one, their attitude changes. "When I need you, mentor, I will call you; otherwise leave me be and let me do my life and ministry as I see fit" becomes their unspoken intention.

For most people, especially prophets, the real motive for wanting mentorship with prestigious people is to brag that this or that one is "my" mentor. The idea of submitting to a mentor is rarely a factor in their minds. However, those who realize that submission is a valid, invariable mentorship requirement tend to panic and dread it so much that they make matters worse when they come under their mentor's wing. They fear the structure, shudder at the assignments, slack up on their service, or simply disregard their mentor's requests, tasks, and lessons. To combat this temptation, here is an intelligent protocol of the spirit world that all prophets need to grasp and respect.

COMING UNDER YOUR MENTOR'S WING

Coming under the mentor's wing can be intimidating in the beginning. Uncertain about what it will cost and require of you makes you understandably a little frightened. Giving up control and letting another tell you what to do and virtually orchestrate your life is a bit unsettling. Once you do submit, you find it is much as you suspected it would be: demanding and often ego-breaking. It takes a while for you to realize that it is also a power-shaping experience. For your mentorship to work, a clear-cut outline of service expectations and requirements should be drawn up. Both mentor and mentoree should agree to it.

In the beginning, if you are serious about your mentorship, prepare to have little time for yourself. Initially you will be obliged to spend a large part of your life with your mentor serving, learning, growing, and encountering. You will be stretched, and that is the name of the game. But if you want to get the best out of your mentorship, be guided by the following suggestions.

QUICK STUDY CHART
COMING UNDER YOUR MENTOR'S WING

- Be honest about your actions, reactions, motives, offenses, and defenses.

- Question your motives and honestly appraise your real self, especially in view of required mentorship duties.

- Explore your fears, doubts, anger, and resistance, particularly as they relate to authority figures.

- Ask yourself how selfishly motivated you may have been, or if you have a real problem in developing that should be promptly handled.

- Ask yourself how interested you really are in being successful in God, and what will you sacrifice for it. Will it be pride? Ego? Your independence?

- Investigate what you expected to get from and give to your mentorship in preparation for your ministry. Was your imagination realistic? What hidden psycho-emotional limitations did you place in the mentorship before it began? When they surface, are you willing to honestly declare them?

- Now that you have given your word, are you going to back out, or will you see it through to what you know the Lord called you to do?

QUICK STUDY CHART
SUMMARY OF PROPHETIC SUPERINTENDENT DUTIES

THE PREMISE UNDERLYING THE DUTIES OF A SUPERINTENDENT OF CHURCH PROPHETICS: ADMINISTRATION AND ACCOUNTABILITY FOR STABILITY

As mentioned elsewhere, the church prophet's job is demanding. Being the superintendent of a church's prophetics is even more so. Take a look at what your duties and responsibilities will be to see how much the Lord is entrusting to you.

- Overseeing local church prophetics
- Collaborating with pastor and other ministers of the church on prophetic tenor and flow of the ministry
- Identifying and calling forth awakening and manifesting prophets in the congregation
- Working with and overseeing psalmists and various sections of the church's life
- Leading and regulating prophetic activities at home, church, and throughout the community
- Installing or participating in the installation of leaders or new prophets
- Attending the church's celebratory and commemorative events such as baptisms, christenings, weddings, etc.
- Sharing pastoral visitation and similar loads as directed
- Establishing and confirming the office and particular functions each prophetic officer should be assigned

- Administrating prophetic executions and supervising prophetic staff as they exercise them
- Arranging for prophetic outlets for prophetic members to service the body: conferences, classes, and special events
- Scheduling prophetic representation as desired by the pastor for each church gathering
- Participating in, scheduling, and overseeing prophetic prayer and intercession in the church
- Augmenting normal church counseling with prophetic guidance and insight
- Identifying and disseminating quality prophetic material in the church
- Contributing to the church's fund-raising and entrepreneurial ventures
- Standardizing church prophetic expressions
- Evaluating emerging prophets and ranking them for use
- Developing and acquiring curriculum for ongoing training and refinement of prophetic ministers
- Interacting with and submitting to the pastor's needs and vision for the church's prophetics
- Scheduling and engaging outside prophetics and prophetic types to come in to minister to and refresh the church, its prophetic staff, and ministers
- Training, ordaining, and cultivating novice prophets
- Correcting errant prophetics and prophetic excess in operation
- Screening prophetic actions and messages, often before they go forth to the body

- Standing and waiting with pastor or church in spiritual conflicts

It is understood that the prophetic superintendent will have a staff to distribute these duties or delegate them as feasible. Just make sure the most sensitive responsibilities remain in his or her control.

WHEN TO CALL IN A PROPHET

Much information has been given you on the subject of the prophetic in general and the church prophet in particular. You have been provided with background information on the ancient origins of the ministry and how it applies today. Nearly everything you need to institute the most efficient and effective prophetic order in your church and reap the fullest of benefits from it is included in this book.

One issue not addressed so far is the use of prophets in the local church apart from the church prophet's ministry. The Lord's persistent promotion of the ministry of the prophet means you who read this book will at one time or another receive a prophet into your church or be one of the prophets a church calls in to serve its needs. It is scriptural to do so, based on Jesus' promise to reward those with like rewards for receiving His prophets. (See Matthew 10:41.) That being the case, the restoration of the office in mainline Christendom means most churches today and in the future will call in a prophet to minister the supernaturals of God on occasion. The question is how to know when to call one in.

Over the course of our discussions we have established how to know whom to call in. What remains then is a means of deciding when a prophet should be called into your church to minister to your people. To begin to answer this question, I suggest you look back to the sections that dealt with the ministries of Zechariah and Haggai and their ministries to Ezra and Nehemiah. From that information alone you get an idea of the situations that arise in which you and your church can benefit from an itinerant prophet's service. Along with the examples given above, I want to add a few specifics that can help you decide on when to expose your church to prophetic ministry.

The first thing you may want to consider is any concrete voids your church may be currently experiencing due to lack of prophetic ministration. What are some of the humanist and demonic conditions surfacing or prevailing in your church? Can you, for instance, see clear evidence of a spiritual attack or devilish infiltration on the wider population? Such assaults usually start at the head and target leadership first. The most diligent leader can get weary or overwhelmed to the point that their guard drops and the enemy takes advantage of their weakened state. Do not be reluctant to acknowledge such problems when they surface, and by all means do not allow Satan to make you feel guilty or ashamed for needing some outside help.

Here are some examples of when to call in a prophet. We will start with marriages. Are the marriages in your church, especially the leaders', dissolving all of a sudden? How about the youth? Is teen pregnancy rampant? Are drug addictions, criminal activity, and incarcerations increased among them? What about the physical health of the flock? Are sickness and disease, especially those of a debilitating or fatal sort, all too frequent? What about employment? Are your members constantly losing jobs? An affirmative answer to more than a few of these can signal a need for prophetic ministry in the church.

However, there are other signs not as crucial but every bit as essential.

To illustrate, are you, as a pastor, finding fewer and fewer financial or promotional breakthroughs experienced in the work overall? Is the fund-raising down while the bills pile up? Do you encounter apathy and indifference from your people all too often, particularly in the area of money? Is the body at large afraid to give or enter into costly ventures with you? What about your ministers, trustees, elders, and leaders? Can you say they have been constant with you to date, or are you noticing a trend of wavering indecision regarding the moves you want to make? Are they confidently and competently handling and completing their assigned projects, or are more and more of their duties going undone or simply being ignored?

How about their spirituality? Is there a steady progress in their ministry callings? Are they constant and diligent with the mandate of God on the church? Are they applying and growing from what they learn? Do they demonstrate effective in-church ministry? Consider your church programs. Are they flourishing, or does it seem as if a bronze sky has replaced the earlier open heavens over you? Could you use a breakthrough in building negotiations, land purchases? If any of these issues affect you, then your church is due for a qualified itinerant prophet's ministry. Just make sure the one you bring in specializes in the issue you need to address. If you are wrestling with civil authorities in the area of zoning laws in your area, you need a prophet with strong judicial influence. That is, one with a particular influence over governmental principalities that has proven itself by amassing a like constituency to appeal to regarding your matters. Any one of these reasons is enough for you to decide to call in a bona fide prophet.

To add to the above, consider the following. If your mandate has been changed or been completed and God is pressing you to do a new thing, then like Ezra and Nehemiah, the time has come for you to add prophetic power to your normal church dispensation. Also, if there are frequent accidents, shortfalls, setbacks, or a powerful strangulation on the work of your ministry, a prophet is needed. Infighting, leadership clashes, recent splits, spiritual harassment, and membership wandering also signal the need for prophetic power to restabilize your church. The most major indication of all is death. If you suddenly find your membership hit often with the death of significant and stable members beyond the aged, a prophet is certainly needed in your church because a death agent has been set to doom it. Lastly, if there is a pressing need for huge financial infusions in the ministry, you need a prophet with an economic stronghold in the heavenlies.

As you can see, the modern church's need for prophetic strength is just as dire, if not more so, as that of the early church. That is why the Lord continues to replenish the office generation after generation. However, after all this information, by now you must want to know where to go from here, and how to get there. The next section will give insights to point the way.

CHAPTER SUMMARY

1. Specific (well-defined) limits should be set on the church prophet institution. These should not compromise the quality of the ministry.

2. A set of guidelines should be used to identify candidates for church prophet.

3. Pastors need to remember that they are also to shepherd awakening prophets in their churches.

4. The supervisor of the church prophet institutions is called a prophetic superintendent or chief prophet.

5. All types of prophetic service thrives on mentorship.

6. Prophetic guidelines for every church should include mentoring guidelines.

7. The person to be delegated the tasks related to the entire prophetic institution should be the chief prophet, also called the prophetic superintendent.

PROPHETIC ACTION ITEMS

1. Gather with a study team to discuss and settle on the best answers to the chapter's opening questions regarding the prophetic institution. Prove how relevant, reliable, and useful your answers are and how they may be used in the formation and establishment of a viable church (or organizational) prophet institution.

PART TWO

GUIDELINES FOR ESTABLISHING A PROPHETIC COMPANY

Chapter 11

GETTING STARTED

This chapter addresses the establishment of the prophet's institution. It covers:

- Getting started
- Prophetic training
- Administrating a prophetic training program
- Entering God's prophetic staff
- A wise word to prophetic trainees

ENTERING GOD'S PROPHETIC STAFF

In understanding and acclimating yourself to God's prophetic staff, you are joining the ranks of a powerful, age-old kingdom organization. Your call to the prophetic launched you into an explosive career of divine service. Its weighty responsibilities are balanced only by the exhilarating joys of moving in and out of God's heavenly terrains as you have never done so before. If you are adequately prepared for it, this season will mature and stabilize you as one of God's prophetic voices when you purpose in your heart to conquer its sometimes turbulent learning curve. The explanations and applications described in this handbook can help you fulfill your call to prophesy and to understand the range of services, functions, operations, and objectives that constitute prophetic ministry. Use this material to learn how to administrate the Lord's spiritualities and to guard and oversee His possession as a prophet in your appointed sphere. If you are diligent, you will prosper your ministry to possibly undergird the prophetics of your community in the future. If you are new to the prophetic, this handbook tells you what is ahead. If you are a seasoned prophet, it will serve as a helpful refresher that takes much of the work out of replicating yourself and your mantle.

POWER AND ASSIGNMENTS

As we have said, prophesying is a divine communication, coming from God through a vessel. Specifically, it is the delivery of God's word to the earth, which may comprise His will, plans, teachings, purposes, and disposition on a matter. Generally God does this through people, though He has been known to use other means: Balaam's mule, angels, visual signs in nature, or dreams and visions. These all constitute the tools of the prophet's trade.

God has community, neighborhood, regional, or district prophets. Novice prophets may start out in one of these areas and later be promoted to city, state, national, or international watchmen—not a rash or hasty move on God's part. (Only the devil is in a hurry.) To God, timing and preparation are critical, and His omniscience makes good use of both. Regarding territories, a body of states or other geographical area may be served by a union of several prophets who guard its supernatural realm, intercede for its protection and safety, and overturn demonic enactments and institutions. They do all of this to stay the tide of satanic onslaughts.

Needless to say, regarding the above, the broader a prophet's scope and the wider his range of influence (sphere of domain), the greater the problems he or she is likely to face. God's wisdom knows this means stronger spiritual endowments are called for if the minister is to do his job effectively. Faculties and capacities are intensified to equip the minister to perform at peak levels when needed. Frankly, the reason God makes these distinctions is because verifying prophets' work responsibilities demands varying levels of dispensation and anointing. Warfare, confrontation, and demonic contact all determine who gets what, at what time, and for what reasons. One need not be a genius to know that national or regional demons are more shrewd, cunning, and powerful than state or community spirits. Consequently, a prophet's dispensation invariably fits the need. God is not given to foolish excess and power for power's sake when dealing with mankind.

Furthermore, the oracular sides of the ministries too are not the same. The amount of verbalization needed to serve a church body is far less than that needed to serve a nation. Visions, communications, perceptions, and the like all differ vastly within the designated territories. Prophetic abilities and capacities are wisely dispensed by God accordingly. When they are upgraded, it is because a promotion is pending and the increased dispensation is needed for the new or higher office's demand.

PROPHETIC TRAINING

Long hours alone with God, surprise demands, and sudden shifts in interaction describe the prophet's training. They are what contribute to a prophet's being able to say emphatically what is or is not of God. True, many believers can do this *sporadically*, but the prophet does it consistently. The higher his order, the more consistently he can do it. Few are chosen to enter into this depth of relationship with the Lord, which is the only way breadth of ability comes about. Such a position never usurps, supersedes, or preempts (or conflicts with) Scripture. For God and His Word are one and the same. The prophet's Scripture training, to supplement his biblical knowledge, integrates the broad field of the life experiences he has had. Whether a prophet has witnessed directly or observed indirectly and what he or she has gone through in life are not discarded by the Lord. He uses them for the prophet's mission and to shore up his supernatural services. Early in the journey, the prophet learns God is not to be taken lightly. Beginner lessons concentrate on the prophet's respect for God and who He is to all the earth.

Respect for the Lord means innately comprehending the wisdom of honoring God's sovereignty. The true prophet will not explain away anything the Lord has done, but will faithfully uphold it. Training and experience have resolved for him that God is just and knows what He is doing—all the time. Regardless of the appearance of the impact of His actions in the earth, true prophets take God's side all the time, without explanation or vindication. They simply know they exist for God, and whatever God says and does is right. As you can see from this description, many Christians are disqualified from this office. They simply cannot help but find fault with God or detract from His Word to appease the world and pacify the saved, instead of glorifying the Savior.

Administrating a Respectable Prophetic Training Program

Perhaps by now you have discovered that your breadth of service as a prophetic minister is diverse. At times you act as an intermediary, and at other times you are an intercessor. If you are a veteran prophet, you are likely to be asked to troubleshoot, solve problems, resolve conflicts, and arbitrate disputes, because these too are inherent to the mantle. However, at all times you are God's spokesperson, and you exist to reveal His thoughts and intents as directed.

In this position, you will be delegated various watchman duties for which you should be effectively trained as a prophetic minister or as a qualified trainer. If you are a trainer, you should establish a prudent training period for all of the prophets you will train. If you are serious about the caliber of prophet you will turn out, you will no doubt immerse your trainees in an intensive preparation program that goes from beginner to advanced lectures, studies, practice, and evaluations. When it comes to administrating your training program, you will want to track each one's learning. You will also want some means of recording attendance and evaluating performance.

Beyond these, as any concerned trainer would, you will want to homogenize your prophetic trainees' knowledge and skills so that they are uniform and your end product is consistent with your founding and development goals and objectives. All graduates from your program should uniformly reflect you and your organization as their preparers. Also, a good prophetic readiness program maintains a record of service on every trainee to verify his or her conformity to the training and ability to meet future service demands. This is particularly useful with candidates for a prophetic company post. Much of this detail is handled by the existing company's prophetic superintendent.

If this is a new company, the one exhibiting the vision and heart for it should be evaluated for the post of superintendent. This person should be chosen if interest is upgraded to a passion for the company and its success in the organization. Once he or she has demonstrated the skill or potential to establish a company of prophets and what its management entails, formal steps should be taken to place the candidate for this position in office. This process should take time and require a proven and verified record of responsible and consistent service to the present or previous organization(s). In addition, several veteran prophets should be consulted and asked to confirm the candidate before entrusting this person with the task of building or leading a prophetic company. If the best candidate proves competent and confident enough to carry out this duty, then the position of prophetic superintendent should be installed, even if only temporarily.

At this point, attention should turn to developing a viable readiness program for the company of prophets to serve the institution. When this has been accomplished, the prophetic superintendent welcomes the institution's incoming prophetic trainees into its program. Upon accepting trainees into the program, a specialized training and service plan should be created for each trainee based on his or her qualifying information. Included in this process should be a way to monitor and record progress, performance, and quality of work. This record should also progressively track and assess the trainee's prophetic capacity in relation to the proposed prophetic company's service criteria. Standards, guidelines, procedures, and such are routinely explained by the prophetic company's superintendent at the new prophets' orientation meeting.

A WISE WORD TO PROPHETIC TRAINEES

If you are serious about your call to the prophetic, you will have already resolved that your readiness to serve in this ministry will subject you to some demanding requirements and unsettling lifestyle changes. A true prophet welcomes these as part of his grounding to fulfill God's purpose and destiny for his life. If your organization follows the Bible's historical pattern, it will have counseled you to arrange your life, responsibilities, and family to accommodate your prophetic education. This wisdom is germane to anyone who enters a serious career training or refinement program. Prophets with a definite call understand that God's summons on their lives is all-consuming. They know the duties of the position for which they are trained will absorb a good part of their existence, and their families should be prepared for it. For this reason and many others, it is prudent to require your trainers to undergo your readiness process themselves so that they can coach others through it as they prepare to serve the Lord.

To cultivate and keep a realistic view of the prophet's ministry, learn to relish the opportunity to go beyond your historical limits and experiences and outdo your personal best at every stage of your development. Allow yourself to grow and soar as the Lord's future prophet and resolve to become strong, capable, and indomitable in your faith and your skills.

Recognize that a quality readiness program should bring out the best in a future messenger of the Lord. The opposite is that a quality program will also weed out those who are not up to the demands of the call. This is normal and necessary to ensure that the Lord ends up with the best of the best at His disposal. No matter how bumpy your initiation to prophetic training may be, over time you will settle down and merge fully with its character, attitude, and disposition if it is a good program. When you complete it, you will be transformed sufficiently enough to join the ranks of the long line of competent and quality prophets who have gone before you.

Chapter Summary

1. Starting a prophetic company takes planning and structure. A clear vision for the end product must be cast first.

2. The Lord has many types of prophets whose assignments range from community to global.

3. Effective prophetic service does not spontaneously happen either naturally or supernaturally. It requires practical training.

4. A prophetic training program should be structured, relevant, measurable, and verifiable. These all involve administration. That is, scheduling, recording, evaluation, and monitoring pre-specified goals, objectives, and outcomes.

Prophetic Action Items

1. Develop an action-based prophetic training guide that integrates (or supports) theory with practice. Detail how you will measure, evaluate, record, and monitor your program based on what you want your end product (trainee) to become and be able to do.

Chapter 12

A HISTORY OF WHAT GOD EXPECTED FROM HIS PROPHETS

In this chapter you will learn historically what God expected from His prophets. It covers:

- Prophetic potency
- The prophet as God's thinker
- Authority
- Leadership authority figures
- Responding to authority figures and peers

PROPHETIC POTENCY

If knowledge is power, then understanding is its potency. Once you understand the purpose of a thing, you gain a greater respect for it and appreciate its values. Hopefully this will be true with your understanding of the ministry of the prophets. For example, there are a lot of presumptions associated with this office. If it is true that power corrupts (or can cause corruption), then here is one office that would most likely bring about such corruption. Innate to mission and consistent with its purpose and requirements are powers, authority, skill, and abilities that can prove intoxicating to the frail ego. Power is a heady tonic on its own; how much more tempting is it to be able to live, roam, and move (almost independently) about the supernatural?

In the prophetic, an unstable person can easily stumble and be induced to sin. For these reasons, the office of the prophet is certainly not the call of the foolish, naive, prideful, or self-centered. In their control, God's power is perverted and put to evil use.

The Bible's record of Israel's first king, Saul, is a good example of this. Saul was obviously prophetic, because he could not seem to ignore the institution. Perhaps his fascination with the prophets began with Samuel, a chief prophet who inducted him into office. The fact that God's prophet anointed him and made him king must have greatly impacted Saul. Add to it that the man was transformed into a king by the singing of a prophetic company and a season in their camp, and things become a little clearer. Saul's heart, however, was not purged, just upgraded to think and act like a king. When he sat among the prophets as they prophesied God's glory, Saul's prophecies were then cursed and he stripped himself naked. The prophetic anointing upon him brought out the worst—not the best—in Saul.

Over time, Saul went from bad to worse, especially after Samuel, the prophet who installed him as king, severed all relations with him. Being embittered by this action and the Lord's rejection of him as king, Saul's enchantment with the prophets turned to hatred, and he persecuted them. Here is a vivid example of the prophetic anointing and power creating a deadly mix. The fruit of such arrogance and presumptions is disastrous for the church and antagonistic to God. This unfortunate blight on an otherwise impressive institution is seen continually throughout Scripture in the false prophets who seduced Israel.

The most amazing thing about the prophet's office is that while it is one of the most abused and violently rejected, it tends to be among the most coveted because of the intrinsic power connected with it. While all the offices and every Spirit-filled believer receive empowerment and enablement from God's Spirit of grace within, the prophet goes way beyond what is corporately distributed to that which is corporeally infused. There is just no better way to explain it than this.

Exceeding the "collective dispensation" of grace for salvation, the people who fill this office receive by the Holy Spirit of God a capacitating imbuement. They are physically restructured within to accommodate the steady stream of God's omnipotence and strength, without which they would react in much the same way that Daniel, Ezekiel, and the other prophets did. When confronted with the majestic holiness and power of God critical to quality performance in ministry, they continually crumbled under His glory.

To prevent their collapsing under the Lord's power, prophets are emotionally, psychologically, and mentally upgraded. God enhances their physical and psychological selves to better apply wisdom and keen understanding to their exercise of Christ's resurrection power. The prophet is not only enlightened of mind, fortified in character, and enriched with supernatural knowledge and wisdom, but he or she literally "oozes" the peculiar texture of the Lord's strength. Here is the reason why prophets can endure hardships that would crush the normal soul and bounce back a thousand times over. A more than rugged constitution, though not necessarily impenetrable, makes these messengers resilient beyond typical human measures and means. The spirits of the prophets within cause them to heal faster, mend quicker, and—under the sentence of the "thorn"—function superbly under stress and duress. Why? Because of the great power that is at work in their souls. It is a power that does not come upon prophets suddenly, and it is not irresponsibly conferred by the Lord. No, a prophet's power and stamina come from the continuous breaking, shaping, remaking, and dynamic power of the Holy Spirit that prepared the vessel for the Master's use. The process is so strenuous and the pruning so severe that many Christians cannot bear up under it.

PROPHETIC READINESS

Prophetic readiness involves a rigorous series of drills, object lessons, and humiliating experiences that challenge, chasten, train, and even scold all newcomers to the office. Regularly this agent of the Godhead is morally crushed to destroy the ego that would rise up to compete or contend with its Maker. Suffering defeats more than victories in the beginning, this servant is God's molded marvel; one of the undefined features that accounts for His submitted prophets' success. All that God puts His prophets through to confirm their faithfulness, allegiance, and endurance, normal Christians never imagine, let alone experience, in their daily human existence. The specially arranged lessons, practices, and correction, along with extensive studies, are what make prophets the unusual people they eventually become.

The Lord's prophetic readiness program puts trainees in touch with the real world they will serve. For this reason, the curriculum consists of a good amount of early rejection, stubborn perseverance, brutal trials, and harsh pressures to toughen the ministers enough to survive and thrive under the strenuous assignments and persecution that come with the position. On top of everything else, prophet trainees encounter constant exposure to the spirit realm, which eventually ends up severing them from this world forever. As time moves on and God moves in closer every year, the prophet in truth becomes a citizen of heaven. These and similar activities all have a huge part in the caliber of minister most prophets turn out to be.

Think about some of the recorded incidents that took place in the lives of our biblical models: Isaiah, caught up to heaven to literally see with his own eyes the glory of the God of Israel; Ezekiel, also coming face-to-face with the Lord upon His throne. Then there are Elijah and Elisha, whose handling of God's power boggles the mind when one thinks of the way the Lord listened to and granted their abnormal prayer requests. And let us not forget Daniel's legendary visions. As an ongoing part of their profession, these human wonders moved and roamed about the supernatural almost at will. However, the privileged calling did not come without a price—a very high price. These examples were included to show that the prophet's anointing is not merely a spiritual, intangible ordeal. There are physical experiences that go with it to evidence the supernatural at work within. Often this evidence goes way past the incidental to produce totally transformative effects in those the Lord entrusts enough to endow so extensively.

Another significant example of God's prophetic upgrade is David's anointing of power to become the king of Israel. It is widely accepted that although David was a king, he was also a prophet and thus underwent the same preparations as his prophetic predecessors. So, how is it that his anointing for royalty translated into his ability to kill lions and bears before he even fought his first war? The answer is his prophetic upgrade and enhancements. Look at Samson. His anointing also enabled him physically to exhibit superhuman strength. Again and again we see physical strength and might accompanying the anointing to move and rule in the Spirit. Over and over the spiritual, the supernatural, and the natural are interlinked as a network of divine bestowals.

New Testament anointing for this office is no less spiritual or powerful. Due to the resident Holy Spirit within, what the Lord does with His prophets appears to emphasize less of the physical and more of the supernatural. However, Peter's miraculous shadow says otherwise, as does Philip's literal translation from place to place to preach the gospel. His physical translations recall Elijah, who was known to disappear at will, and Ezekiel, who preached in Jerusalem while exiled in Babylon. Besides these, there is Paul, who understood his unusual capabilities as the power of the risen Christ at work in human vessels. (See 2 Corinthians 4:7.) When it comes to the Lord's amazing power at work within His ministers and His strength at their disposal, the glory was always meant to go to the Lord. Instead of just being able to perform Herculean feats with their arms and hands, the New Testament offices now tap into the truth behind all those physical displays of the Old Testament: the word of the living God. The New Testament minister simply speaks and God's Spirit does the work by manifesting or physicalizing any word spoken by him, as Jesus said in John 14:10.

THE PROPHET AS GOD'S THINKER

By now it should be evident to you that the prophetic office requires thinkers. God has His greatest successes with people who think. That is, people who use their heads in harmony with their emotions, their will, and their individuality in unison with His Holy Spirit. Otherwise, apart from being a divinely inspired thinker, the prophet's mouth is incompetent and unreliable.

A thinker may be born with the capacity and faculty for intelligent, sensitive, and reasonable thought; however, the ability to put these qualities to productive use to God's advantage takes learning. Whether Christians like it or not, instances of supernatural acquisition of utilitarian knowledge are rare. Even in the instances where they seemed to occur, it was the multiplication of some sort of core knowledge that was built upon.

A thinker, for the record, is also one with vision, imagination, and creativity. A thinker has analytical skills and the capacity for sound judgment in making decisions. Thinkers are people with sagacity who weigh matters carefully and are governed and guided by the wisdom of careful deliberation. Thinkers must be strong-willed, self-restrained deliberators who meditate and contemplate to the fullest extent the repercussions, impacts, and outcomes of their and others' actions. They must, if they are prophets, have a sense of the practical plans associated with their words and deeds. Thinkers tend to be purposeful people, motivated by wisdom and endowed with great mental focus. God's thinkers are high conceptualizers gifted with innovative ideas and capable of intense mental activity. For thinkers, concentration is not usually a problem; they can often will themselves to concentrate on what they deem important and vital. Moving chiefly by design, thinkers have excellent deductive powers and well-disciplined reasoning faculties. Their ability is to withdraw from a matter—to stand away from it for the time it takes to purview it from all sides. In the meantime they exercise great restraint in delaying responses and reactions until meticulously and methodically weighing and evaluating all aspects of the matter under consideration.

The church of Jesus Christ all too often diminishes the Lord's glory in the minds of others because believers refuse to think. Many of them do not even know how to think and are unfortunately "emotion-bound." God, however, is a thinker. He thinks more quickly and astutely than we do, but He is unquestionably a deliberate, methodical, and contemplative thinker. To become a credible prophet, you must resolve to become a thinker, too.

THE PROPHET'S OFFICE IS LEADERSHIP

Leadership is a key component of the prophet's service. The office by nature is that of leading and guiding in addition to prediction and revelation. This being the case, the prophet's training must include some teaching on the subject of leadership, especially the leadership of God's people—taking them from the world to God, from sin and Satan to righteousness and Christ. These are all seemingly incidental duties, often receiving low priority on the Christian workman's agenda. In reality, though, they are not trivial.

People are followers by design, a trait deposited by God at creation to direct their hearts toward Him and effectively steer their lives to eternal salvation. This aspect of human nature explains why God dubbed His people *lambs* and *sheep*. The terms convey His intimate knowledge of all mankind—that they are driven to be led. This is so, whether they follow God and His righteousness or not. The inclination to follow someone in a flock or pack-like manner is an established fact in human history. We see this in the masses' compulsion to be led away with fads, fashion, and new philosophies. Anyone with an inkling of authority can attract a following within his or her field or range or influence due to this tendency. The world's opposition to God and His righteousness necessitates His appointment and training of His own leaders. He does so to identify and employ those most likely to obey Him because they desire His rule. God's chosen will acquiesce without fail to His reign over those they lead.

AUTHORITY

As we have already established that a prophet is a leader, the fact that he must exercise authority is a given. Authority frightens many people, however, mostly because of its function, purpose, and roots. Simply speaking, authority is the lawful right to enforce obedience, to give orders, and to direct the behavior or conduct of others over whom one has charge. Loosely stated, authority is synonymous with power. However, it is more accurate to say that authority is established by power, because power can exist and be exercised apart from lawful authority; it is "applied force" or the threat of it. Only in an environment where the conference of power exists can authority be firmly established. Where there is no power, there can be no authority. Without power, authority has no basis to exist, having no enforcement outlet to maintain and effect its ends.

Although authority is frequently abused, it is nevertheless a necessary factor in leadership. Otherwise there is no mechanism of influence or control to ensure those who start out with a mission or charge will put forth genuine and quality effort to bring the vision to pass on a consistent basis. Something has to motivate people to do their part, to shoulder their load, and to follow the plan when they would just as soon not, or would rather do it their way. Furthermore, authority and power are effective in dealing with those who would oppose or endanger a movement or deter other workers from their labors. Incidents of anarchy, rebellion, and resistance are redressed through the use of authority. (See Proverbs 29:19 and 20:30.)

Consider, in viewing the essential place of authority, the accounts of Ezra and Nehemiah, who had both received charges from the Lord God of Israel to repair the temple and rebuild the wall of Jerusalem. In order for them to do so, being captives to another nation, they needed the authority to initiate the work, and even to enlist the help of other people. They derived their authority from the decree of Cyrus the king, who had the power to allow or disallow their actions. His authority included enforcement power so they could complete their task in the face of opposition, hostility, or revolt. This authority to legitimize, enforce, and protect the God of Israel's restoration plan was actually the reason Cyrus was born and attained power in the first place, as said by the prophet Isaiah. The authority Cyrus had was derived from God Almighty. (See 2 Chronicles 36:22–23, Ezra 1:2–8, and Isaiah 44:18–45:4.) By his divinely appointed position, this king authorized the Jews to begin the work God had commanded Cyrus to see to before he was conceived. If the king were not in agreement, the very attempt by the Jews to rebuild God's house could have gotten them killed. In this case, it was the other way around. Cyrus' decree meant that anyone who opposed the work could be killed.

Authority is critical because few people, when in groups, can agree or remain in harmony for extended periods of time. Personal pursuits, preferences, and perspectives inevitably surface to divide and confuse them. Fear of being bossed around, taken advantage of, or abused makes them begin to doubt the validity of their associations and leads them to contend with the leaders.

It is a known fact that groups of people without a leader cannot come into one mind on issues and maintain that focused agreement for any length of time. Someone will have to keep his eyes pointed toward the goal, set the priorities for success, and keep victory ever before the group. If not, when tedium, longevity, setbacks, and obstacles begin to take their toll, group members will challenge the work and attempt to escape using any means they can. The possibility of this occurring increases greatly when groups have to value and prioritize more than one issue at once, or if they are to decide the most effective way of tackling a mass endeavor. All these reasons are likely to stress a group. The larger its number, the greater the prospect of stressing a group's bond of cohesiveness, decreasing the likelihood it will complete the job at hand without leadership.

Once the suitable person has been identified and appointed as the leader, a large part of the distracting factors previously hindering the work disappear. The leader's presence and skill see to it. However, such a person must be invested with the authority to do what it takes to benefit those who trust him or her to enforce the will of the majority on the few opponents. Trust, consequently, is a large part of leadership. The people must perceive an atmosphere of safety, integrity, fairness, and ethics to relax their guards and establish unity. A sense of safety and well-being must foster within all followers the belief that justice, equity, and balance will prevail with those to whom they entrust their leadership. Because of this, any delegation of authority has to convey these to those who follow, or else the entire structure is vulnerable.

Authority, as we have said, implies power that can negatively affect a group's support of its leaders. Still, an element of force is needed to ensure compliance, conformance, and performance demanded by the authority. Without it, there can be no motive for obedience, and as a result, little or no success. The vision is not realized because the goal is not achieved.

When strong leadership is absent or undefined, only the fruit of failure, disillusionment, and disappointment are experienced. Followers become bitter and cynical and their leaders confused and insecure. Everyone walks away from such ventures defeated and jaded when there is a breakdown of authority, which is native to leadership. Only in an environment where leaders are clearly established and respected can efficient means of completing projects occur. It is the leaders who discover and release that efficiency.

Christian leaders need to understand that every delegation of God is accompanied by a corresponding degree of power, supernatural more than natural. As the manifestation of the Son of God showed us, the problems of earth have spiritual origins and their roots can only be handled on the supernatural plane. That begins with sound, responsible, prophetic authority!

LEADERSHIP AUTHORITY FIGURES

Traditionally, more than a few aspirants and newcomers to leadership struggle with authority figures. They dislike being told what to do unless they agree with it and feel their positions are as vital to their organization's mission and goal as their superiors', whether or not they know the mission and goal. To avoid yielding to their authority figures, followers invent all sorts of excuses, complaints, and criticisms that run the gamut of unjustified reasons for disliking or distrusting a superior. In the end, the problem often turns out to be just plain old rebellion.

On the other hand, new leaders frequently tend to isolate themselves and their work in a vacuum, choosing to ignore or disdain what the other members of their staff do or did. Showing unmistakable apathy in what they do affects their followers. Rudeness, broken promises, late submissions, and neglected details often frustrate a new leader's good intentions and dull what started out as a wonderful achievement. These behaviors on the part of a new leader are rooted in an attitude that sees leadership as wholly prestigious, not as necessarily accountable or responsible. Leadership positions for them are for celebrity status and are not offices of trust or duty.

The other side of the coin is the leader who cannot get along with his or her peers. Many times, new leaders feel that pleasing the boss or the head of the organization is enough. Meanwhile, when it comes to those who work alongside them on their level as peers, they tend to mete out respect or disrespect based on their like or dislike for one peer over another. Or, they may demonstrate their appreciation of a particular peer's position in relation to their own on the grounds of merit. Neither of these makes a harmonious or productive work environment, not to mention the seething resentment and retaliation they can breed in offended workers.

When left unchecked, such an atmosphere can foster vengeful sabotage as wounded peers strike back at one another through their jobs. Productivity and profitability are the first to take the hits as a tit-for-tat environment renders the workplace and its workers ineffective. Pettiness and pranks can abound as the spirit of healthy competition takes an ominous turn. Internal feuds can severely damage an organization's standing with its constituency and risk the loss of valuable workers and leaders. Every one of these behaviors is detrimental to any organization's success. If prophets are oblivious to these behaviors, the results are tragic. Prophets are leaders and should be schooled and experienced in organizational dynamics and workplace harmony.

Arrogant attitudes and isolationist or divisive tactics adversely affect all workers' performance and cause strife and contention, which slow progress and cost business. Prophetic leaders should be aware of the signs of these potential detriments in those they oversee and discover quickly how to remedy them. Should they appear in you, you have a greater obligation to alleviate them from your leadership attitudes and motives. Make no mistake about it: prophetic rivalry is more deadly to an organization than any other problem because of the dual spheres it affects. The prophet's most uncelebrated role is to undo something with the word of the Lord that already exists. *"Therefore have I hewed them by the prophets; I have slain them by the words of my mouth: and thy judgments are as the light that goeth forth"* (Hosea 6:5). *"I have also spoken by the prophets, and I have multiplied visions, and used similitudes, by the ministry of the prophets"* (Hosea 12:10). *"And by a prophet the Lord brought Israel out of Egypt, and by a prophet was he preserved"* (Hosea 12:13).

What do all these passages add to our discussion? They show the power of prophets' words and will. Prophets' words kill, judge, reveal, attack, or reward. These officers cut and heal, destroy and build with their mouths. They see visions and discern and interpret similitudes as well as rescue, deliver, lead, and preserve. Collectively, prophetic faculties wield effectual power in the spirit. That is a tremendous amount of power, and to have the prophets of any organization collaborate or collude to mount an assault on it has deadly consequences. The prophets are to be the solution that overturns such misconduct and restores the harmonious balance in the institutions that they serve. They are not to be their adversaries. Prophets are to work with their authority figures, covering them with prayer and intercessions. They are to cooperate with leadership and not so pity the people that they unwittingly overthrow it. Prophets over an organization should include in their services classes that help leaders get their message across to the staff and motivate the staff to support and trust their leaders. The prophet should under no circumstances foster or tolerate competition between himself and the leaders he or she exists to protect.

RESPONDING TO AUTHORITY FIGURES AND PEERS

The following is wisdom to help prophets get along with their authority figures and peers. New leaders must accept that a chain of command, whether it is documented or not, does exist in all organizations. The church is no different. It does not matter how much religious people like to pretend otherwise; every organization has its hierarchy of positions and ranking leaders who fill them. New ministers should not expect to start at the top of their organizations unless that is what they were engaged to do. For that to happen, it is generally accepted that previous experience, education, and success qualify people for their levels of position. Therefore, prophets need those who ascended ahead of them to help them escalate at the right time to higher positions.

Often the person to help promote a younger prophet is the immediate supervisor, professional coach, or mentor. For this reason and many others, he or she should be respected. Supervisors know the history of the world you are entering and have a proven track record with those with whom you will work. They understand the lines of authority and the sentiments of the leadership circle you are joining. Your new position's supervisors, coaches, and mentors can recall their sting, discern their motives, and detect their nonverbal signals. They can help you skirt trouble, avert crises, and avoid offending any of those above you so that they will not uniformly shut you out. This is particularly helpful with the key influencers, and you should take time to learn who these people are and what they do. As you learn about them, take time to figure out what makes them so influential, since not all of them are in leadership positions. Acclimating to your new position should include being on the lookout for what the group likes, responds to, or attacks. Trust your trainers to know this, as they took the time to become well-versed in the beliefs, ideologies, preferences, and strategies that identify your organization before you arrived.

Believe your trainers are capable people whose wisdom should be sought and respected. Acknowledge their achievements and value their skills. Avoid beginning your season with these people by forcing your stories and experiences upon them. Better yet, connect with them to learn and grow. Pay attention when they start telling you the rules of the game.

Your stories and testimonies can come later. In the beginning, follow James' advice, and be swift to hear and slow to speak.

The Bible says in Ecclesiastes 8:4 that where the word of a king is, there is power. This is a profound remark. People in authority have power. All people in authority have some power and you cannot see it on them as you would a suit of clothing. The word of a king holds power; what a simple-sounding statement. Yet it is replete with implications. Leaders who have been in their positions for some time know people. They have friends, competitors, allies, and friendly enemies that could be of use to you later. See beyond your impatience or disrespect and esteem them because you do not know the extent of their reach, even if it is to just one significant person. The world is smaller than you think and your world with this person may be smaller yet.

Be an asset to your leaders. Make yourself valuable to those you work for, because this is the best way to properly relate to authority. As a prophet, you have much negative history to overturn, so plan to show the positive side of the mantle. That does not mean you should distort your prophecies in the process. However, refuse to spend time fuming in secret about what you dislike about your leaders or nursing some real (or imagined) hurts. When you allow this, you risk having them surface when you least expect. Negativity will leak out as unpleasant sentiments at the most inopportune times with disastrous consequences. It is wise to weigh your feelings and confirm that they are accurate before jumping to conclusions about your leaders' remarks. Take the time to clarify what you think you heard, and question why it offended you. Be honest about why you became offended. Ask your leaders frankly (if possible) if you heard them correctly, and if so, what they meant or intended by what you heard. Wait to hear what they say and listen. Make sure when you talk with your leaders that you open the conversation by calmly presenting your case, and always confirm that you heard or interpreted their remarks accurately throughout the discussion. Above all, be obedient, endeavor to fulfill your duties, and to do so with excellence.

Whenever your leaders correct you, be honest about whether or not correction is deserved. If the correction is warranted, admit it, fix the problem, and resume the relationship. It if was not, schedule a time to discuss the matter calmly to learn what is considered improvement and the best steps to achieve it. This is sage counsel that coheres with what the Bible tells us to do. It admonishes us to keep our heart with all diligence because out of it come the issues of life (Proverbs 4:23). As a prophet, keep your heart clear when dealing with your supervisors and managers. No matter how right you may feel you are, take time to ponder the cost to you of forcing certain issues with them. Will it be worth it in the end? Will your actions make your life better or worse in the end? Who has the most to lose? The biggest, most significant question of all is, why are you so affected by a certain situation in the first place? What are your real motivations for making a big deal out of something and what do you want to prove or accomplish by it? In short, what are you defending? Be curious about what causes you to jeopardize your position, disrupt relationships, and discredit your reputation on a particular issue. These may all be answered by doing a little probing of your own heart.

The entire outcome of your leadership service is seated in your heart. How you really feel about people, authority, work in general, and your organization's structure will all show up in your emotions, and a leadership promotion will definitely bring it to the surface. Your emotions are so important that more than intelligence is needed to balance your sentiments. Other emotional restraints are required to help you transition from a voluntary servant to an official prophet in the Lord's kingdom. You must mature in your outlooks, attitudes, and reactions to serve Him as a recognized kingdom functionary. None of this can truly happen until the Lord replaces your present heart with that of a leader—a prophetic leader in particular. Afterward, you will be enabled to function competently in your new sphere of service.

CHAPTER SUMMARY

1. Prophetic potency and power can unsettle a weak soul.

2. Saul exemplified what happens when pure prophetics meet a corrupt soul.

3. Because God is a thinker, prophets too must be thinkers.

4. Leadership is a key component of prophetic service.

5. Prophetic leadership presupposes prophetic authority.

6. Respect for any offices includes professional respect for those that occupy it. One cannot claim respect and obedience to an office and contemptuously treat those who fill it.

PROPHETIC ACTION ITEMS

1. Come up with a twenty-point practical behavior and conduct code for prophetic service. Show how it is to be applied form the top down, the bottom up, and peer to peer.

Chapter 13

DIVISIONS OF PROPHETIC AUTHORITY

This chapter expounds on divisions of prophetic authority. It covers:

- Prophetic groups
- Prophetic classes
- Prophetic realms

PROPHETIC GROUPS

The prophet's mantle is manifested in two groups: executive (or governmental) and administrative (supportive). Think of it this way. While all levels of government have leadership authority, their authority is not equal. Local official authority is not the same as state authority, and state authority is subordinate to the federal authority. Also, anyone with global reach would have the greatest authority of all.

The office will always have a group of chief prophets and a group of subordinate prophets. Chief prophets are distinguished by their assigned territory, class, and realm.

They are designated chiefs because of the responsibility they have for overseeing and securing the Lord's prophetic force.

While both groups appear equal in their office among the fivefold officers, the chief prophet has a wider territory and therefore a wider range of authority. In addition, chief prophets have high, well-groomed organization, leadership, and governmental skills with which to empower and cover the prophets in their care. Chief prophets also possess excellent teaching skills, which are used to train and refine novice and subordinate prophets for God's service. Furthermore, chief prophets' target ministry groups are high-ranking and made up of people of great stature, power, and authority. It is obvious from this brief duty description that those appointed to this level of service are stringently screened and rigorously trained. The chief prophet should be promoted after years of rigorous training and strenuous tests. Loyalty demands, obedience exercises, and resistance to intense opposition qualify a prophet for this level of public service. Few people will pay the price to stand in it.

Subordinate prophets fit three categories: new or novice, trainer or moderately equipped, class- or realm-assigned. Of the three, the first two are candidates for promotion. The last one is class- or realm-assigned because it is a God-ordained subordinate position. Other types of leadership prophets come under the heading of apprentice prophets. Their duties, though significant, revolve around serving a senior prophet to gain the experience and confidence needed to execute the ministry. Subordinate prophets have less authority within their assigned area. However, they are vital to the organization and are no less valued by God than the chief prophets they serve.

Elijah and Elisha are examples of the chief/subordinate relationship. Moses and Joshua are another. Samuel with his school of prophets, as well as Elisha after Elijah's departure, are two more. Peter, James, and John over the remaining twelve apostles and Paul are additional examples. While some prophets are loners, isolated for special, divine dispatches for which they were created and prepared, most prophets have an ordained chief within their territory whom they are assigned to serve. Scripture and history show that more prophets served in companies than alone. This current independence and alienation from one another, aside from being contrary to Scripture, is detrimental to God's overall prophetic mission. If there is no established school or study group for a subordinate prophet to serve under a chief prophet, then he or she should seek other credible means of getting trained and becoming accountable. As Elisha poured water on the hands of Elijah (meaning that he served him) and Gehazi served as assistant to Elisha, in like manner, contemporary prophets need to put in their time under their designated chiefs. The time can be as long as twenty years or as brief as three months. The decision, however, is God's, not man's. Three years, though, appears in Scripture to be the reasonable minimum amount of time a subordinate should expect to serve. However, it seems that prophets are not thoroughly equipped until they serve ten years. Fifteen to twenty years appears to be the norm.

PROPHETIC CLASSES IDENTIFIED

The eight prophetic classes operate within the ten prophetic realms listed below. They show the human field of duty assignments the prophet is likely to be placed in.

- Business
- Health
- Societal
- Special Groups
- Ecclesiastical (church and ministers)
- Domestic (family)
- Ministerial (clergy)
- Financial
- Political
- Industry

The following eight fields are the official areas of a prophet's ministry to God and territory of service. From them, you will see how the boundaries, though geographic, will overlap in execution.

The prophet's work requires teamwork, and Christ's community of the ministers for this reason should be diligent about assisting and supporting one another's endeavors. Since prophets are very symbiotic, they need each other and actually thrive on their company members' mantles. That is another reason why their classes of service should be clearly defined.

The prophetic classes themselves designate the area of expertise, field of knowledge, and range of faculties a prophet has been equipped and groomed with for his or her service. These decide the territorial boundaries, prophetic groups, and prophetic assignments associated with a particular world of humanity. The elements of each class apply to the stationary and itinerant prophet. Furthermore, these eight classes are influenced by the prophet's realm of service as well as his or her traits and talents. They refer to the realm of human life to which the prophet is most commonly assigned by God. The only way to get the most out of each group of prophets is to know where their highest concentration of activity lies.

Prophets, like any other professional guild, are most effective in areas and situations where their gifts and equipment are best suited. Proper placement increases the prophet's greatest breakthrough power on a consistent basis. People ministered to by properly placed prophets—those standing in their designated place within the office—are likely to experience more deliverances, broader prophecies, greater blessings, and extensive prayer breakthroughs more quickly because the prophet is ministering within his or her capabilities. This is mainly because the prophet is wholly unified in ministry and better aligned with the Holy Spirit's attestations. When the prophet's anointing is compatible with his or her realm, class, group, and assignments, the results are startling. The Spirit's cooperation with the messenger is astounding and compatibility with his or her mantle's realm enables the prophet to enjoy success and his or her following continually reaps the bountiful harvest of the Lord as a result.

PROPHETIC CLASSES EXPLAINED

JUDICIAL

A Judicial Prophet is one whose focus and perception center on matters of lawfulness, propriety, protocol, ethics, and morality. Righteousness and integrity are this prophet's summons to the people of God. Wisdom in problem-solving, decision-making, human conduct, and behavior motives is strong in these prophets. They are mainly oracular. Their faculties will include a significant measure of the native abilities of judicial aptitude. They tend to be able negotiators, accomplished arbitrators, and sage counselors. Their judgments tend to be sound and their discernment keen.

MILITARISTIC

Militaristic Prophets emphasize the raging, ongoing battles with the forces of darkness. They have a keen insight into the strategies and tactics of Satan and innately understand how to deal with them. These ministers have a fierce countenance and a low tolerance for compromise and mingling with sin. These are the prophets of supernatural breakthrough, and they are mainly of the power class. These prophets are likely to have a significant measure of native abilities, including sensitivity to spiritual things, apprehension of the role and place of prophecy, and a great sense of practical application.

ECONOMIC

Economic Prophets are concerned with the financial condition of the people of God. Their emphasis is on thrift, spending, prudent buying, and wise economic consumption. Their itinerary includes circuits of congregations and ministry organizations, where they communicate these subjects and supernaturally loose the wealth of the churches and the financial stability of their congregants. They are often oracular. These prophets will most likely exhibit the native abilities of unusual judicial aptitude, heightened spiritual discernment, and outstanding leadership ability. They tend to make good treasurers, able fund-raisers, and sound businesspeople.

GOVERNMENTAL

Governmental Prophets are concerned with the righteousness of those in their territory as it pertains to God's holiness. They are committed to Christ's standard of living as expressed during His earthly pilgrimage. The Word of God is unusually clear to these prophets as a stand-alone judge. Its applications are not difficult for them. Such prophets are discerning and discriminating, and they have policy-making and regulatory skills. All of these are useful to God in His organization, restoration, or restructuring of His church. Also, these prophets prove to be wise counselors to secular administrations that are interested in the Almighty's integrity and ethics in their government. Their sagacity can be invaluable in forecasting outcomes of pending legislation. These prophets are most likely to possess the native abilities of influential governmental ability, peculiar interpretive skill, impressive elocution/oration, and unusual judicial aptitude.

CONFRONTATIONAL

Confrontational Prophets are those who always seem to be on the attack. With axe-like words, they cut down sinfulness, apostasy, and indulgence in the body. There is a harsh edge to their messages, and because of this, they are shunned more often than any other prophet. These people are usually of a stern countenance, and their words carry strong rebuke and chastening weight. Warning of impending judgment and demanding repentance from sin are their dominant ministry calls. They are generally oracular prophets with power. The native abilities of heightened spiritual discernment, capacity for revelation discovery, and sensitivity to spiritual things are likely to attend to this mantle.

EXECUTIVE

Executive Prophets are those whose business and administrative acumen make them competent managers of God's temporal matters. They are able to advise the body on its business, management, industrial, and entrepreneurial ventures. This mantle is also equipped to warn entrepreneurs of the dangers of indiscretion, abuse, excesses, poor supervision, and weak leadership. In addition, they are sagacious and predictive enough to prophesy trends and recognize if and when an organization or individual is to take advantage of them. These prophets also have strong leadership aptitude and make able teachers of their disciples. The native abilities associated with this class of prophet include comprehension of prophetic matters, apprehension of role and place of prophecy, capacity for revelation discovery, and peculiar interpretive skill.

POWER

Power Prophets are messengers whose ministry is replete with the supernatural signs and wonders of God. They are literally *dunamis* vessels ordained to exercise and exert discretionary spiritual power in many situations. Their place is critical in the body of Christ because extraordinary miracles are a must where they are assigned. This prophetic class's main objective is to manifest the supremacy of the risen Christ's powers. Outstanding leadership ability, heightened spiritual discernment, and great sense of practical application are some of this mantle's native abilities.

ORACULAR

As said elsewhere in the text, Oracular Prophets are those whose ministry is more verbal and communicative than powerful. These prophets are more likely to be researchers, lecturers, teachers, and writers. Their ministries generally have strong teaching and motivational components attached to the mantle. They are often founders of educational institutions and schools of the prophets. The native abilities that are most likely seen in this class of prophets include potential for inspired utterance, strong literary skill, peculiar interpretive skill, and extraordinary wisdom and insight.

The explanations given here are presented as a guide. They do, however, answer a host of questions surrounding the wide range of capabilities and applications we see today in Christian ministry. The characteristic features of the mantle apply no less in the classes. Qualities and anointing like predictive insight, interpretive skill, teaching, preaching, and revelation are still critical elements of the staff and mantle of prophetic officers. In addition, the prayer work, intercessory responsibilities, and watchmen's correctional or exhortative duties are not reduced by class assignment. It should be pointed out that God can cross His prophetic classes, intermixing His messengers' assignments to enable prophets to handle greater loads. Higher prophetic assignments call for this, and thus such prophets display a variety of aptitudes, knowledge, and skills.

These discussions answer the question of the messages one prophet receives over another. Topic concentrations from God center on information related to their assignments.

ABOUT PROPHETIC REALMS

In respect to prophetic realms, the following explanations can help you understand how they fit into God's prophetic scheme. The word *realm* refers to:

1. A royal domain
2. A domain of knowledge
3. A regional sphere of domination
4. A system of government
5. A sovereign's territory of rule

The prophetic realms are:

1. Domestic
2. Ministerial
3. Financial
4. Political
5. Industrial
6. Business
7. Health
8. Societal
9. Special group
10. Ecclesiastical

The **Domestic Realm** is where prophets deal extensively with family matters. These prophets are articulate and sensitive to marital breakdowns and insightful in spouse selection and treatment of family issues. They are especially empowered to facilitate conception and child-rearing and are able to overturn family life deterioration. Such prophets have a strong appreciation for the place of the family in successful earthly life. Thus, they are called to minister to the organizations that specialize in watching over, praying for, and reaching out to the families of the earth. Their ministries bring with them the word and power of God.

The *Ministerial Realm* speaks of a prophetic ministry to clergy. These prophets are sent to ministers, especially pastors, and work well alongside ecclesiastical prophets. They are empowered to serve them and guide their endeavors to shepherd and oversee God's people. Such prophets know the importance of balanced teachings and firm leadership to the Lord and His body. They understand flock sanctification, enlightenment, and maturity, and are sensitive to the deceptions and seductions of the world that can veer a shepherd and his church off God's ordained course. Prophets of this realm quickly recognize sin and its pitfalls and respond promptly with God's ordained plan, strategy, and ideals. Prophets assigned to the ministerial realm are firmly committed to the Lord's worship and holiness. Prophets of this realm are typically assigned a circuit of churches for which they pray and intercede, nurture, and feed. That is when they are not assigned to one congregation or its church prophet. These prophets provide the spiritual undergirding that upholds ministers and ministries. With them comes the supernatural strength that fortifies the labors of a shepherd and guards his or her open links with God.

The *Financial Realm* is where prophets with expertise and experience in monetary matters are placed. They teach the body about God's views on money, wealth, financial stability, and overall prosperity. Such prophets have an anointing to achieve financial breakthroughs, teach money management and its related subjects, and cause spiritual and material abundance, although the former manifests the latter.

The *Political Realm* is where prophets are set as watchmen to guard and patrol the political front of a society. They are astutely aware of shifting tides of public sentiment, cultural trends, and demonic strategy. Their ears are open to hear the sugarcoated plans of deception that eventually dupe a society into compromising or dropping its moral and ethical standards. These prophets are able to hear from the Lord regarding who is entering and exiting a community or region's political offices. Alert and informed, this class of prophet garners political favor, is effective at lobbying and other political actions, and easily gathers the prayer support, political clout, and believer action needed to sway pending matters God's way. They quickly recognize infiltrations and proposed actions that could adversely affect the church and God's will. This realm should be adequately staffed in order to avoid weakening a nation whose political views expose it to God's judgment. The teaching, preaching, and persuasive oratory skills of this prophetic class are extensive as their normally charismatic demeanor aids their potential to communicate God on the political front in a nonreligious or similarly inoffensive manner.

The **Industrial Realm** is the realm where prophets with strong ties and influence in the labor force are appointed. They are usually well versed in industrial operations and production. These prophets not only reach souls in this realm but are able to aid the body of Christ in establishing and maintaining such companies under God's auspices. Their mantle is equipped to help believers in their realm start companies where godliness, integrity, and ethics are valued and maintained. Their skill and expertise will include organization, structure, productivity, and agriculture, along with the other activities associated with successful industrial ventures that glorify the Lord Jesus Christ. Prophets in this realm can be dispatched to any industry and tend to serve well as organizational prophets. The above areas are given as examples.

In the **Business Realm**, the prophet's main audience is businesspeople who need or belong to the Lord and who are instrumental to His divine purposes. Business skill, as with all the other classes, is a tool for this mantle. It is a means by which the Lord can be preached and presented in a light that entrepreneurs and executives can understand. Such prophets can be useful in management and administration and provide vital technical and executive know-how to Christ's church and the world. Those who are in a consulting capacity are examples of this group. The wisdom of the Lord in this mantle is applied to the operation of the business to aid God's children in their appointed means of providing for their temporal needs. Also, business trends and movements, and shifts and upsets, along with impending or possible downfalls, are readily apparent to this class of prophet. Their foresight, acumen, and sagacity allow these messengers to warn endangered or detrimental enterprises. Such prophets detect problem areas and suggest solutions to them from what they receive from God to convey. A powerful, predictive element foresees and foretells of probable difficulties early on, in hope of averting any catastrophes.

The **Health Realm** is where prophets have peculiar insight into the needs and functions of the human body. They have an understanding of the harmful agents that can affect them. Piercing prophetic sight reveals developing issues in the body often before they surface. Diet programs, preventive medicine, and health maintenance procedures are uniquely clear to this prophetic class. Their anointing also gives them revelation into certain illnesses and their causes. Revelations, of course, come with wisdom to instruct the sufferer on how to treat the problem. This is not medical care or therapy, although health professionals can surely be among this prophetic class. It is

God's omniscience applied to the area of health in an effort to stay the onset of sickness and disease, because many illnesses have spiritual roots that can be treated by the inclusion of spiritual insight and prophetic astuteness. This ability works powerfully with all types of health care providers. When the prophet is not in the medical field, then it is through prayer and intercession that these work. However, as our Savior showed us, people who are healed should still show themselves to a physician.

The *Societal Realm* is where the prophet has a strong leaning toward the social services. Helping to deliver souls enslaved to drugs, alcoholism, deprivation, and neglect is what he or she is inclined to do. These prophets have strong deliverance features attached to their ministries. They are also great believers in post deliverance follow-up, and are therefore likely to have rehabilitation centers and special service agencies of their own or integral to their ministry circuit. Giving the spiritual support needed to affect the natural existence is what they do. Shelters, transient homes, and vocational training are all of interest to these prophets. Supporting and supernaturally girding those who found and operate these facilities, or strengthening and aiding the church or ministry that does so, is what the prophet is further equipped for, as well as intercession, counseling, and life coaching.

The *Special Groups Realm* can employ a number of prophets from several groups and all classes. This is where a prophet is given a message to deliver under the anointing for a particular group. These groups may be men only, women only, single parents, youth, recovering addicts, divorced people, or professionals. They may be suited to any category of human culture. These prophets have a special tenderness toward those of their designated group and may engage in or sponsor a variety of programs to meet their needs or prepare others to do so.

The *Ecclesiastical Realm* is the realm of church authority. Prophets in this realm deal primarily with churches and are adept at interpreting right conduct, proper behavior (that which sanctifies), and the characteristics of holiness as they pertain to the church at large or individuals in particular. They are strong in doctrine and tend to be highly scholastic theologians. Ordinarily stern in their preaching, this prophetic class is skilled at fusing teaching with prophecy. They are strong in revelation of the Scriptures, and the talents and abilities of these ministers authenticate and verify sound doctrine in application. Such prophets establish and maintain godly standards in service, training, and conduct, especially focusing on other ministers around them and fellow prophets.

As with the classes, these realms are meant to be a guide to understanding God's placement and emphasis of prophets. It is good to remember that the Lord is over all the earth and the church, being spiritual, has its members scattered throughout it. Therefore, as the Great Shepherd, He must cover the needs of His entire body. With the prophet's office, He does this in innovative and practical ways. God desires that His people never have an occasion to miss hearing from Him or tapping into His vast resources. So prophets, like all the officers and many of His servants, are dispersed throughout the world, covering every stratum of human life with the practical and supernatural resources of God.

CHAPTER SUMMARY

1. The prophetic is divided into two distinct groups: executive and administrative. That is, governmental and supportive.

2. At least ten classes identify the subdivisions of God's prophetic service.

3. Prophetic divisions also assign the classes of prophetic service to specific realms. In addition to the ten classes of prophets that may exist, there are ten geospherical realms.

PROPHETIC ACTION ITEMS

1. Build a profile of what you believe to be your prophetic type, class, and realm, and state why you think your profile reveals you as a prophet.

Chapter 14

PREPARING THE PROPHET TO SERVE

This chapter explains how to prepare the prophet to serve. It covers:

- Shaping the prophet for service
- God's ways and means of prophetic preparation

SHAPING THE MINISTER FOR SERVICE

Prophets, like all other ministers, are a set-aside group of servants dedicated to God. Their set-aside, or consecrated, status is achieved by God on a two-tiered arrangement. First, the position itself is extracted from the masses of God's societies and orders and placed in a separate vocational department category. Afterward, the people are actually selected, and upon being designated to fill this or that office, are endowed accordingly. Intrinsic signals are instilled in prophets to eventually summon them to the Lord's service, and subsequently to His chosen field of ministry for them. The entire composition of the minister for this purpose is geared toward the end that he or she hears, responds to, and obeys God's ordained mission in life. As we have learned earlier, native abilities are how God does this. Having groomed a future prophet over the specified number of years that God deemed it would take for the messenger to get ready, He activates the signals that translates into the call to ministry. He then moves into His preparatory stage and the task of training the servant to begin working.

At least six means are used by God to bring a minister into His service. These methods are employed by the Lord secretly and silently throughout the anointed's life until he or she is brought to the stage of presentation. This is the point where the person is ready to be extricated from the masses and delivered to God for ministry. Various things start to occur to lead a potential minister to separation and consecration. Once initiated, it involves numerous jolting breaches in a person's life that can be distressing and disturbing. In anticipation of these, upsets are likely to have been felt early in life. Tragedies, conflicts, and hostility many times greet God's future servant at young ages. Turbulence and crises can characterize the youth's experience. Instability and inconsistency may have marked his or her existence from childhood. What determines this is the dynamics of the ministry call. The rule is, the more dynamic the call, the more fiery and intense the severing process. It can seem to the future servant that everything is against him or her. Every major aspect of prospective messengers' worlds can be turned upside down to equip them for the demands and backlash of the call. Such people become familiar with struggles, defeat, suffering, and hardship during youth or adolescence.

This method has a goal for God, one that ensures the one divinely appointed will, at the appropriate time, answer God's call and take his or her place among the ranks of His laborers.

Chosen before the foundation of the world, many of these people take up God's challenge at a young age. However, the actual service may come years later. From the moment they hear about God in truth and understand what they have heard, the mechanisms placed in them for that very purpose at conception are activated. It is as though they awake out of a slumber-like state and begin to follow the Lord's voice to enter the position of their call. Throughout the making and shaping process, His induction can demand—and in the end achieves—a complete about-face in life. The servant jumps off the treadmill of life and onto the course set by the Creator almost rashly, impulsively. Appearing unreasonable in their resolve, future prophets stymie their friends and associates. They frustrate employers and confuse, and often alienate, relatives for reasons even the called ones are unsure of at the time. All they know is that an urgent prodding within insists they abandon all and follow Jesus. So they resolutely go about the business of cutting cords, breaking ties, and disengaging themselves from the world.

Selling off property, settling accounts, closing comfortable and convenient doors forever, these people take up their crosses to follow Jesus. To where they do not always know. Why? Because it is what they must do. The time has come for them to enter into the reason they were born, to fulfill the purposes for which they were saved: to present themselves as living sacrifices for the Lord's service.

The next stage following this is getting ready for the Master's use. Here is where God's shredding and shedding takes place. Hearts aflame with devotion and hungry for the fullness of God, they go through the strenuous, stinging process of letting go of the world and the flesh. God appears to be in hot pursuit of everything that makes them, them. He is on their case relentlessly, and they don't know why. Now separated from family and friends, the trainee servants go into the wilderness to confront themselves and to meet their God. These are cruel, hot days and bleak, cold nights. With no one to divert their attention from the task at hand, all newcomers to the Lord's service must now sit face-to-face with God. As God begins to teach them, they all grow frantically aware of the excruciating chipping and nipping away at their personhood. Under the blaring light of the truth, in the reflection of Jesus, the novices are forced to see themselves as they are: narrow-minded, cruel, insensitive, thoughtless, selfish, and deceitful. They are compelled to recollect things they would just as soon forget. To have unkind, ungodly words replayed by God and to relive unrighteous thoughts and imaginations for cleansing and service is painful. Constantly, in this wilderness, future servants are cut off from every customary anesthetic. They must make one agonizing revisit after another to the rooms of their past lives. Pains, hurt, abuse, hostilities, fears, and angers resurface. All are presented piece by piece to show how and why these trainee servants became what they are before God. Each piece acts like the main course of an elaborate dinner having its own appetizer (motive and will) and dessert (reason and advantage).

Every part of the trainee is shattered under the process. Tears, anger, bitterness, resentment, hatred, and defense each take their turn through the roller-coaster ride of emotions the experience provokes. It's excruciating, but somehow the servant knows it's for his or her own good. Each inwardly understands he or she will be better for the emptying.

As the time passes by, the turnstile of memories and recollections seems to never cease. The servant wonders how

Christ ever wanted him or her in the first place, let alone needs him or her in His service. What could possibly be offered to such a holy and righteous Savior? After all they have been through, these future servants are convinced that they certainly have nothing of value to offer this just God. After seeing all that was within, the trainees are sure there is nothing worthwhile to give God. At this stage, the Lord's devastated inductees are ready to toss themselves away, being broken and hopeless now without life's normal props. Little do these future prophets know that, at this point, God has His new agents right where He wants them. All the while, the future vessels of the Lord's voice are painfully seeing themselves as God does—in truth—and it may be jolting.

In God's presence, under His holy hand, future prophets are no more than a feeble, puny, hopeless, and unreliable rejects, apart from God. That is the message the Lord wants to get across. Here is when the virtues of Christ are poured in. Similar to the meticulous and elaborate ritual undergone by the Levitical priesthood, these new creation ministers are made ready for service. Love, mercy, wisdom, and grace are filling the breaches and broken gaps in these vessels. Every cracked hole is filled as though it had never been broken. Warped outlooks, biased opinions, and perverted viewpoints are straightened to allow the path of truth to flow freely through the messengers. Carnal appetites and desires are replaced with the heavenly; every selfish yearning and pursuit is excised in order to align the prophets' existence with the will of God. Holiness adorns the messengers, and truth fills the Lord's temple. The structure is recomposed of love and every furnishing tool of the Holy Spirit. To get the prophets ready, every supply now comes from above as the stringent lessons and orientation process impress upon the newly renovated servants that this is life from now on. Now they are ready, ready to be taught and groomed. Ready to learn. Death has moved out, and life has moved in. God is on the throne of these lives, and Christ reigns in their hearts. It is done. Now the vessels are *"meet for the Master's use"* (2 Timothy 2:21).

The renewed ministers are then brought to the Lord to receive their charges. They are taught their mission, its approach, and God's standards, will, and way. They are made to comprehend their boundaries, privileges, limits, and so on. As these newcomers submit to God, the Lord exalts them, sending them out to use and exercise all that has been implanted within to take on part of the Son's mission for the Father.

WAYS AND MEANS OF PROPHETIC PREPARATION

God has different ways of readying a soul for His call and service. There are at least seven of them, and the combination of several or all of them may be used during the course of a person's life. The mix used depends on the years God allows the messenger to pursue his own course before pulling him out of mainstream life and setting him on the course of his duty to the Creator and Savior.

All ministers are ordained by God for His service before the foundation of the world. Jeremiah 1:1–10 frankly states this, as do Galatians 1:15 and Isaiah 49:1–5. These and many other Scriptures emphatically show God's ordinations are from before the womb to let us know the womb is the crafting place of a person's equipment for God's ministries. To bring us into His service requires several stages of life:

1. Life experience
2. Structured training
3. Apprenticeship
4. Dramatic induction
5. Divine confirmation
6. Supernatural enlistment
7. Childhood induction

Life Experience is the first stage, and the largest of them all. It gives prospective ministers the broadest base of knowledge and the widest frame of reference to draw from upon entering the ministry. Naturally the education process from this preparation branch starts at birth. Every component—parents, home life, environment, school, joys, pains, pleasure, and suffering—serves as a tool that etches the proposed minister's fundamental self for the remaining years of his life, determining what he or she will do forever. The situations and events that occur mold the attitudes, beliefs, and so on, affecting what is to come. They form the instruments in God's hands that will be used by Him for service to Him. Ideally, that service will be through His Son Jesus Christ and salvation. However, whatever path the person chooses, he or she will always be clay in the Maker's hand. Past encounters, experience derived from certain events, and exposure to different situations all come together to generate the skill, proficiency, and reservoir of inherent knowledge the person draws from once in God's service. History and retrospection play the most vital roles in this preparation branch.

Moses' years of service with the Egyptians, Paul's long tenure with the Sanhedrin, and Jeremiah's rearing in a priestly household are examples of this.

Structured Training comes under the umbrella of formalized education. It goes beyond rudimentary study. This preparation branch speaks to vocational study geared toward equipping the minister for eventual religious service, and therefore is designed with the rigors and demands of the ministry in mind. Such training pulls from large portions of life experience and links significant aspects of its teachings to what the minister will ultimately be doing. For good reasons, practice and application make up a good amount of its delivery. Object lessons, simulation exercises, and relevant case studies figure prominently into this branch of the prophet's readiness program. It always involves a teacher, mentor, and steward-type relationship with the learner. Different developers that contributed to the minister's education all leave a portion of God's handprint on that person's soul, in or out of the classroom. Elijah and Elisha, Samuel and Eli, and the school of prophets they trained to staff Israel's prophetic offices continually are examples of this.

Apprenticeship is closely related to structured training in that it is the intern arm of the learning process. Once actual study has been completed, theory is translated to practice. Apprentices are thus assigned to work as subordinates or juniors in the field where God will use them. Apprenticeships can last many years and are dictated by the call, field, and territory in which the laborers will subsequently work. For example, Elisha poured water on Elijah's hands for twenty years before installation to office. Joshua served Moses for over forty years to become successor to his mission: to bring Israel into the Promised Land.

Dramatic Induction speaks to the prophet being suddenly, and often radically, pulled into service. The motives for this method are varied and can be as simple as God needing to have a speaker immediately and finding none reliable in a particular region, or His having to utter a rebuke to established prophets and therefore needs a fresh messenger groomed and trained outside of His present systems. Amos' induction appears to fall under one of these categories. (See Amos 7:14–17.) The call of the twelve apostles of Jesus also fit this category.

One minute, it's business as usual, the next, the person's entire life is upside-down. God's reason for this approach typically centers on a new move for which He desires to use a new staff of prophets. Paul's Damascus road encounter with Jesus of Nazareth illustrates this perfectly.

Divine Confrontation is what the prophets Isaiah and Ezekiel and the apostle Paul encountered. The theme of such prophets' message is the holiness of God. Their words concentrate on His hallowed glory. Usually the prophetic stance is one of awe and reverence for the Most High—the kind the majority of God's people cannot fathom. Moses' fresh from the burning bush experience conveys this outcome of a face-to-face with Jehovah most eloquently. God chooses particular ministers for this type of induction to confirm eternity, qualify the afterlife, and to help them grasp the depth of human sinfulness in contrast with the Maker's holiness. His aim is to equip them to centralize these teachings in their ministries to their respective groups.

Supernatural Enlistment combines the previous two and includes the servant's inexplicable exposure to supernatural agents and other supernatural elements of God's creation. Where others may have led spiritually silent and dormant lives, these people seem inundated with glimpses of the supernatural for what they perceive to be no reason at all. Many times it starts at an early age and continues throughout the course of life. Samuel's prophetic introduction to God to offer judgment to Eli exemplifies this.

Childhood Induction may seem to fit every worker in God's kingdom, and in the broadest sense it does. However, there are those chosen to be reared in prophetic or priestly households, as opposed to those called from the households of Egypt who must be trained, post adolescence, to serve the Lord. Through childhood induction, children are exposed to God and His kingdom, ways, and work from infancy. Their parents are generally faithful, devout believers who, knowing their charge concerning the child, take his or her spiritual and religious development seriously. They are told by God who and what the child is to Him and what their responsibility as parents is to the Lord are as far as the child is concerned. In situations where the parents are not devoted to God, the child is adopted, formally or casually, by devout tutors for this purpose. They may contribute to the child's spiritual training indirectly (as a family friend) or directly (as legal adoptive parents), taking on the task of grooming the youngster for the Lord's service.

Sometimes these people inherit the task through the death of the natural parent. Other times the parent willingly relinquishes the child's spiritual development to them, not knowing it's the will of the Lord. Hannah, for instance, gave Samuel to Eli so he could groom him as a prophet for the Lord. Moses was reared by royalty to be a prophet to regents. Daniel was among the nobles of Israel to be a royal prophet in Nebuchadnezzar's house. As childhood induction itself goes, Samson, Samuel, John the Baptist, and Jesus Himself all fit this category.

CHAPTER SUMMARY

1. Prophets are groomed by God from the womb to enter His service at the appointed time.

2. The Lord uses no fewer than seven concrete means to ready a prophet for his future use.

PROPHETIC ACTION ITEMS

1. Recall the course and events of your life and compare them with the seven methods discussed. See if you can recognize the one the Lord used most with you, or a combination of one or more of them. Explain the results as they contributed to making you who you are today and bringing you to this point in your prophetic journey.

Chapter 15

FALSE PROPHECY

This chapter addresses the subject of false prophecy. It covers:

- Features of false prophecy
- Traits of false prophecy
- Exploring false prophecy
- Recognizing false prophecy
- Screening your prophecy
- Guarding prophecy

FEATURES OF FALSE PROPHECY

Any discussion of the prophetic and definition of prophets would be wanting if it did not address people's number one problem with it—false prophecy. Throughout the ages, beginning with Cain's countering of Abel's representation of God that led to the younger brother's death, false prophecy has been a problem for God. (See Luke 11:49–51.) Actually, the serpent's deception of Adam and Eve in the garden of Eden predates this.

False prophecy has some very unmistakable features that all begin at two places:

- The flesh
- The devil

Perversion of the Lord's word always has its roots in the world. Do you notice how the order is flesh first, and then Satan? This is because in his or her heart, a person must have already decided to forsake or ignore God, or His truth in general. Once that decision has been made, the door of spiritual power that maintains and executes that decision is opened. The spirits of rebellion, disobedience, unbelief, and delusion all enter to see that the person is enslaved to the *chosen* sin that supports the decision. (See Isaiah 66:1–4.) It is at this point false prophecy arises to strengthen the seduction and block all hints of repentance. But how does one know? So you will not be deceived, look first at the list of synonyms for the word *world*, because *all* false prophecy promotes and glorifies the world, something James 4 and 1 John 2:15–17 condemn vehemently. What a believer actually turns to or defects to is always rooted in the world. Reviewing the following list helps you make good decisions when you encounter false prophecy. Look for any of these terms in slick advertising campaigns or other promotions designed to tempt you. When you see them in print or hear them preached, you will know where they lead to and whose program they really propagate.

TRAITS OF FALSE PROPHECY
FORTY WAYS TO DISCERN FALSE PROPHECY

The following statements reflect the hidden agenda of all false prophecies. What they share is a veneer of good deeds and positive motives that make one wonder what could possibly be false about them. Here is where the astute (and resolute) prophet must hold his or her ground. Despite the positive nature of the objectives, it is their motives and mission out-comes that must be suspect. How God-inspired are these cosmo-humanitarian aims? Are they steeped in carnality? Do they seek to replace the Creator's plan and truth? Is there an underlying intent to divert the souls recovered to and from the Lord? Is there a fundamental seething against Him spear-heading these good intents? Here is the greatest test: Does it exhibit the antichrist spirit? Does it aim to assault, discredit, scorn, or otherwise overthrow Jesus Christ, His kingdom, or deity? If so, then regardless of its humanitarian stance, it is not meant to serve the true and living God.

Read the list of traits below and measure them against the questions just posed. False prophecy has one or more of these goals in mind. It aims to motivate or achieve any one or all of the following without the wisdom or involvement of the Creator:

1. Clamors for peace on earth
2. Calls for the elimination of world hunger
3. Proclaims religious unity of man independent of God the Creator or the new birth (ecumenism)
4. Exalts the flesh (humanism)
5. Divides the flesh from the spirit (carnality)
6. Exalts the primacy of man
7. Defiles the worshipper
8. Eliminates sanctification
9. Blocks holiness
10. Causes retreat from God
11. Fosters carnal indulgence; appeases carnal appetites

12. Turns to the world (secularism)

13. Makes flesh (humanity) its strength

14. Leads to, or culminates in, immorality, immodesty, or hedonism

15. Is self-serving and indulgent

16. Makes provisions for the flesh instead of God

17. Ignites strong cosmopolitan influences

18. Exceeds the realms and boundaries of Scripture

19. Ignores the cross and salvation

20. Compromises God's righteousness—misconstrues or otherwise diminishes or subjugates it

21. Causes wavering and double-mindedness

22. Diminishes or humanizes Christ's deity (by ignoring or overriding)

23. Dismisses the Lord's sovereignty

24. Conflicts with or counteracts scriptural truth

25. Clashes with established and revealed prophecy

26. Grieves or quenches the Holy Spirit

27. Causes isolation from the saints

28. Interferes with worship and service to God

29. Condones sin; sympathizes with flesh's whims

30. Perverts doctrine

31. Sparks heresy

32. Negates the new birth—crushes the new creation

33. Makes salvation a matter of the flesh and gender

34. Spawns greed, envy, and lust

35. Breeds, or culminates in, irresponsibility or recklessness

36. Precludes the will and ordinations of God

37. Coincides with, and endorses, worldly views and philosophies

38. Empowers, exalts, and protects the devil and sin

39. Is consistent with, or closely linked to, desires, temperaments, or beliefs of the old man

40. Is impossible to find in Scripture, or to be substantiated by it

41. Fosters demonism, painting it as benevolent

42. Shields rebels from God to prevent acknowledgment of sin, His justice, and righteous judgment

EXPLORING FALSE PROPHECY

All of the above brings us to the meaning of false prophecy. The word *false,* as you well know, means "erroneous, untrue, wrong, mistaken, deceitful." These amplify the root problem with false prophecy. It is:

- Erroneous revelation or prediction
- Untrue revelation or prediction
- Wrong revelation or prediction
- Mistaken revelation or prediction
- Deceitful revelation or prediction

However, the simplest way of looking at false prophecy is to see it as "not the word of the Lord." But why is that such a big deal? Going back to our previous discussion, prophecy is God's communication of His eternal chronology of events, scripted for His programs and our benefit. Reasonably, then, we can deduce that anything not in His program would not (indeed could not) be uttered by Him. If it is not uttered by God, then by whose inspiration do false prophets speak? The answer, of course, is Satan. Scripture confirms this, identifying him as Baal. Jeremiah, as did the other prophets, told us of the prophets of Baal—those who prophesy by the power of Satan.

False prophets receive their inspiration from demons dwelling within them, using their vocals to declare Satan's aims, wishes, and plans. They obtain their communiqués from the counter journals of Satan, seeking to imitate, as well as frustrate, God's predestiny archives. Satan's goal is to interject his proposals into the fixed ordinations of his Maker. Being the god of this age, he has the authority to devise and implement plans for his subjects—something he seized illegally from Adam in the transgression. However, he strives to push these plans off on the chosen elect of God and endeavors to use them to usurp God's word.

The devil plans as things unfold, desiring his own program of intents for humanity to rival what the Lord has eternally appointed. Since he is but a creature—a fallen messenger—he cannot have eternal perspective or foreknowledge of what happens on the earth. Consequently, he schemes as he goes along, for the most part, planning and intruding into the Lord's programs. Whenever his efforts hint at foreknowledge, it is because of his long history of experience with manipulating God's creation, as well as anticipating the basic nature of God and humanity. This answers why he is so repetitious and somewhat mundane in his activities. But what has all this to do with false prophecy? Much.

What false prophets declare or predict, they receive from Satan's plan book—what he hopes to accomplish and can accomplish apart from God's intervention. In fact, true prophecy—God's—is quite helpful to him, as he can use God's revelations to formulate his own plans and fortify his work. They aid his frustration and obstruction attempts and, in an atmosphere of unbelief, do much to advance his programs.

False prophecy is a lie, because only God is true. It is the sum of the devil's dark, egotistical imagination. It is error because it seeks to interject the counterfeit into God's ordinances. Even people who are unaware of Satan's use of them can be unwittingly used by him to prophesy falsely. The prophets of old encountered this and were permitted by God to understand why. They learned how, like false prophets, unwitting souls too were moved by their own hearts. Greed, vanity, bribes, selfishness, and covetousness all inspired them to surrender their members as instruments of unrighteousness to do the devil's bidding. Even emotionalism can serve as a solid conduit for false prophecy. The promised reward of the pleasures of sin is another. Therefore, rash, impulsive, indulgent, impatient, and egotistical types are very inclined to make ready vessels of false prophecy occasionally or consistently. Their penchant for private interpretation, bias, and subjective reasoning all contribute to their being effectively used by seducing spirits. Covetous, greedy, insatiable, and glory-seeking people make reliable ministers of false prophecy.

The first major false prophet the Bible records, aside from the serpent in the garden, is Lamech. (See Genesis 4:16–24.) He interjected what amounts to justifiable homicide and bigamy into the culture of man outside of what evolved from Cain's city, which he built to rival his father's. Around this time, especially after Cain's banishment, false religion (worldly religion) began to flourish; and since that time, false prophecy has prospered and grown to be the vast institution it is today. Currently the branches of the tree of false doctrine are numerous, targeting everything from the planets and stars to the earth and animals. Every kingdom of God's creation has been integrated in some kind of worthless ritual for false religion. The deviant doctrines seem to be as plentiful as the tongues of the nations. Yet the genuine prophet can rest assured he or she has the capacity to discern even the most subtle deceptions and refute them, thereby protecting the flock of God. The only way to do this is by studying to become an approved worker of the Lord Jesus Christ, one who rightly divides His words of truth. However, false prophecy can, and often does, prosper successfully in the church of the Lord Jesus Christ. (See Acts 20:24–32.) This is mostly because there are those who relish private interpretation and wander easily off the path of truth, defining Scripture to suit their own ends.

Modern-day false prophets or demonic messengers are known as psychics, clairvoyants, fortune-tellers, tarot readers, mystics, and spiritualists. It is hard to miss them as the airwaves and media are now flooded with their advertisements and messages. They have become popular because they offer something people crave and need most in these last days—answers. Answers from the spiritual, unseen forces manipulating or maneuvering the natural world. This job, Isaiah 19–20 tells us, is the work of God through the prophets He assigns to His people. If you read 2 Chronicles 33:1–13 and 2 Kings 21:1–15, you will learn several things about this. Among them is what is presented today as popular insight and innocent counseling. They recall the tools and intents of the same ancient eastern religions condemned by Jehovah for natural Israel. Look at 1 Chronicles 33:6. Soothsaying, witchcraft, sorcery (magic), mediums, and spiritists are all condemned by God and cursed by Him. He forbids His people to even entertain them. Yet, modern-day advertisements have these people brazenly peddling their message as hope for a better life on earth. Still, the end result is the same: death. Death by deception, in fact. Since the false prophecies rival God's ordinations, they cannot help but fail, being overruled by the eternal and living word of God.

RECOGNIZING FALSE PROPHECY

Prophecy, God's divine communications medium, was designed to give voice to His thoughts and actions in our world, not to entertain or appease those to whom it comes. When prophecies are uttered outside the Almighty's legitimate script decreed on a life, it is designated as false prophecy. Deuteronomy explains it best:

> *But the prophet, which shall presume to speak a word in my name, which I have not commanded him to speak, or that shall speak **in the name of other gods**, even that prophet shall die. And if thou say in thine heart, how shall we know the word which the Lord hath not spoken? When a prophet speaketh in the name of the Lord, if the thing follow not, nor come to pass, that is the thing which the Lord hath not spoken, but the prophet hath spoken it presumptuously: thou shalt not be afraid of him.*
> (Deuteronomy 18:20–22, emphasis added)

This passage begins an extensive list of what constitutes false prophecy.

- First, it speaks in the name of other gods. Do not be confused by this statement and think that it does not apply today. Besides the inrush of other gods' names into the world, what they peddle and promise is just as indicative. Anything that is prophesied that distorts the Lord's character as revealed in His Word, or purports to remove the hearer from His will or household, reflects the words of another god.

If the word or subject of the prophecy does not follow after it has been declared, this is a peculiar distinction that can go unnoticed. The passage reads, *"follow not, nor come to pass."* They appear to be repetitive statements so that you would only try a prophecy based on its coming to pass. However, the Hebrew terms from which they were translated convey two different intents. For *"follow,"* the Hebrew word *hayah* is used, and for *"come to pass,"* the word *bow* is used. *Hayah* essentially is talking about existing. Thus, if the thing (spoken by the prophet) does not exist, or in the case of *bow*, which means "to come or to go," doesn't appear or arrive, it is presumptuous.

The Lord is making an important distinction between the two terms and apparently their separate prophetic events. Prophetically speaking, He is telling His people first of all that what a prophet says must *exist*. That is, it must be somewhere in his or her life or sphere of life. An example would be to prophesy something to a person who has no capacity to become what is prophesied, regardless of how many times the prophet wills it to be. (See Ezekiel 13:17.) Where verse six of that passage says the prophet hopes he can make the word come to pass. This is witchcraft because it is rooted in two things: divination (fortune-telling for pay) and spiritual manipulation (intending to coerce creation to perform or produce the word apart from God's authority or approval). Prophecies can only come to pass when they exist on the person's Psalm 139:16 book of life. This is because the sum of the hearer's talents, abilities, and faculties must exist for a prophecy concerning them to be fulfilled. For instance, to predict a person will be a world renowned opera star when he or she cannot sing is false prophecy. The Lord would not say such a thing because He did not equip the hearer for it. Prophecies of this sort ignore or shipwreck God's word of destiny on a life. Since He neither wrote nor spoke it, there is no place for the prophecy to come to pass.

- Second, the prophet's word must be appointed to the person's life, or else, again, it cannot arrive at any time. The words of the prophecy must be empowered by God's will and authority to come to pass. That is, to engineer themselves, the events that cause it to be must also be written on a given hearer's page of life. Generally speaking, there are telltale signs in their interests, past exploits, experiences, or opportunities (or abilities) that hint at the word's potential to come to pass. These are two separate ideas, although they appear to be one and the same.

A prophecy must speak what is and not what the prophet hopes or fantasizes to be. To assure this, there must be some reference or hint of such an occurrence in Scripture, such as auto-powered vehicles like Ezekiel's living creatures or light-emitting beings and materials as with God's heaven and angels. These two anomalies of the day did not exist for the people of the age, but they did exist in God.

- Third, the prophecy must be empowered by God's authorization to take effect in the person's life. For instance, Elijah embodied the power to make fire come down from, and to close up, the heavens. He was imbued by God with the biopneumatic material to impregnate a barren old woman by prophesying. It was part of his mantle and his ministerial covenant with the Lord as a prophet. Elisha, his successor, also had such power. He was authorized by God to cause lead to float, to slaughter people who offended him or his God, and to command the elements to obey. This authority was integral to his mantle as a prophet. Therefore, his words along these lines were self-evident because they had always come to pass or shown immediate signs of being able to do so at the prophet's command. The phrase *immediate signs* is a key in this explanation. The Hebrew word *bow*, used by Moses in the Deuteronomy reference, suggests that some sort of sign regularly accompanied or immediately followed the prophets' words so that when they spoke the Lord promptly acted on their prediction by manifesting a present, unmistakable sign of the word spoken.

The two tests of a prophecy—existence and appearance—are individual ways of distinguishing prophets who just love to hear themselves talk. They delight in prophesying for the sake of prophesying. The Lord calls such prophesiers *presumptuous prophets* and suggests that because of this character flaw, He does not listen to what comes out of these messengers' mouths. Notice that He did not say the person was not a prophet, only that he or she had no power or influence with God due to the habit of saying whatever comes to mind. The

Ezekiel 13 reference solidifies this explanation well. It speaks of how the prophets are led by their own spirits and when they prophesy falsely in the Lord's name, they hope that they can somehow make their words come to pass. To do so requires magic, which of course has no power to coerce the Almighty.

More recognizable signs of false prophecy or divination are unbelief, apostasy, and libertinism, all damaging behaviors and responses that are addressed elsewhere in this handbook. Moreover, spiritual errors and prophetic blunders are incontrovertible outcomes of prophesiers who delight in just seeing (or claiming to see) in the spirit realm and saying what is seen (or imagined) as prophecy, regardless of whether the word can be verified as God's or not. To such prophets, the fun is in the prophesying, not in the other safety measures that protect God's reputation and His people's faith.

Opening the doors, hearts, and ears to their prophetic gifting is the main objective for these people. Prophesiers of this type use their prophetics to vocalize anyone's real or imagined spiritual hurts or offenses, or they take up others' causes just to generate outlets for their ministries. They contrive all sorts of prophetic antics to ingratiate themselves with people who appear influential enough to showcase their ministries. God's involvement or affirmation of them, as with Balaam, on the other hand, is inconsequential.

Errant prophesiers succumb to impulses of gift-driven prophesying and a gift-defined prophetic ministry. Surrendering to purely charismatic prophecies makes such prophesiers strong candidates for delusion and divination, another danger of errant prophecy. In addition, it opens the way for rebel spirits to manufacture the materialization of words the

Lord neither wrote nor authorized on a life. Even though they cannot halt the Lord's will on a life in its time, they can interject a host of frustrations and hardships along the way. Unnecessary trials, setbacks, and delays can result as the false starts connected with the false word triggers them. All of these situations explain why servants of this critical medium of God's communications should be strictly regulated, something the Lord has been doing progressively since He revived the prophetic more than two decades ago.

God needs the prophetic. He relies on it because He has no alternative to it. Therefore, He must purge and protect the institution for His own sake. According to Joel 2:28–29 and Acts 2:17–18, the Lord provided Himself no other avenue or recourse for getting spiritual information and truth across to this natural world outside of prophecy. As we have seen from the dearth of spiritual wisdom, insight, and true revelation suffered by our own and previous generations, without the prophets, much of what God says and does may never be delivered to those that really need it. If the Lord does not communicate through His prophets, the task is simply left undone or perverted by psychics. We have seen both of these outcomes in our times.

SCREENING YOUR PROPHECY

Now that you have gone through all this information, a typical question would be how to tell if what you have been receiving from the invisible realms and voices is from God. This is an understandable response. That the question is raised in your mind is a positive statement to your personal integrity, and integrity is where it must begin. Generally, persons who are new or young in this ministry do not think to interrogate their souls as to the veracity of the information they receive and put out as prophecy. Often they just run with what they receive and give little regard to the possibility of its being dispatched by someone other than the Most High God. This practice was shunned vehemently by ancient prophets of God. The writers of Scripture harbored no such misconceptions. They knew that many voices (spirits) are in the world to deceive those who receive not the love of the truth. The Bible speaks often about deceivers, with Paul writing to Timothy that seducing spirits and doctrines of devils were real. (See 1 Timothy 4:1.)

Besides other spirits that inspire false prophecy, prophesiers should be very aware of the prospect of their own hearts', literally emotions', inclination to deceive them also. It can falsify prophecy in two ways: by picking up and clinging to thoughts that are not from God, or by fabricating images and ideas that qualify as divination because the person wills something greatly desired to be. The distortions of the human soul typically find it easier to be persuaded by what is not of God than to wait for Him to verify what *is* of Him. The prophets of old learned this early as part of their training.

Furthermore, the information unclean spirits can emit in general, and that the prophets can pick up on, can adversely affect the prophets' nature, even if only by symbiosis if they are not careful. The possibility of impure prophecy was a great concern of Bible prophets for these reasons, and no part of their being, they knew, would remain unaffected by it if they ignored the signs and seductions of divining spirits. They acknowledged that if they left their suggestions and infiltrations unnoticed or unchecked, their likelihood of being contaminated was as real as those so infected.

Dreams, visions, intellect, insight, and perception faculties were all open to the spirit world once a prophetic person's supernatural endowments were awakened and made known. From that time on, the bliss of ignorance gave way to protection and defense. Both became bywords for ministry life. Protecting their minds, hearts, and souls from anything that could render their faculties and gifts unusable to God became the ancient prophets' highest priority. Every effort was made to ensure all their prophecies were true and sprung exclusively from God's base of the truth. Modern prophets should accept that their predecessors witnessed false prophecy and false teaching on a national scale. Routinely they were the objects and observers of their fruit. As a result of what they were exposed to, God's ancient prophets never took the issue or potential of false prophecy lightly—a position many of today's prophets would do well to adopt.

The fundamental aim of any prophecy from God will not deviate from the nature of the Lord. When a nation sins against Him, He judges it. When His children do the same, He judges and chastens them that they may not be destroyed with the world. God forgives sin, but He has been shown throughout Scripture to still deal, in His own way, with its actual deeds. (See Psalm 99:8; 89:24–37; 2 Samuel 7:12–16; and Hebrews 12:5–6. Also refer to 1 Corinthians 10:1–10.) The prophet who receives a word from the Lord must not try that word by his own emotions, personal preferences, viewpoints, and patterns of belief. Instead, he or she must deny the natural self and face squarely and objectively God's truth. Each time a prophet is tempted to compromise, he or she must ask the following sober question: Am I accustomed to thinking God is like me, or that I am just like God?

Read Psalm 50:21. It bitterly disdains this notion. If a prophet maintains it, he or she is prone to release false prophecy. If a prophet is one who finds it difficult to separate his feelings from God's wisdom, the inclination to "prophe-lie" is great. Other probing questions that may shed further light on the subject include: Does the prophet tend to sacrifice righteousness and truth for brotherly love and imbalanced tolerance of the sin-ridden variations of all humankind? Is he or she the sort who feels salvation and the new birth are subordinate to the human experience and must be reconciled with the real life of man? Perhaps the prophet believes in his or her heart in the universal salvation of all mankind, or in the contention that the entire human race will be saved and restored in the end, regardless of its treatment of and response to God. Maybe the prophet finds it impossible to rise above his or her empathy with carnal suffering to be a minister who maintains allegiance to God, His Word, and His truth. Or lastly, does the prophet in his heart tend to lean on the human side more than the spiritual side and manipulate truth to cause it to line up with his or her five senses? These and possibly many other questions have to be resolved within prophets before they can accurately and objectively take up the mantle of prophecy, or ever hope to boldly confront and refute false prophecy. If not, the prophet has little hope of discerning or challenging the deviations from revealed truth that God gave us His Son, His Word, and His Spirit to uphold.

Today's moral decay and corruption, added to sin's brazen-ness, have caused many of the righteous to be cowered. Con-temporary Christians have allowed themselves to be backed into a corner like whimpering animals under threat of attack. They have bowed to the rising revolt against the truth of God and have bought into the philosophy of preferential service to the Creator, adopting free-style independent thinking, whether or not it can be substantiated by Scripture. They have greatly succumbed to popular sway. The most detrimental of all is large-scale acceptance of the belief that God's use of human writers constitutes an invalidation of the Scriptures. Deeming the Scriptures no longer authentic and thus unreliable as doctrine and guidance for man, people think they are free to "do God and Christianity their way." Surrender to these seductions has caused the ministry of the prophet to be suspect and largely rejected by the church and the world.

Therefore, the task of screening prophecy is made even more difficult since the minds and psyches of modern prophets and the church alike have been oriented to these convictions. Weeding them out takes stringent effort on the part of bona fide prophets and intense working of the Holy Spirit. But it can be done, and has been done, in prophets the world over. There are those who have forsaken all and seriously taken up their crosses to follow Jesus, though not without a price. The price of alienation, isolation, rebuke, and reviling awaits every one of them. The reason is John 3:21. But the prize of Christ for them far outweighs it all. Trusting Christ, they gladly relinquish the elements of their prior life that make for contaminated prophecy and questionable doctrine, flinging off the garments of society to joyfully don the Lord's mantle of truth. In doing so, they receive the gifts they truly desire: high discernment, increased enlightenment, and strong judgment, so that they may, without a blink, screen and validate the moves and deposits of the Spirit of God placed within them accurately and convey without wavering the true Word of God.

GAUGING PROPHECY

The absence of sound techniques and principles to help people gauge prophecy and verify its truth has put prophets' credibility at risk. Hearers of the word of the Lord should be taught that prophecy has scheduled seasons to perform, and then shown how they can be assured of its fulfillment at the appointed time. Without these tools, many people are motivated to simply abandon their words and discredit their prophesiers. Sometimes this is justified; most times it is not.

In Scripture, false or errant prophesies do not outweigh the true ones. Therefore, the over-magnified fear of false words being imposed on true believers is unwarranted. To counteract this, I use a pet formula to measure the degree of spiritual error one is likely to encounter in God compared to the amount of truth. Of course it is not all-inclusive, but it can offer a pretty good gauge to project the rate of God's truth dispensed to the believer from the lie. You may appreciate it. Here is how it works.

There were twelve tribes, yet in the book of Revelation only one is lost. That is the tribe of Dan. Christ chose twelve apostles and, according to the book of Acts, only one was lost—as foretold by Jesus. That was Judas Iscariot. In carrying this principle over to the seven churches, of all those with which Christ had an issue, only one was threatened with complete dissolution—that was Ephesus. He said only to them that they were in danger of having Him remove their candlestick out of its place. I use this pattern to explore how much of what God does fails, or better yet in His vernacular, is given over to the devil.

What the above principle means to you who give and receive prophecy is that God permits very little error to get through to those who honestly desire and pursue His truth. (Ezekiel 14:16 explains it best.) Whatever error does get through, the Lord permits for two reasons. One reason is to enable you to hone your instincts in discerning the truth from the lie. The Lord wants you to learn to protect yourself from the latter. The second reason is what Ezekiel 14 shares: the desires of people's hearts have turned to idols that caused them to be estranged from Him. For these reasons, prophets need to be well versed in the Scriptures and articulate them well enough to depict their prophecies with the correct imagery. Verifiable prophets are eloquent enough to translate their chosen imagery and revelation to the right audience at the right time.

What all this means is that prophets must be highly trained communicators. They must be adept at choosing and employing the most precise words to convey God's thoughts visually and intelligently. This suggests the need for an extensive and thorough learning development program that demonstrates how, and why, spiritual words work. The better programs will have strong public speaking and other communications components attached to them.

Moreover, the best program would show prophets and their hearers why spiritual words have physical objectives that do not limit them to strictly spiritual reactions or behavior. In fact, prophetic words are designed to be ignitions or determiners of human response and conduct. Heavenly communications publicized on earth and dispersed for human beings are not interested in sheer ethereal responses.

In the next chapter, I introduce you to the features and functions of the prophetic company.

Chapter Summary

1. False prophecy has two sources.

2. There are more than forty traits of false prophecy.

3. Five factors identify a prophecy as false.

4. Summarily false prophecy is "not the word of the Lord."

5. Recognizing false prophecy takes wisdom, knowledge, discernment, and skill.

6. There are practical ways for you to screen your prophecy.

7. There are many intelligent ways to gauge prophecy.

Prophetic Action Items

1. Explore several significantly sized prophecies and compare their themes, message, and foundation against this chapter's discussion to see how they stack up as true or false prophecy. Use modern and Bible prophecies for this assignment.

Chapter 16

THE PROPHETIC COMPANY

In the previous chapter, I examined false prophecy at length and ended the discussion with a promise to introduce you to the prophetic company. Here, I will do just that. As you read on, you will learn:

- What a prophetic company is
- What a prophetic company does
- What prophets do for God's institutions
- How to establish a prophetic company
- A prophetic company's structure
- Standard prophetic company personnel
- The Bible's view of a prophetic company
- Core prophetic service requirements
- The prophetic office and the prophetic company
- Uniform standards for the prophet
- The institutional prophet
- Duties, responsibilities, and service guidelines of the prophet

WHAT IS A PROPHETIC COMPANY?

A prophetic company is a community of prophets who are members of a local church body or other organization whose primary purpose is to provide prophetic care, service, prophecy, and oversight to its membership. These activities include special high-level prophetic coverage to its founders and leaders. The prophetic company is generally assembled with people of varying prophetic minds, callings, dimensions, and backgrounds to blend a healthy mix of diverse spiritual mantles. Ministerial diversity is important to prophetic companies to help avoid prophetic monopolies, overly spiritual symbioses, or non-productive affinity groups that can render the revelatory and predictive functions of the company ineffective.

WHAT THE PROPHETIC COMPANY DOES

The prophetic company fulfills the duties and responsibilities of prophetic ministry as directed by a church's senior leadership. The model it uses includes the one developed from the early church depicted for us in Scripture, with adjustments for modern applications included. All the functions of a prophet's mantle are beneficially employed as expressed in this handbook. The delegations and applications of the prophetic company's supernatural faculties are concentrated on in this chapter.

WHAT PROPHETS DO FOR GOD'S INSTITUTIONS

Prophets are not just for the church. The apostle Paul made this plain in 1 Corinthians 14 when he discussed the nature, purposes, and functions of prophesying. He mentioned how the unbeliever or sinner can be positively affected by God's medium of divine communications when entering a gathering of Christ's members. Throughout the New Testament, the medium of prophecy is discussed, along with the entire complement of the Lord's spiritual operations exercised by His church. So accurate is the conclusion that prophets belong in the stratum of earthly existence that it is substantiated by the dreadful trends of the modern world. The world has replaced God's absent prophets with its own version of spiritual communicants. Devils and their agents now occupy the Creator's spiritual and supernatural posts in society to answer its need to know tomorrow's answers today. The church's neglect of its duties to the Lord in this world has left sinners on their own to figure out how to reconnect with their spiritual roots. A natural rejection of the Lord's truth and resentment of His church left them with only one recourse. It motivated them to turn to the darkness for their supernatural light.

Today, we are seeing a resurgence of 1 Kings 12:26–13:5. God's people are abandoning their true roots for the ways of the world. History is repeating itself. The reason is found in Lamentations 1:9, which says she did not consider her destiny. Prophets on the horizon in this dispensation face the same challenges, as satanic counterfeits try to convince the world that it no longer considers or desires its destiny in Christ Jesus.

Psychics, clairvoyants, and other false facsimiles of the Lord's supernatural staff have seated themselves in His prophetic voices' vacated seats. As it stands today, they perform the majority of earth's supernatural tasks. Despite having been ordained from Pentecost, this was not meant to be. On the other hand, Creator God's will is that prophets be present and vocal in every area of human life. People should be able to hear from the Creator on all planes and have the opportunity to conform their behaviors, alter their plans and visions, and align their purposes to benefit from His creation-inscribed will for their lives. Thus, every institution and organization on the planet would do well to install its own godly prophetic staff.

The reason the word *organization* is used in this and later discussions more than *church* is so that Christian ministries and enterprises can consider the advantages of having, along with their own staff of intercessors, a company of prophets to attend to their supernatural business. If they are going to attempt to become affected by apostles, it stands to reason that they should also seek to be covered and guarded by prophets. With its own prophetic guard, an organization can not only expedite a Christian enterprise's endeavors, but it can also minimize or alleviate altogether nuisance and resistance from satanic blockades put in its way. However, installing this institution in one's organization takes forethought, much wisdom and counsel, shrewdness, and strategy. A handbook such as this one can certainly aid the process.

Using this guide as a tool, a company or para-church ministry can establish an in-house prophetic company using institutional rather than ecclesiastical prophets. With the help of the proper screening tools and general training, such an entity can efficiently and effectively install a worthwhile prophetic guard with the force and competence to enhance its organization's performance and increase its overall potential to prosper.

HOW TO ESTABLISH A PROPHETIC COMPANY

The purpose of the prophetic company is the establishment of a divinely appointed staff of ministers to serve as hearers, seers, interpreters, appliances, and intercessors for an organization. Prophetic ministry is a functional layer between Christ's universal church organizations' headship and its members under the auspices of the Holy Spirit. As a company prophet, you become part of an insulating shield between the ministry's senior leaders and the people they exist to serve. You are a guard, watchman, prophesier, revelator, and a number of other duties that you by now realize are integral to the prophet's mantle. Once you are appointed, you should be immediately enrolled in your organization's prophetic company training. Your required leadership and prophetic orientation classes should be satisfactorily fulfilled or nearly complete to qualify you for trial placement on the company's senior staff. Your probationary period should not commence until your prophetic superintendent has approved the first phase of training success. To confirm this, he or she should review your individualized training and service plan with you.

A PROPHETIC COMPANY'S STRUCTURE

The prophetic company normally consists of a minimum of five leadership and service positions. These may be expanded as needed by formal resolution of those in authority over the company. However, if the work is small, no more than three to nine prophets should be installed at any given time. Too big a company over a small church can dwarf the pastor's influence and dominate the ministry's effects. The basic structure of a viable prophetic company should consist of various spiritual personnel to staff the company. The following is a brief description of what each staff member does and how each company position interrelates with the others. From there, some of the rationale of what each member of the staff should perform is given to help you recognize yourself and understand what your peers, colleagues, and authority figures are responsible for performing. The positions' order and descriptions essentially depict their ranks and possible lines of authority and accountability. View the chart below to comprehend the nature of the prophetic company's leadership and its most recommended form of government.

LIST OF STANDARD PROPHETIC COMPANY PERSONNEL

- Apostles
- Senior Pastor
- Prophetic Company Superintendent (also called Chief Prophet)
- Assistant to the Prophetic Superintendent
- Staff Prophets (also called Company Prophets)
- Scribe
- Scribal Assistant
- Psalmists
- Seers
- Dreamers of Dreams
- Prophesiers
- Messenger Prophets
- Governmental Prophets
- Senior Intercessors
- Prayer Warriors

THE BIBLE'S VIEW OF A PROPHETIC COMPANY

For the purposes of shaping your mind and preparing your spirit to establish and/or serve in a prophetic company, the following explanations are provided to give you practical terms that express the symbology of your future prophetic service. It is based on how the conquering monarchical era of the Bible saw its ministers and agents. These applications were even attached to the prophets like Deborah, Joshua, Samuel, and Moses. Thus, a prophet was seen in Scripture as a predictive, revelatory authority who also functioned as:

- a soldier, a member of a military force
- a specially trained adult in the use of a particular weapon
- a capable fighter to serve the king permanently
- professional soldiery including cavalrymen, or troops
- a guarding soldier assigned to protect a particular person or thing
- a charioteer who fought from a chariot
- a commander who led other soldiers
- a centurion, a non-commissioned officer commanding at least a hundred men
- a sergeant serving as the local policeman, enforcing the law, with punishment pronounced by the magistrate

The above was given to help your mind shift to Scripture's idea and intent for professional prophetic ministry. To aid your ability to do so, the following guidance is given.

PREPARING TO SERVE AS A COMPANY PROPHET

WISDOM FOR THE INSTITUTIONAL PROPHET, THE ORGANIZATIONAL PROPHET, AND THE INDEPENDENT PROPHET

Preparing to serve as a company prophet is a bit different from learning how to prophesy. A company prophet has a function very dissimilar in function from that of the independent prophet, discussed elsewhere. The company prophet makes the decision to cease going it alone and to come under an order and structure many modern prophets find repressive due to their traditional view of the ministry.

Independent prophets who execute merely a predictive ministry equate to the typical freelance prophet. This freestyle messenger cannot fathom what an institutional organization prophet gains by becoming part of a group. However, the principle of the law of large numbers as well as the adage that says there is safety in numbers come to mind as the two most obvious benefits.

NOW THAT YOU ARE AN INSTITUTIONAL PROPHET

The first order of business is that your historical mind on your prophetic service should shift. If reading this material makes it unquestionably clear that you are prophetic, bear in mind that even though you may have served the King of kings as an independent prophet for years, all that must change.

Now that you are becoming a part of a prophetic company, your predestined membership on the Lord's universal prophetic staff is being narrowed to a designated position in your company of prophets. Your views and attitudes toward working with teams, workgroups, and prophetic presbyteries may need to change from what was acceptable as an independent to what is required of an institutional prophet. An institutional prophet serves an organization by performing specific prophetic functions. He or she now occupies an office and may no longer freelance as one who merely exercises the gift of prophecy from time to time. Henceforth, you will learn to mainstream your prophetics with those of the company and be answerable to its superintendent.

Accountability, reporting, screening, and other spiritual administrations become integral to your service as you enter and execute the office of the prophet above exercising the gift of prophecy at your discretion. You will find in response to this action that the Lord will no longer interact with you in your prophetics as before. He may even seem to withdraw from you for a while as though what you two once shared has become insignificant or obsolete. Of course, that is not true. What the Lord is doing is preparing you to serve as a professional *nabi*—a prophet accountable to a company and not just to the Lord directly. Therefore, expect Him to now direct you to those He has put in charge of your ministry's prophetic service. These would be the head of your organization and your prophetic superintendent. Initially, this may disturb you, but if you study Scripture you will remember that this is routinely how God handles and works through His prophets. Once He has established a viable organization through which to work, He concentrates His instructions to the head of a prophetic company (such as Samuel, Nathan, Jeremiah, Isaiah, and Daniel).

The head of the organization, in this case the company superintendent, has authority to delegate various tasks and details connected with the Lord's instructions to the most capable prophet in the company. The reason for this is that God works through His offices and the authority figures that have been installed to execute them. Most of the church has lost sight of this factor of divine order over the years. Our Lord is the God of government, law, and order. Therefore, as much as possible, He will initiate His kingdom actions with the heads of whatever legitimate institutions He has at His disposal. Here is where you will have to shift your mentality from that of an independent prophet's mind-set to an organizational mind-set. Your training and probationary period are to help you do just that. In addition, this handbook was designed be used throughout your development and thereafter to facilitate your adjustment to your new prophetic life.

THE PROPHET'S OFFICE AND THE PROPHETIC COMPANY

The prophet's office, as stated earlier, predates all time and history, although is has existed for eons in God's service. Despite what you may have come to believe from popular religious doctrine, the mantle of the prophet is to serve the Lord above His people. That is the reason one of its definitions is that of a deity's spokesperson. If God does not speak, you as His mouthpiece have nothing to say in His name. As we established in earlier discussions, the genuine prophet's office does more than prophesy, in particular; it does more than predict the future.

The prophets of old performed a myriad of divine, secular, sacred, and professional duties in office that ranged from telling the future to installing monarchies and their monarchs. As a result, if you are going to be an effective company prophet, you must see your service as requiring more than predictive prophesying and the skill set needed to fulfill it beyond seeing and saying. See your prophetic company post as an official function ordained by the Lord and attached to your organization. Accept your call to the prophet's office like all of the offices of 1 Corinthians 12:28 and Ephesians 4:11, as the possession of the Lord Jesus Christ. All the ministries God bestowed in the organization began with and are installed by Him. As a result of these truths, yours is a place of spiritual authority over which the Lord Jesus Christ, God's Son, supervises. Therefore, He is your real evaluator.

Your eventual success or failure is a matter of record to Him as well as to your company leader. Do not neglect your duty and accountability to Him as one of His preordained prophets. The organization supervises your divine service on His behalf, but He alone controls it. Remain prayerful and attentive to what the Lord has groomed you for over the years of your prophetic development. Recognize that all He taught and instilled in your was to prepare you to serve Him as you are about to do in your prophetic company.

SUMMARY OF CORE PROPHETIC SERVICE REQUIREMENTS

- Corporation and Company Prayer
- Organization Events
- Leadership Support
- Special Assignments
- Future Company Prophet Prospects
- Scheduled Company Prophet Duty Assignments

- Counseling
- Prayer Groups
- Mentorship
- Spiritually Undergirding the Flock
- Prophetically and Ministerially Interacting with Peers and Leadership

UNIFORMING AND STANDARDIZING THE PROPHET

The task of uniforming all the standard functions, features, activities, and abilities for the office is a massive one that can take years to accomplish. Careful study lets one easily see that all prophets, like any other professional group, share commonalities that are exclusive to them or particularly concentrated among them. These should be isolated, organized, and applied to what prophets do for God and His people in the world. Such a giant leap toward uniformity cannot help but foster unity in this office. This author's initiative in this cause was the development of *The Prophet's Dictionary*. It lays a solid foundation for future work in this area and can serve as a suitable platform for gathering and creating related tools to accredit this ministry. In addition, after the dictionary, this author developed a number of standardized assessments to help you better define and refine the prophets in your sphere of authority. The hope is that, with these tools, fearful prophets and even more fearful Christian leaders can embrace this vital ministry as an integral part of mainstream Christian service. Of course, this requires the prophets submit themselves to screening, and after that adequate, specialized training in order to win the confidence of the church at large.

At present, only a few of the Lord's contemporary prophets consider formalized education a must for their ministry. This is unfortunate, since a quality educational training program for any subject does two necessary things: it equips and perfects. Using well-defined goals, objectives, and outcomes, quality readiness programs declare what they set out to do, accomplish it, and then inform the student how to recognize its accomplishment upon completion. Every program's objective, through its chosen materials, is to speak what learners need to understand and perform adequately in their chosen fields of study and proposed service. Ideal learning materials should tackle the strengths and weaknesses of the field, including its proponents and opponents. It should factor in what people respond to most or dislike about a particular field of ministry. Good readiness programs address how the learner may counter, conquer, or override his field's sources of opposition and best profit from its opportunities. These may be competitors with equal or similar strengths and values or former leaders in the field who have not kept up as they should with changing trends and user or consumer needs and views. At the least, these should motivate learning and teaching programs that prepare people for God's real ministries and the actual world in which they will serve.

WHAT PROPHETIC COMPANIES GENERALLY DO

It is almost universally understood that the work of the prophetic company in an organization is predominantly prophesying. However, many people make the mistake of thinking that is all prophets do because of the prevailing view of the prophetic. Tradition has it that the prophetic is strictly a verbalizing ministry. It seems that much of the previous teachings on the subject emphasize the obvious: prophets utter what they see or hear from ethereal sources. I have soundly refuted this notion throughout this text.

Beyond the previous misconception is the error that claims the manifestations of the Holy Spirit in 1 Corinthians 12:3-11 are gifts that are equal to the official prophet's mantles. Further exacerbating the problem that prophets face is the contention that any and all spiritual gifts are randomly bestowed—that they are indiscriminately bestowed on individuals to be appropriated at will by whosoever will. Problematically, the manifestations of the Spirit are treated the way that the gifts of the spirit in Romans 12 are intended. These two mistakes have caused the prophetic to be seen exclusively as wholesale verbalizing what anyone who wills senses to be God's thoughts. The problem with these prevailing views is that the other very important functions of the mantle are ignored, which prevents the body of Christ from deriving any appreciable benefit from them.

The prophet is endowed with enormous resources with which to serve, protect, and advance Christ's body. These resources are meted out to each prophet in the same way all gifts and talents are, according to each one's abilities. There is no more of a blanket prophetic ability that is the same for every prophet than there is for any other divine bestowment, spiritual or otherwise. Prophetic capacities are not equal and should not be practiced by everyone as if they are. As you go through the prophetic functions to follow, keep this in mind. Below are twenty specific tasks required of prophetic companies.

SAMPLE PROPHETIC COMPANY GUIDELINES TO ORDER AND GOVERN YOUR INSTITUTION

1. PROPHETIC COMPANY PRAYING AND INTERCEDING

Company prophets should not evade their responsibility for building, increasing, and maintaining the essential prayer guard the organization needs. That means each company member is to actively participate in all prayer vigils, routine and impromptu, and be prepared to lend their mantle's support to its effectiveness and success.

- Prophets are not to sit in prayer groups and refuse to pray. They must not exhibit resentment for having to be there or emit a contentious spirit to signal their disturbance.

- Company prophets must not behave unseemly to publicize their displeasure at being in attendance at any required gathering or refuse to respond when called upon at such meetings.

- Company prophets must not, on the other hand, dominate any gathering with untimely prophecy or spiritual harangues or any other action that tends to render spiritual meetings unproductive.

- Company prophets are required to keep the peace, maintain order, and uphold the leader in charge of the session.

- Company prophets are to use their authority and influence as representatives of the organization to continually unify the company's strength and exhibit harmony and maturity when on duty in any official (or unofficial) capacity.

- Company prophets are to exhibit discernment and respect for the gatherings they cover, while evaluating and monitoring all prophetic expression.

2. PROPHECY

Company prophets are to continually bring the word of the Lord to the body as assigned. They are to remain in constant studious communion with the Holy Spirit to ensure fresh and current revelation is ministered to the body. Prophecy stagnation and redundancy assume the prophet has been out of touch with the Lord and therefore been forced to fall back on gifting and experience to meet congregant or organizational needs.

3. PROPHETIC COUNSELING

Designated members of the prophetic company may be permitted to counsel those to whom they are assigned in the body from the prophetic wisdom the Lord has placed in their mouths. Such counsel may only be based upon the unction of God's Spirit and the Holy Bible. Prophetic counseling is not meant to be therapeutic in any way that suggests that the company or its members are qualified to treat non-spiritual, ecclesiastical, doctrinal, or moral disorders.

Refer counseling situations immediately to the chief prophet who in turn will take the appropriate steps to see that the people needing more clinical attention are directed to the appropriate practitioners. Company prophets may not suggest in any way that their counseling is an alternative to serious clinical therapy of the sort that may only be legitimately done by certified licensed professionals in the field of mental health and its related services.

4. Prophetic Company Leadership Interactions

The prophetic company, as an institution in the organization, may constitute a dimension of its spiritual authority. As such, all members of the company are answerable for their decisions, actions, and judgments when functioning in their official capacity as spiritual representatives of the church. However, not every member of the prophetic company is to be viewed or treated as an authority figure apart from the corporate authority the entire company holds. Only those members of the company who hold official authority titles may exercise their delegated portions of spiritual, practical, and organizational authority up to the limits of their position.

5. Intercession

The prophetic company is responsible, through personal and company prayer, for continually standing in the gap for the church and its membership to defend, guard, propel, and position it to excel in its assigned region and endeavors. The chief prophet is to assign a member of the company to oversee the organization's intercessors. This prophet's position is intercessory supervisor.

6. Intercessory Supervisor

The intercessory supervisor should oversee all of the organization's intercessory activities, products, and operations. The intercessory supervisor is to appear at all intercessory sessions. When this is not possible, the intercessory supervisor is to assign an assistant (temporary or permanent) to fill in whenever scheduled intercessory meetings encounter a scheduling conflict. The intercessory supervisor is to maintain a separate journal for intercessors, handle all supervisory, evaluative, and disciplinary activities, and maintain records of these activities to report to the chief prophet at regularly scheduled meetings.

7. PROPHECY INTERPRETATION AND TRANSLATION

Prophetic company members are to receive and hear the word of the Lord directly and from other prophets or prophesiers to ascertain its authenticity by rightly dividing God's word using Bible truth and the prophet's spiritual faculties. They are to apply God's wisdom to communicate or clarify prophecy in ways their audiences can comprehend and act on in obedience to the Lord.

8. VISION INTERPRETATION AND APPLICATION

Prophetic company members are expected to understand and apply the prophetic medium of visions and interpret their imagery to deliver the word of the Lord. This also pertains to symbols, signs, and tokens. They are to study Scripture to cement the word as God's by identifying Bible passages, profiles, precedents, or patterns that substantiate the dream or visions.

9. DREAM INTERPRETATION AND APPLICATION

Company prophets are expected to understand their own and others' dreams to see if they are Holy Spirit-inspired and safe to release to the body or the intended target or audience. Company prophet training should include what God may say through the medium of dreams and visions. They are to be equipped for this by studying Scripture to cement the word as God's by identifying Bible passages, profiles, precedents, or patterns that substantiate the dream or visions.

10. PROPHECY CLARIFICATION AND CONFIRMATION

Prophetic company members are to hear and evaluate prophecy from within the group and within the body to clarify what is or is not from the Lord and to confirm those who deliver prophecy regularly as accurate. Of the many goals for this function is the company prophet's eventual validation of consistently accurate prophesiers as potential prophets or prophetics in the making.

11. PROPHECY SCREENING

Company prophets are to review written prophecies or prophetic messages and approve them before they are given to the church or its leadership to ensure only the true word of God is delivered.

12. REMEDIATING PROPHETIC ERRORS AND PROPHECY

When guest prophecies are uttered, as needed, company prophets are to evaluate guest ministers' prophecies, critique questionable words to judge them as errant or not, and correct or refute them so the body does not act on error, ill-timed words, or soulish prophecies masked as revelation from God.

13. ORGANIZATION PROPHETIC DEVELOPMENT

The prophetic company and its assigned members are to present the prophetic to the church, answer its related questions, and overall equip them to hear from God, understand what is heard, and act on it wisely.

14. DELIVERING PROPHECY TO WORSHIP SERVICE

As assigned, each company member is to contribute to the prophetic atmosphere of the church. Weekly words are to be prepared after prayer and ministry to the Lord and uttered to the organization at regular gatherings when a company prophet is called upon to do so.

15. IDENTIFYING POTENTIAL PROPHETIC VOICES FOR THE CHURCH

As it is the duty of all leadership to interact with the sheep and to get to know them, the prophetic company has the privilege of recognizing prophetic potential in certain members who may be developed for future service to and in the company. Through continuous interactions company prophets spot those who may eventually be used in the company. Such discoveries should be referred to the chief prophet or assistant and may not be declared to the person until approval and other screening and proving activities have taken place.

16. IDENTIFYING POTENTIAL INTERCESSORS

It is incumbent upon all the members of the company to notice spiritual maturity and stability among all the members of the body, and it is a primary function of the chief prophet and the assistant to identify potential intercessors and approach them for preparation and readiness to serve on the church's intercessory corps. Both leaders should be on constant lookout for quality intercessors whom God may have sent to the body to pray for it. The intercessors corps is the primary pool from which candidates for the position of company prophet should be drawn. The decision to qualify and appoint a candidate to the prophetic company's eligibility program is jointly that of the intercessory superintendent, who makes the recommendation, and the chief prophet.

17. Identifying Novice and Potential Company Prophets

While the church or organization has its own means of educating its ministers in general, the company prophet superintendent and his or her assistant are to encourage company prophets to grow in their ability to replicate themselves and so contribute to the replenishment and expansion of the group. Therefore, they should look for prospective students to qualify for the prophetic education program and eventually serve in the church's prophetic company.

18. Protecting and Warning Leaders of Impending Spiritual Events, Assaults, and Infiltration

Here the watchman functions of the company prophet are called upon. This function cannot be fulfilled if the prophets are not prayerful or studious. Watchman requirements place great demand on the company's regular prayer gatherings and other prophetic assemblies scheduled to allow each prophet to minister, learn, counsel, and receive guidance in the position. Watching may take the form of a spontaneous prophecy, a written word, a shared vision or dream, or a Scripture revelation that speaks prophetically to the messenger during study and devotions. Occasions of the delivery of such words, once confirmed, are at the discretion of prophetic company leadership.

19. Uniting to Compel Victory and Spiritual Obedience to the Church's Visions and Endeavors

Here the intercessory functions of the prophetic company are brought into action. Regularly scheduled prayer, concentrated prayer vigils to address stubborn situations or resistant demonic forces, frequent prophecy outlets, and intense personal devotions all unite to enable the prophets of the church to relentlessly attack long-standing and new problematic areas of the church's existence. In addition to their spiritual maneuvers, company prophets should not overlook the value of team and leader collaboration. At times, to focus all spiritual efforts, it is necessary to consult with the entire ministry to identify the issues, assess their threat, an devise the best strategy for dealing with it.

20. *Maintaining Up-to-Date Journal of Company and Personal Prophetic Activities*

Generally a journal of prophetic activities should be kept to record the company's prophetic activities, log the events of warfare or intercession, and its strategies. Also to be included in the journal are God's revelations along the way and chronicles of the high features of the conflict and battles, conquests, and how they were ultimately won. This requirement is consistent with the Bible's mention of the "Book of the Wars of the Lord" and the very presence of the prophet writing in Scripture. These no doubt began as the prophet's journal that the Lord invoked as canonized Scripture.

MANDATORY PROPHETIC DUTIES, RESPONSIBILITIES, AND SERVICE GUIDELINES

For a prophet company to serve well, there must be mandatory obligations that are not negotiable. Here is an example of such obligations:

All members of the prophetic company, in addition to the prophets themselves, are responsible for attending all scheduled prayer meetings. This includes the psalmists, seers, and prophesiers. Like the prophets, they are to stay prophetically keen and astute enough to render prophetic service on call. They should be ready to participate in all prophetic gatherings as instructed and satisfactorily complete all scheduled training and development. Company prophets are to be and remain members of the church in good standing and carry out all chief prophet (company superintendent) instructions. Prophets are to interact positively with organization membership, support pastoral efforts to nurture and stabilize the flock, and minister the word of the Lord responsibly.

Prophets are to minister the Lord's word according to the guidelines for delivering prophecy contained in the policy manual and the Bible. They are also to remain in fellowship with one another to maintain the unity of the group and keep conflicts and disharmony to a productive minimum. Prophets are to observe the standard of decorum for the position and adhere to nondisclosure and confidentiality guidelines. All prophetic company members are to respect and cooperate with church leadership and properly represent the ministry in all their professional and public activities.

These guidelines were given as a sample of how to organize and govern your prophetic company. They are excerpted from the manual I developed and use with my prophetic company. You will certainly have many other things to add to your company handbook. Take the time to build it before your company gets into full swing. Of course, in your handbook of policy, you want to include guidelines for attendance, a code of conduct and behaviors, disciplinary measures, arbitration, and appeals. Make sure you have well-defined confidentiality rules and disclaimers.

CHAPTER SUMMARY

1. Prophetic companies serve under senior church leadership.

2. The prophetic company itself is a sphere of leadership in the churches.

3. The prophetic company staff is diverse and consists of representation of all spiritual ministries in the body.

4. A good prophetic company carries out at least eleven core requirements to serve and cover their assigned churches.

5. Standards for the prophetic company should be uniform.

6. Itinerant and independent prophets must change to belong to and competently serve a prophetic company.

7. A minimum of twenty responsibilities are required of the prophetic company.

PROPHETIC ACTION ITEMS

1. Profile the knowledge, intelligence, and skill levels a candidate for prophetic duty needs to qualify and then to serve.

2. Decide with your group the extent of training and other readiness methods needed to carry out the duties of a company prophet.

PROPHETIC COMPANY BRANCHES

PRAISE AND WORSHIP
PROPHETIC PSALMODY

ORGANIZATION
PROPHETIC EDUCATION

PROPHETIC COMPANY
ARCHIVE DEPARTMENT

PROPHETIC COMPANY
EVENTS AND
CONFERENCES

DEPARTMENT OF CHIEF
OF APOSTLE PROPHET

MINISTRY OF DREAMS,
VISIONS, SYMBOLISM

PROPHETIC
COMPANY
SERVICE TO
ORGANIZATION
LEADERSHIP

PROPHETIC COMPANY
INTERCESSORY ALLIANCE

PROPHETIC COMPANY
FIELD AND AFFILIATE
MINISTRIES OUTREACH

PROPHETIC
COMPANY TRAINING,
ORIENTATION, AND
REPLENISHMENT

Prophetic Company Organization Chart

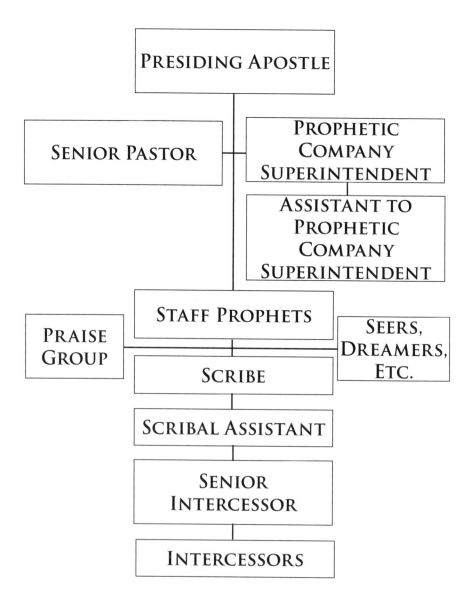

Appendix A

THE MINISTRY OF
PERSONAL PROPHECY

A Q & A FORUM

Amid all the controversy surrounding the prophetic, another issue that may be greatly misunderstood is personal prophecy. Opinions range from viewing it as being unnecessary to deeming it entirely biblical. When God first restored the prophetic, He introduced it through prophecy so that people could relate the fastest. Initially, prophetics centered on the gift of prophecy, essentially predicting the future. The negative side of the coin is its extreme, merely fortune-telling. Over time, prophecy matured to include the prophetic's other functions. However, the most beneficial side of prophecy is what God says prophets and prophecy are to do for us. That is, they are to profit and prosper us according to Jeremiah 23:32 and 2 Chronicles 20:20. Both passages make a good case for personal prophecy. After all, who would not want profitability and prosperity in life?

Historically, Scripture shows that God uses prophecy to predict the future, reveal the past, announce impending world events, and direct our life paths. Through prophecy He appointed leaders, installed and dethroned kings, fertilized barren wombs, and established kingdoms. With prophecy, God waged and won wars and transformed fearful souls into courageous giants, even using it to bring His only begotten Son to earth. As you can see, prophecy is an indispensable tool for God and mankind, and no era really existed without it, despite its abuse from time to time.

Moving past puberty, the prophetic today motivates many to learn it. Now what remains is understanding how to receive personal prophecy and to recognize and respond to genuine prophets. People are asking very probing questions about it. Below are some answers to these questions that address personal prophecy's major concerns.

Question #1: *What is prophecy?* The most succinct definition of prophecy, used in *The Prophet's Dictionary,* is "God's communications media." Prophecy is God's means of talking to us to reveal His mind and actions.

Question #2: *Why is prophecy needed?* Prophecy allows our invisible and inaudible God to publicize His thoughts in our world through people.

Question #3: *Whom is prophecy for?* Prophecy is for its communicator; in our case, the Lord. Communication between the Creator and His creation began with God, who remains unknown apart from tangibly contacting us. True prophecy reveals His future for us. Despite what traditional doctrine preaches, the Scriptures emphatically show that He wants us to inquire of reputable prophets to unveil to us His eternal answers for our lives. Daniel 2:28 frankly makes this point.

Question #4: *Should "personal prophecy" be practiced?* Yes, because people desire to know the future for many reasons, most of them good. Also, the Lord needs them to know it. Prophecy helps us plan life better, arm ourselves for its upsets, and equip ourselves to take better advantage of coming opportunities that God arranged before time. With prayer and Bible study, it can be an amazing tool.

Question #5: *Why should people receive personal prophecy?* God desires people to know His future for them so that He can guide their life decisions. Ecclesiastes 3:11 says the Lord put eternity in our hearts. Why? So that He can lead us throughout life. Job 33:14–16 adds that He sealed our work in our hands for us to seek His plans for our lives because, as Acts 15:18 declares, God has known from eternity all of His works. Prophecy answers our unknowns.

Question #6: *What is the biblical basis for personal prophecy?* Scripture is full of examples of personal prophecy to individuals, families, and nations. From God's prophecy to Adam that he would surely die in the day that he ate from the forbidden tree, to the book of Revelation's end of the age, prophecy reigns. Creation, future leaders, and answered prayer all started with prophecy. It is the single medium that keeps the Almighty in touch with His creation and keeps God in control. Jesus reiterates how He came to earth according to the prophecies made concerning Him. (See Psalm 40:7 and Hebrews 10:7.) The purpose of prophecy is to bring God's eternal word to pass on time, as stressed in Scripture at least fifty-five times. Evidence of that word's coming to pass is its physicality in events, objects, or actions.

Question #7: *What value is personal prophecy to people and why does God permit it?* We cannot know tomorrow except if someone from the future reveals it to us. God is outside our time and holds all tomorrows in His hand. Psalm

139:16 says He wrote a book for every life that He made, and recorded every life before it began. Genesis 5:1's book of Adam's *generations* and Matthew 1:1's book of Christ's *generation* suggest this. See *The Prophet's Dictionary* under their headings. True prophecy is not empty words prayed or uttered by gifted people describing what they see. Rather, it taps into Creator God's library and sees a page or chapter of a person's life book written long before time began. God permits and perpetuates prophecy to steer our lives to His eternal existence and to refine us and make us flourish along the way. He also uses prophecy to assure that the gifts and talents He deposits in people are properly and prosperously used as He intends. According to Exodus 18, Moses performed this function for Israel as he told them the work they were to do.

Question #8: *Should people seek personal prophecy?* Scripture does not say God's people are not to inquire of Him by His prophets. In fact, it appears to say the opposite. Jesus said to receive a prophet in the name of a prophet in Matthew's gospel; Paul encouraged Timothy to use the prophecies that commissioned him to wage a good warfare. Later he told Timothy not to neglect the gift he received by prophecy. (See 1 Timothy 1:18 and 4:14.) Why else would he instruct his young protégé thusly, except that prophecy is a powerful means of conquering this life?

When questioning the propriety of seeking a bona fide prophet, consider this. If it is okay for you to seek counsel, prayer, intercession, professional or casual advice, but why is it taboo to inquire of God from a prophet? You can seek words of wisdom or knowledge from someone's prayer, hear God through an advisor or a therapist, and benefit from a friend's wisdom, but you may not seek a prophet. That does not seem to make sense. Meanwhile, as pointed out previously, Exodus 18 says Moses let God's people inquire of him all day. As a prophet, he judged, taught, and instructed Israel according to God's law. Later, in Exodus 18:20, Jethro's counsel shows that Moses addressed their lifestyles and careers, clearly doing so by ministering personal prophecy.

In 1 Samuel 15, Saul visited the prophet Samuel to learn what happened to his lost donkeys. Samuel was not surprised that Saul sought him on such a mundane issue. Furthermore, Samuel's company of prophets suggests people sought them routinely for life's answers.

Question #9: *Does Scripture allude to or record anything akin to a prophetic presbytery?* A prophetic presbytery is strongly implied in Scripture based on several mentions of a company of prophets, also expressed as "the sons of the prophets." These groups of stationary or itinerant ministers identify a body of prophesying voices who served from the palace to the villages. Jeremiah's conflict with Hananiah in Jeremiah 28 further reinforces this practice as an apparent presbytery of prophets was summoned by the king to advise him on an impending military campaign. A similar example is seen with Ahab and Micaiah in 1 Kings 22, and Paul spoke of a prophesying presbytery in 1 Timothy 4:14.

Question #10: *What are the means of receiving personal prophecy?* Aside from gaining audience with a prophet or encountering one with the gift of prophecy, other ways of receiving prophecy include dreams, visions, prayer, Scripture study, and casual conversation with highly spiritual or especially wise people. Most notable among these is the conscientious intercessor. A last and most typical way to receive a prophetic word from the Lord is through the manifestation of the Holy Spirit, taught in 1 Corinthians 12:7–11. This action is not the same as one exercising the gift of prophecy. The manifestation is as the Spirit wills; exercising one's gift of prophecy is not dependent upon the Holy Spirit's initiatives.

Question #11: *What about false prophecy?* Of the more than five hundred times the word *prophet* appears in Scripture, there are only about twenty-one mentions of false prophets, perhaps because less than 10 percent of the prophetic actions recorded were false. Of the more than thirty prophets identified in Scripture, including major and minor prophets, only a handful of false prophets are named: Jezebel, Noadiah, Jannes and Jambres, and Balaam, to name a few. That is not to say that there were no others, but it implies that false prophets and false prophecy were less of a threat than today's popular teachings communicate. *Divination*, the word for false prophecy, is in the Old Testament about twelve times. While false prophecy is a concern, more damage is done by uneducated or overly sensual prophets such as those given little opportunity to perfect their skill before now.

For those who believe the Old and New Testaments are separate with different rules, here is a thought. Jesus relied on ancient prophets and prophecies for His ministry. So, if part of the Old Testament applied to the New, then—except for the ritual laws abolished by His cross—it applies equally today, especially in relation to prophecy. Otherwise, where and how do we draw the line?

LIST OF PROPHETS

T his list does not name or identify every prophet Israel had because some were only mentioned. It is included to show the interesting connection between the prophet and his name as it relates to either the theme of his message or the time (condition and climate included) of his service. As there are no accidents or coincidences in God, the meaning of each messenger's name has significance.

NAME	MEANING
Aaron	Bright
Abijah	Brother of Yahweh
Abraham	Father of a Multitude
Agabus	He Loved
Amos	Burden Bearer
Anna	Grace (fem. of John)
Azariah	Yahweh Has Helped
Barnabas	Son of Exhortation
Daniel	God Is My Judge
Deborah	A Bee (industrious and fruitful)

NAME	MEANING
Dodavah	Beloved of Yahweh
Elijah	Yahweh Is God
Elisha	Yahweh Is Salvation
Enoch	Dedicated
Ezekiel	God Strengthens
Gad	God's Fortune
Habakkuk	Embrace
Haggai	Festive
Hanan	Merciful
Hanani	Gracious
Hosea	Salvation
Huldah	Weasel or Mole (hidden away)
Iddo	Festal
Isaiah	Yahweh Is Salvation
Jacob	Supplanter
Jahaziel	God Sees
Jeduthun	Praising
Jehu	Yahweh Is He
Jeremiah	Yahweh Establishes
Joel	Yahweh Is God
John	Yahweh Has Been Gracious
John (The Baptist)	Yahweh Has Been Gracious
Jonah	Dove
Joseph	May He (Yahweh) Add

NAME	MEANING
Joshua	Yahweh Saves
Judah	Judah (Hebrew) Praise
Malachi	My Messenger
Micah	Who Is Like Yahweh
Micaiah	Who Is like Yahweh
Miriam	Obstinacy, Stubbornness
Moses	Drawn Out
Naham	Full of Comfort
Nathan	Gift
Noah	Rest
Obadiah	Servant of Yahweh
Obed	He Has Restored
Paul	Little One
Peter	Rock or Stone
Samuel	Name of God (asked and heard of God)
Shemiah	Jehovah Has Heard
Silas	Wooded
Urijah	Yahweh Is Light
Zadok	Righteous
Zechariah	Yahweh Remembered
Zephaniah	Hidden of Yahweh

Glossary of Key Terms and Phrases

1. **Agency**—An extension of an organization in a remote location authorized to transact business on its behalf.

2. **Agent**—An authorized representative of an organization.

3. **Biblical Prophetics**—Prophetics based on and operated in accordance with those described in the Bible.

4. **Church Prophet**—A prophet stationed in the local church.

5. **Commission**—A charge, calling, or assignment where delegated authority is given to a person or group dispatched to act on behalf of an organization, country, or company. Involves proxy, ambassadorship, and ministry.

6. **Divination**—Fortune-telling and predicting by fallen angels.

7. **Divine**—To tell fortunes and predict the future under the influence of an unclean spirit.

8. **Dreams**—Visual images communicated to a sleeper.

9. **Features and Functions**—Traits and their corresponding operations.

10. **Foundations Studies**—The basics of a subject or discipline.

11. **Functionary**—One who serves at the behest of an authority and on its behalf.

12. **Mentor**—One who trains and nurtures another for a profession.

13. **Ministry**—Service to a deity or religion. May also be to a country or government.

14. **Mishemereth**—The watch, duties, and station of a prophet.

15. **Nabi**—An official prophet.

16. **Nastar**—The encircling effect of prophet covering.

17. **Office**—A position of trust, responsibility, and delegation of derived authority.

18. **Officer**—A person who occupies an office.

19. **Official**—The legitimate actions of an officer carrying out an office.

20. **Prophecy**—A statement of what will be before it happens.

21. **Prophet**—A spokesperson for a deity; one who invokes the gods.

22. **Prophetic**—That which proceeds from the prophet's work and authority.

23. **Prophetic Attributes**—Traits that characterize prophets, revelations, and predictions.

24. **Prophetic Authority**—The rule, governance, and influence of the prophet.

25. **Prophetic Delegations**—Tasks, assignments, and authority received by prophets.

26. **Prophetic Function**—The professional operations of a prophet.

27. **Prophetic Guard**—A force of prophets assigned to a church for its spiritual protection.

28. **Prophetic Jurisdiction**—The spherical territory over which a prophet watches and governs.

29. **Prophetic Mantle**—The empowered cloak prophets of old wore to identify themselves as prophets.

30. **Prophetic Ministration**—The service and dispensation of a prophet.

31. **Prophetic Orientation**—Introductory teachings that expose one to and acquaint one with prophets and the prophetic.

32. **Prophetic Sphere**—A specific area of human and earthly existence over which a prophet has sway; knowledge and information that communicate the disciplines of prophetic ministry.

33. **Church Prophet Superintendent**—The head of a local church prophetic organization.

34. **Prophetic Task**—Prophetic work assigned by God.

35. **Prophetic Territory**—The physical and spiritual region of a prophet's clout.

36. **Prophetic Ward**—The literal station of a prophet's ministry or assignment.

37. **Protocol**—A system of proprietary rules and precepts that govern activities.

38. **Prototcratic**—Rulership of first founders or superseding authorities.

39. **Psalmist**—A singing prophetic, one who rhymes and sings predictions and revelations.

40. **Realm**—A designated area or division on earth.

41. **Seer**—One who sees what is ordinarily unseen by the natural eye.

42. **Sod**—Hebrew term for closed-chamber deliberations of high powers.

43. **Sphere**—An invisible area or arena of dominance.

44. **Symbol**—An image or mark meant to signify something else.

45. **Territory**—A land division.

46. **Vision**—Images that communicate a message from unseen sources or the mind.

Books Researched and Studied

Genesius' Hebrew-Chaldee Lexicon of the Old Testament
H. W. F. Genesius
Published by Baker House Books, 1979

The Dictionary of Classical Mythology, Religion, Literature and Art
Oscar Seyfert
Published by Gramercy Books, 1995

Prophecy in Ancient Israel
J. Lindbloom
Published by Fortress Press, Philadelphia, 1965

Studies on Women at Mari
Bernard Frank Batto
Published by Johns Hopkins University, 1974

The Hebrew-Greek Key Study Bible
Spiros Zodhiates, Th. D.
Published by AMG Publishers, 1984

Dictionary of Symbols
Jack Tresiddor
Published by Chronicle Books, Duncan Baird Publishers, 1997

International Standard Bible Encyclopedia, Electronic Database
© 1996 by Biblesoft

Nelson's Illustrated Bible Dictionary
Thomas Nelson Publishers, 1986

The New Unger's Bible Dictionary
Moody Press of Chicago, Illinois, 1988

The Lost Books of the Bible and the Forgotten Books of the Bible
Published by LB Press, Cleveland, Ohio, © 1926

ABOUT THE AUTHOR

Paula A. Price is vastly becoming the international voice on the subject of apostolic and prophetic ministry. She is widely recognized as a modern-day apostle with a potent prophetic anointing. Having been in active full-time ministry since 1985, she has founded and established three churches, an apostolic and prophetic Bible institute, a publication company, a consulting firm, and a global collaborative network linking apostles and prophets together for the purpose of kingdom vision and ventures. With an international itinerant ministry, she has transformed the lives of many through her wisdom and revelation of God's kingdom.

As a former sales and marketing executive, Paula blends ministerial and entrepreneurial applications in her ministry to enrich and empower a diverse audience with the skills and abilities to take kingdoms for the Lord Jesus Christ. A lecturer, teacher, curriculum developer, and business trainer, she globally consults Christian businesses, churches, schools, and assemblies. Over a twenty-year period, she has developed a superior curriculum to effectively train Christian ministers and professionals, particularly the apostle and the prophet. Her programs are often used in both secular and non-secular environments worldwide. Although she has written over twenty-five books, manuals, and other course material on the apostolic and prophetic, she is most recognized for her unique 1,600–term *The Prophet's Dictionary,* a concise prophetic training manual entitled *The Prophet's Handbook,* and her most recent releases, *Divine Order for Spiritual Dominance,* a tool for five-fold ministry, and *Eternity's Generals,* an explanation of today's apostle.

Beyond the pulpit, Paula is the provocative talk-show host of her own program, *Let's Just Talk: Where God Makes Sense.* She brings the pulpit to the pew, weekly applying God's wisdom and divine pragmatism to today's world solutions. Her ministry goal is to make Christ's teachings and churches relevant for today. "Eternity in the Now" is the credo through which she accomplishes it.

In addition to her vast experience, Paula has a D.Min. and a Ph.D. in Religious Education from Word of Truth Seminary in Alabama. She is also a wife, a mother of three daughters, and a grandmother of two. She and her husband, Tom, presently pastor New Creation Worship Assembly in Tulsa, Oklahoma.

Test Your Spiritual IQ

Introducing the Standardized Ministry Assessment Series
How do I test my Spiritual IQ?

Use our standardized ministry assessments to help determine where you fit—whether in ministry or business; find out how equipped you are for your calling, and evaluate your readiness. Our assessments are essential tools for Christian ministry that aid in assessing the potential and proficiency of those claiming or exhibiting ministerial aptitude or giftings in action.

What are the assessment types?
Purpose for Destiny (PFD)

Have you ever asked yourself, "*What was God thinking when He made me*?" Are you a leader with members who seem like square pegs in round holes? If so, the **Purpose for Destiny Questionnaire** is ideal for you or your team.

Minister's Assessment Questionnaire **(MAQ)**

The MAQ is for any minister, leader, or gifted individual called to serve. It is an assessment created to identify the various features of five-fold ministry at work in an individual, as exhibited and/or practiced by the ministries featured in Ephesians 4:11 and 1 Corinthians 12:28–29.

Prophetic Aptitude Questionnaire **(PAQ)**

For prophets, intercessors, psalmists, seers, prayer warriors, and the like, the PAQ is an evaluative assessment tool to help Christian leaders evaluate those entrusted to their prophetic oversight or tutelage and to determine where their prophetic ministers may best serve. The PAQ is ideal for individuals interested in understanding their prophetic identity.

Apostolic Assessment Questionnaire **(AAQ)**

The AAQ is for apostles—seasoned and new; prophets—new and veteran; and pastors and church leaders inclined to apostolic ministry. It pinpoints whether you are called to serve officially in apostolic ministry or operate in the gifting. The AAQ reveals your strengths, weaknesses, and areas that need training and development.

What is the value of these assessments?
- To connect ministers with identity and calling
- Join leaders with a profitable tool for ministry selection
- Unite students with guidance and direction
- Link readiness programs with accurate evaluation of their trainees

How can I schedule myself or my group?

Individuals may register to take their selected assessment at a host site in their local area. Ministry groups, professional teams, or schools may register their group to receive a proctored assessment by one of our teams, or register to become a host site.

For more information, visit www.drpaulaprice.com
or call (918) 446-5542 to speak with an assessment representative.

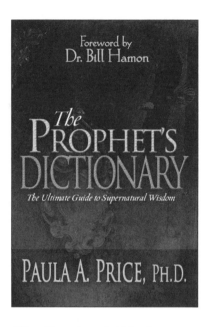

The Prophet's Dictionary:
The Ultimate Guide to Supernatural Wisdom
Paula A. Price

The Prophet's Dictionary by Paula Price is an essential tool for laymen, prophets, prophesiers, pastors, intercessors, and dreamers of dreams. As the ultimate all-in-one dictionary and reference book, it contains over 1600 relevant definitions of terms and phrases for the prophetic realm of Christian ministry. Here you will discover how to correctly interpret and apply God's prophetic words, distinguish between true and false prophets, understand God-given dreams, and develop your spiritual gifts. Also included are prophetic visions and clues to interpreting their symbolism, imagery, and signs.

This one-of-a-kind resource is a book no Christian should be without!

Hardcover ISBN: 978-1-60374-035-7 • Trade Paper ISBN: 978-0-88368-999-8

www.whitakerhouse.com